CURRENT ISSUES IN THE
ECONOMICS OF WELFARE

CURRENT ISSUES IN ECONOMICS

General Editor: David Greenaway, University of Nottingham

Series Standing Order

If you would like to receive future titles in this series as they are
published, you can make use of our standing order facility. To place
a standing order please contact your bookseller or, in case of
difficulty, write to us at the address below with your name and
address and the name of the series. Please state with which title you
wish to begin your standing order. (If you live outside the United
Kingdom we may not have the rights for your area, in which case we
will forward your order to the publisher concerned.)

Customer Services Department, Macmillan Distribution Ltd,
Houndmills, Basingstoke, Hampshire, RG21 2XS, England.

Current Issues in the Economics of Welfare

Edited by

Nicholas Barr
Senior Lecturer in Economics
London School of Economics

and

David Whynes
Senior Lecturer in Economics
University of Nottingham

MACMILLAN

First published 1993 by
THE MACMILLAN PRESS LTD
Houndmills, Basingstoke, Hampshire RG21 2XS
and London
Companies and representatives
throughout the world

ISBN 0–333–55694–1 hardcover
ISBN 0–333–55695–X paperback

A catalogue record for this book is available
from the British Library.

Printed in Hong Kong

Contents

    A. J. Culyer   153

9   The Economics of Education: Changing Fortunes
    Howard Glennerster   176

10 Political Economy, Applied Welfare Economics and
    Housing in the UK
    Duncan Maclennan and Kenneth Gibb   200

    END-NOTES   225
    BIBLIOGRAPHY   229
    NAME INDEX   248
    SUBJECT INDEX   252

List of Figures

List of Tables

Series Editor's Preface for *Current Issues in the Economics of Welfare*

The *Current Issues* series was piloted by *Current Issues in International Trade*, which was published in 1985. This was produced to meet a specific need, namely to provide accessible and digestible overviews of frontier topics for undergraduate students. Since that pilot, seven further *Current Issues* volumes have been published covering microeconomics, macroeconomics, labour, international money, money and finance, public sector and development economics. These follow a similar format to the pilot – nine or ten essays, one of which provides an overview, whilst the remainder are devoted to current issues.

As series editor the main challenge I have faced throughout is finding suitable editors for each of the volumes – the best people are generally the busiest! I believe, however, that I have been fortunate in having such an impressive and experienced team of editors with the necessary skills and reputation to persuade first-class authors to participate. I would like to thank all of them for their cooperation and assistance in the development of the series. Like me all of them will, I am sure, hope that this series provides a useful service to undergraduate and postgraduate students as well as to faculty.

Current Issues in the Economics of Welfare is the eighth volume in the series. Its editors are Nicholas Barr and David Whynes. Both are experienced editors and have worked extensively in this field. Their experience and reputation has resulted in them assembling a first-rate line-up of contributors addressing an excellent range of topics. Recent years have witnessed extensive reforms in the delivery of health care, education and other social services. As a result the role of the state has been the subject of extensive discussion. The editors commissioned papers on health, education, poverty, housing, pensions and other topics. The result is a comprehensive reader on the economics of welfare which not only passes muster in its own right but complements very effectively *Current Issues in Public Sector Economics*.

I found this an impressive and informative volume. I hope that readers find it equally useful.

University of Nottingham   DAVID GREENAWAY

Notes on the Contributors

A. B. Atkinson is Professor of Political Economy at the University of Cambridge.

Nicholas Barr is Senior Lecturer in Economics at the London School of Economics and Political Science, on secondment to the World Bank, Washington, USA during the time this book was written.

A. J. Culyer is Professor of Economics at the University of York.

Christian Dustmann and **John Micklewright** are, respectively, Lecturer in Economics, University of Bielefeld and Associate Professor of Economics, European University Institute, Florence.

Howard Glennerster is Professor of Social Science and Administration at the London School of Economics and Political Science.

Andrew M. Jones and **John W. Posnett** are Senior Lecturers in Economics at the Universities of Manchester and York, respectively.

Duncan Maclennan and **Kenneth Gibb** are Professor and Research Fellow, respectively, at the Centre for Housing Research, University of Glasgow.

David Piachaud is Professor of Social Science and Administration at the London School of Economics and Political Science.

David Whynes is Senior Lecturer in Economics at the University of Nottingham.

1 Introductory Issues

NICHOLAS BARR and DAVID WHYNES

It has traditionally been thought that the welfare state is about distributional objectives, that it has been studied mainly from non-economic perspectives, and that it is a subject about which economics has little to say. That view, fortunately, is now changing (Atkinson, 1987), in part because of recent theoretical developments, particularly the economics of information, and in part because of the breakdown of the post-war consensus about the welfare state. Economics, it turns out, has much to say on the subject; and a large part of the argument concerns the welfare state's important efficiency functions, which are a major theme of this book.

The organisation of the book and the main strands of argument are set out in section 1.4 of this chapter. First, though, it is helpful to discuss some background matters. Section 1.1 considers what we mean by the term 'welfare state', and section 1.2 examines its diverse and frequently conflicting purposes. Section 1.3 looks at the long and convoluted historical development of the welfare state in the United Kingdom. Given this history, it would evidently be a mistake to regard the welfare state as a purely modern device. Moreover, and although much of the empirical contents of later chapters are drawn from the UK experiences of recent years, it would also be a mistake to regard the welfare state as something uniquely British. Similar institutions, aimed at dealing with essentially similar problems, exist in all the OECD countries. Thus the theories and concepts to be explored are not peculiar to the UK alone, but are relevant to the analysis of state welfare provision in all advanced industrialised economies.

1

1.1 DEFINING THE WELFARE STATE

Many important concepts are hard or impossible to define (examples include poverty and inequality); others (e.g. the concept of utility, or the size of the government sector) can be given precise analytical meaning, but face major or insuperable measurement problems. The welfare state is one of those concepts which defies precise definition. Richard Titmuss wrote (1968, p. 124): 'I am no more enamored today of the indefinable abstraction "The Welfare State" than I was some twenty years ago when . . . the term acquired an international as well as a national popularity.' There are three areas of complication.

1. *Welfare derives from many sources in addition to state activity*: individual welfare derives from at least four sources.
   - *The labour market* is arguably the most important, first in the form of wage income. Full employment is a major component of welfare broadly defined. High levels of employment and rising labour productivity have been a major equalising force since the Second World War. In addition to wage income, firms (individually or on an industry-wide basis, voluntarily or under legal compulsion) provide occupational welfare in the face of sickness, injury and retirement.
   - *Private provision* includes voluntary private insurance and individual saving.
   - *Voluntary welfare* occurs both within and outside the family, where people give time free or at a below-market price, or make voluntary charitable donations in other forms.
   - *The state* intervenes by providing cash benefits and benefits in kind. In addition, by offering various forms of tax relief, it contributes to the finance of occupational and private provision.

2. *Modes of delivery are diverse*: though a service may be *funded* by the state, it does not necessarily have to be publicly *produced*. The state can produce a service itself and supply it to recipients at no charge (e.g. school education, or health care under the national health service); or it can pay for individuals to consume goods produced in the private sector (e.g. free drugs under the national health service); or it can give indi-

viduals money (either explicitly or in the form of tax relief) to make their own purchases (e.g. tax relief for contributions to approved private pension schemes).

3. *The boundaries of the welfare state are not well defined*: though the state's role should not be exaggerated, neither should it be understated. Public health and environmental policies are typically not included, even though their purposes are very similar to activities which are included.

Welfare is thus diverse in the source and also the manner of its delivery. Nevertheless, the state is the most important single agency involved in Britain and in most industrialised countries. The term 'welfare state' can thus be used as a shorthand for the state's activities in four broad areas: cash benefits, health care; education; and food, housing and other welfare services.

Cash benefits have two major components.

1. *Social insurance* is awarded without an income or wealth test (i.e. benefit is not limited only to low-income individuals/ families), generally on the basis of (i) previous contributions and (ii) the occurrence of a specified contingency, such as unemployment or being above a specified age.
2. *Non-contributory benefits* take two forms. So-called *'universal'* *benefits* are awarded on the basis of a specified contingency, without either a contributions or an income test. Major examples in Britain are Child Benefit, the National Health Service and most school education. *Social assistance* is awarded on the basis of an income test to help individuals and families who are in poverty, whether as an exceptional emergency, or because they are not covered by social insurance, or as a supplement to social insurance.

In practice the British welfare state can be taken to comprise, at a minimum, the following list. Cash benefits follow the pattern described in the previous paragraph. National insurance is payable to people with an adequate contributions record; benefits cover, *inter alia*, unemployment, sickness (short and long term) and (much the largest) retirement. Non-contributory benefits include child benefit (a weekly cash payment to the parent or guardian of every child), and income support (paid on the basis of a means test to those with little or no other income). The major benefits in kind are the national health service, education, and housing.

1.2   THE OBJECTIVES OF THE WELFARE STATE

The objectives of social institutions, as in any other area of economic policy, are efficiency, equity and administrative feasibility. In this context, however, it is useful to adopt a more detailed categorisation. As discussed later, they can be in conflict. Some writers deny that one or more is an appropriate aim, whilst others would argue that a number of the objectives actually have no practical meaning.

(a) *Efficiency* as an objective has three aspects.

Objective 1: Macro efficiency: the efficient fraction of GDP should be devoted to the totality of welfare state institutions.

Objective 2: Micro efficiency: policy should ensure the efficient division of total welfare state resources between the different cash benefits and different types of benefits in kind. The pursuit of micro efficiency may necessitate state intervention in private markets.

Objective 3: Incentives: where institutions are publicly funded, their finance and the construction of benefits should minimise adverse effects (i) on labour supply and employment, and (ii) on saving.

(b) *Supporting living standards* also has various components.

Objective 4: Poverty relief: no individual/household should fall below a minimum standard of living. Since there is no analytically satisfactory way of defining a poverty line, the definition of the minimum standard and of what constitutes 'adequate' access to welfare services is largely normative.

Objective 5: Protection of accustomed living standards: no one should face an unexpected and unacceptably large drop in their living standard. This is a major objective of unemployment benefits and most health-related benefits.

Objective 6: Income smoothing: institutions should enable individuals to reallocate consumption over their lifetime. Individuals can redistribute from themselves at one stage in the life cycle to themselves at another (an actuarial private pension scheme). Alternatively, there could be tax-funded provision, with no pretence of individual contributions, to groups whose stage in the life cycle suggests that they are likely to be financially constrained (e.g. benefits for families with young children).

Objectives 5 and 6 are different aspects of the broader aim of *economic security*. Objective 5 concerns unexpected reductions in living standards (i.e. it is mainly an insurance objective); objective 6 concerns predictable falls in income (i.e. it is more a savings objective). Both objectives therefore have an efficiency as well as an equity dimension.

(c) *The reduction of inequality* as an objective, in contrast, is almost entirely an equity issue.

Objective 7: Vertical equity: the system should redistribute towards individuals/families with lower incomes. This aim is contentious. All income-tested benefits contribute to it to some extent; so, second, do non-means-tested benefits whose recipients disproportionately have lower incomes (e.g. the flat-rate state pension). A third form of redistribution arises where more benefit per pound of contribution is paid at lower incomes, which can occur in a number of ways: any flat-rate benefit financed by a proportional contribution redistributes progressively (e.g. flat-rate pensions); so does the redistributive formula built into the US social security retirement pension; so does 'free' provision of a tax-funded service (e.g. health care under the national health service), so long as the service is not used even more progressively than the contributions which finance it.

The success or otherwise of benefits in reducing inequality is assessed by inspection over time of aggregate inequality measures, though with all the usual caveats (discussed in Chapter 6), including the conceptual difficulties raised by such measures, and deficiencies of the data on which they are based.

Objective 8: Horizontal equity: differences in benefits should take account of age, family size, etc., and differences in medical treatment should reflect only factors which are regarded as relevant (e.g. whether or not the patient has dependants), but not irrelevant factors like race.

6 Introductory Issues

(d) *Social integration*: so far the objectives have been conventional economic ones. Some commentators include broader social goals.

Objective 9: Dignity: cash benefits and health care should be delivered so as to preserve individual dignity and without unnecessary stigma. Beveridge emphasised the importance of contributions in this context: 'The popularity of compulsory social insurance today is established, and for good reason; by compulsory insurance, . . . the individual can feel assured that [his] needs will be met . . . by paying . . . a contribution, he can feel that he is getting security not as a charity but as a right' (UK, 1942, para. 296).

Objective 10: Social solidarity: cash benefits and health care should foster social solidarity, a frequently stated goal in mainland Europe. So far as possible, benefits should depend on criteria which are unrelated to socio-economic status, e.g. retirement pensions and the national health service.

(e) *Administrative feasibility* has two aspects.

Objective 11: Intelligibility: the system should be simple, easy to understand, and as cheap to administer as possible.

Objective 12: Absence of abuse: benefits should be as little open to abuse as possible.

1.3 THE ORIGINS OF THE WELFARE STATE IN THE UNITED KINGDOM

The term 'welfare state' appears to have been brought to prominence, if not actually coined, by William Temple, Archbishop of York, in 1941. In his book *Citizen and Churchman*, Temple compared the 'welfare state' which he hoped would emerge after the Second World War – a state established to serve the common interests of citizens – with the 'power state' exemplified by Nazi Germany, established to serve the interests of tyrants (Temple, 1941). The term gained popularity in Britain and spread rapidly to the other Western countries. In so doing, however, the religious and moral connotations of Temple's original exposition became transmogrified into economic imperatives for the state provision of welfare services. It became traditional to date the birth of the UK welfare state to 5 July 1948, the appointed day when comprehensive national insurance and free medical care became available (Marsh, 1980).

Whilst the post-war legislation enacted by the Labour government of the time undoubtedly delineated the structure of state welfare in operation today, very few of the reforms were truly original. Only in the case of the National Health Service can such a claim be sustained. By contrast, the majority of welfare measures were simply new manifestations of established practices, some with histories dating back many centuries. Such a proposition does not deny the radical nature of the Labour government's attempt to create a comprehensive suite of social welfare policies, but it does imply that a search for the origins of such policies must begin well before the modern era. In examining these origins it will become apparent that many of the arguments employed in contemporary political debates over the 'proper conduct' of welfare provision have equally long histories.

I

Our modern, intuitive understanding of the welfare state embraces government activity in the fields of poverty relief, education, housing and health care. Of these, the relief of poverty was the first to be the subject of legislation, although initiatives were first taken at a purely local level. Vagrancy and begging had been endemic in Britain, as in all agrarian societies, from time immemorial, Christian charity being the essential remedy. By the sixteenth century, however, population growth and the beginning of rural depopulation transformed poverty in towns from a fact of life into a potential social problem. In response, local governments began to adopt broadly similar policy responses. Parish councils and Justices of the Peace began to levy taxes or 'poor-rates' on residents, and the monies so raised were employed to support the local poor. The form of relief depended upon the classification of the pauper; thus the old and infirm were sheltered in almshouses, the insane were placed in asylums, the able-bodied were provided with employment, the young were offered training, and the indolent (those refusing employment) were punished in 'houses of correction'. Rowse (1950) notes that both Ipswich and Norwich had such institutional structures in place and operating by 1570. Equivalent institutions in London were functioning even earlier, and the names of London's asylum for the insane – Bedlam – and its house of correction – the Bridewell – became generic. Such local initiatives became the models for national policy, as established in a series of parliamentary statutes culminating in the Poor Law Act of 1601.

The Elizabethan, or 'Old', Poor Law survived essentially unchanged for two centuries and it is worth noting that its philosophy appears remarkably modern. First, it acknowledges that the support of the poor is the responsibility of the community and, second, it recognises that poverty has a diversity of causes necessitating a diversity of solutions. Inflation was added to the list of diverse causes in 1795, following the widespread adoption of a system of relief first implemented by the Justices of Speenhamland, Berkshire. Quite simply, the Speenhamland system guaranteed 'every poor and industrious man' a minimum income related both to the price of bread and to the number of household dependants, with earned wages being supplemented by disbursements from the poor rate revenue where necessary (in Birch, 1974, p. 86). In essence, this is the modern system of Family Credit, although benefits in the latter are not index linked.

The period following the Napoleonic War was characterised by rising prices, rapid population growth and political disturbance. Concerned with the situation, and especially its association with poverty and poverty relief, the government of the day instituted a Royal Commission to investigate the workings of the Old Poor Law. Philosophically, the 1832 Commission was utilitarian, and the resulting 1834 Poor Law Amendment Act – the New Poor Law – reflected this ideology. Two changes of principle were incorporated into the new Act. First, the administration of poverty relief was removed from the hands of existing local government and entrusted to Boards of Guardians. The authority of each Board extended over a group or Union of parishes, and Boards were themselves subject to the authority of a central government body, the Poor Law Commission. The intention was to reduce local corruption, incompetence and inefficiency, and to encourage cross-national uniformity of practice. Second, whilst assistance to orphans, the elderly and the infirm was to continue much as before, the treatment of the able-bodied poor became governed by the principle of 'less eligibility'. As the receipt of state welfare benefits was presumed to have a disincentive effect on labour effort, the quantity and quality of assistance made available to the claimant was intended to leave him or her in circumstances overtly inferior to those resulting from employment. As a means of enforcing this principle, public assistance was made conditional upon the claimant's entry into the 'workhouse', the house of correction formerly reserved for the indolent.

The increased centralisation of the administration of poverty relief was intended to facilitate the monitoring of standards, although the inspectorate was given neither the authority nor the resources necessary to fulfil its task. In consequence, the quality of poverty relief at the local level remained variable. Some Unions, anxious to minimise the costs of poverty relief, consigned *all* their poor to a general workhouse, in contravention of the 1834 Act. The exposure of conditions in the Andover workhouse in 1846, and *The Lancet*'s report on the sick poor of London in 1865, shocked even the hardened public opinion of Victorian times. In other cases, however, Unions maintained the earlier and less penal system of relief outside the workhouse, simply because they found it cheaper to do so. In the most prosperous areas, where the tax base was high and the incidence of poverty low, the poor found themselves in receipt of relatively humane treatment (Rose, 1972).

Even as the New Poor Law was being implemented, a range of further measures were initiated which served to broaden considerably the scope of Victorian social policy. The first Factory Act regulating conditions and hours of work for women and children had been passed in 1802. A Royal Commission into perceived abuses of this Act resulted in a more stringent statute in 1833, and further Acts followed in 1844, 1847, 1853 and 1878. Each was designed both to improve conditions further (most notably, to effect reductions in hours of work) and to close loopholes which employers had managed to find in preceding Acts. Public health became the object of government policy in 1848, with the passing of the first Public Health Act, prompted by a cholera epidemic and two detailed official reports on health conditions in the 1840s. Under this Act, local Boards of Health were given responsibility for water supply and the cleansing of streets. Prior to 1875, towns such as Liverpool and Glasgow had petitioned Parliament for permission to clear and rebuild their slums and insanitary areas.

The passing of the Artisans' Dwelling Act in that year, however, granted explicit clearance permission to all local authorities.

In 1833, Roebuck proposed to the House of Commons 'that the education of the people is a matter of national concern; that, as such, it ought to be the object of the most immediate, continued and sedulous attention on the part of the Legislature'. A grant of £20 000 was voted, although not without considerable opposition; William Cobbett opined that the sole benefit of the expansion of public education would be to 'increase the number of schoolmasters and schoolmistresses – that new race of idlers' (in Evans, 1978, pp. 89–90). Likewise, the 1839 Whig initiative to establish teacher training, to centralise the administration of education and to establish an inspectorate provoked a hostile response, especially from the Tories and the established Church who felt that the latter should be entrusted with the monopoly. Opinions were very soon changed, however, and the Elementary Education Act of 1870 empowered local Schools Boards to provide elementary education, financed by a combination of fees and local and central government funds. Subsequent Acts made school attendance compulsory for children aged between 5 and 10 years (1880) and virtually free (1891).

Economists frequently construe the nineteenth century as the 'age of *laissez-faire*', largely because the period coincides with the formal articulation of a pro-market economic ideology on the part theorists such as Ricardo and Malthus. However, it is more accurate to interpret the social reforms of the period as the triumph of utilitarianism, a philosophy which recognised both the virtues of capitalist efficiency and vices of market failure. To remedy the latter, self-help had to be complemented by collective action in the form of a strong but benevolent government. The progress of utilitarian social reforms was greatly assisted by government paternalism, especially amongst the Tory faction, and by the efforts of tireless individuals – Edwin Chadwick, for example, was a Factory, a Poor Law and a Board of Health Commissioner. As noted above, opposition to reform was never absent; indeed Lord Melbourne, the Home Secretary at the time of the New Poor Law, was quite convinced that all Benthamites were fools (Roberts, 1960).

From the point of view of welfare administration, the social reforms of the nineteenth century created a framework which we can recognise today. First, although social reform proceeded in a piecemeal fashion, regulation in all areas became centralised. By the mid-1850s, the central government had established inspectorates for the Poor Law, asylums, charities, factories, prisons, the constabulary, education and public health. Second, a series of Acts towards the end of the nineteenth century created a system of local government with social responsibilities. In 1871, the administration of the Poor Law passed to the Local Government Board. The Act of 1888 established sixty-two administrative counties and sixty county boroughs, each with a defined range of tasks, including public health, education and public works. This administrative structure survived largely unchanged until 1974.

II

The so-called 'Liberal Welfare Reforms' of 1906–14 were a product of distinct pressures which had been building up over the previous half-century. These pressures were many and various. First, the gradual extension of the franchise brought matters affecting the mass of the population onto the political agenda. Although neither of the principal political parties – Liberal and Conservative – appeared to espouse social reform openly during the nineteenth century (possibly for fear of precipitating electoral competition over welfare legislation), the 1906 general election did return twenty-nine Members of Parliament for whom such reform was deemed vital; these individuals subsequently formed themselves into the Labour Party. Second, public attitudes towards poverty were modified as a result of the cumulative marshalling of evidence. The experience of recruiting soldiers for the Boer War, for example, suggested that poverty and ill health were far more prevalent than had been supposed, even amongst social groups not statutorily considered to be paupers. Third, the decrease in Britain's economic fortunes relative to the newly industrialising nations such as the United States and Germany towards the end of the nineteenth century caused widespread political concern, and the view accordingly emerged that support for the less advantaged might be seen less as a drain on consumption resources and more as an investment in labour. A better fed, better educated and healthier workforce could contribute towards the enhancement of national efficiency. Fourth, self-help institutions such as friendly societies amongst groups of workers had already evolved spontaneously, and these provided a

model for government policy. Regular subscription to these
societies enabled individuals to claim in times of unemployment or
when it was necessary to purchase a course of medical treatment.
Finally, some politicians who supported the reforms were evidently driven by a philosophy which accepted that a function of the
state in a market economy was the guarantee of economic security.
Others were more pragmatic, accepting social reform to forestall
social revolution (Hay, 1975).

The Liberal reforms were concerned with several areas of social
policy. With respect to children, local authorities were empowered
to provide school meals for the needy (1906) and to introduce
regular medical inspections (1907). The 1908 Children Act made
the willful neglect of children by parents a punishable offence. In
the same year, the Old Age Pensions Act provided non-
contributory pensions to the elderly poor. In his 1909 Budget
speech, Lloyd George announced his intention of introducing,
first, voluntary labour exchanges to improve the efficiency of the
labour market, second, a fund to finance public works during times
of generalised economic depression, and third, a limited scheme of
unemployment insurance. The first two were enacted in that year,
although unemployment insurance had to wait until the 1911
National Insurance Act, when it was combined with health insurance. In exchange for a regular premium, paid into the National
Insurance Fund jointly by employer and employee, certain classes
of worker could obtain financial benefits to cover periods of unemployment and the purchase of medical care.

Although they embody the rudiments of the welfare state of
today, it is incorrect to interpret the Liberal reforms as completely
radical. First, they were far from novel in inspiration, countries
such as Germany and New Zealand having already introduced
state insurance schemes. Second, the reforms ran, at least initially,
in parallel with the earlier Poor Law structures. The workhouse as
a potential repository for the poor in general was not abandoned
until the Local Government Act of 1929 (whereby the work of the
Guardians was transferred to Public Assistance Committees of
local authorities) and was only fully eliminated in 1948 (Thane,
1978). Finally, the reforms were essentially limited in scope and
further legislation was necessary to broaden their applications.
The first national scheme of *contributory* pensions, for example,
was introduced in 1925. Although unemployment insurance cover-

age was extended in the 1920 Act it soon became clear that the Insurance Fund was incapable of dealing with the permanently high levels of unemployment being experienced during the economic depression. A series of piecemeal amendments was enacted and the consolidating 1934 Unemployment Act finally separated unemployment insurance from support for the long-term unemployed. With respect to the former, contributions to the Fund became the equal responsibility of worker, employer and government. As regards the latter, benefits were to be paid from the Consolidated Tax Fund and entitlement was to be assessed with respect to household need.

Housing was a particular focus of social policy during the interwar period. The Housing and Town Planning Act of 1919 embodied some important changes of principle with respect to earlier legislation. Local authorities were given the duty, as opposed to the facility, of remedying housing deficiencies by public building programmes, subsidised if necessary by central government. An Act of 1923 gave financial incentives to the private sector to expand the scale of house-building, whilst the Act of 1924 increased the local authority grant on condition that it was employed to build homes to be let at controlled rents subsidised from local revenues (rent control had been introduced as an emergency measure during the First World War). As a direct consequence of these Acts, more than 3 million homes were built between the wars (Sleeman, 1973).

III

As Barr (1987) notes, the '1945 Labour government was armed with a large Parliamentary majority and a stack of White Papers, many of which had met with Conservative approval during the wartime coalition' (p. 30). The 1943 White Paper on education, for example, proposed the creation of a Ministry for Education responsible for ensuring that local authorities provided free primary and secondary education for all until the age of 15 years. In 1944, three other White Papers appeared, relating to national insurance, employment policy and a national health service. The first proposed the harmonisation of insurable poverty relief into a single contributory system and drew heavily on arguments advanced by William Beveridge (UK, 1942; Cmd 6404), the novelty of the proposals being the consolidation of earlier piecemeal methods into a coherent strategy. The second was strongly influenced by the economics of John Maynard Keynes and proposed that governments commit themselves to the maintenance of economic stability and full employment, if necessary by means of deficit financing. The third White Paper envisaged the universal provision of free medical care, to be financed from general taxation.

The proposals for education and health care were rapidly translated into the 1944 Education Act and 1946 National Health Service Act, respectively. Those pertaining to insurance were implemented in the National Insurance Act of 1946, whereby contributing parties were eligible for flat-rate benefits in cases of unemployment, maternity, sickness, widowhood and retirement, a death grant to cover funeral expenses also being available. Coverage was to be compulsory and contributions were to be flat rate. Entitlements to benefits in the event of industrial injury were covered by a separate Act of the same year. The 1948 National Assistance Act created a safety net for those whose needs were not met by the insurance schemes. It established a National Assistance Board to provide means-tested benefits for those not in employment, thereby taking over the residual functions of the local Public Assistance Committees. The 1948 Act also formally repealed the Poor Law which had, in one form or another, been on the statute books for some 350 years.

Although many individuals were ultimately responsible for the shape of the post-war welfare state it is impossible to ignore the specific contributions of Beveridge's administrative theories and Keynes' economics. George and Wilding (1976) label both writers as 'reluctant collectivists' and the designation is appropriate. Each described himself as a Liberal and saw his theories as bringing to the operation of a capitalist society the necessary moral or economic constraints to permit that society to continue to function. Without such constraints, each felt, capitalism would break down owing to a variety of market failures – demand deficiency, production inefficiency, severe income inequality – and the political and economic benefits of market society would be lost. Thus Beveridge: 'We want to have free competition upwards; we decline to allow free competition to run downwards', and Keynes: 'The important thing for government is not to do things which individuals are doing already, and to do them a little better or a little worse; but to do those things which are not done at all' (ibid., pp. 54, 58). It is accordingly not unreasonable to see the welfare state of Keynes and Beveridge as 'an unequivocal attempt to patch up capitalism' (Whynes, 1985, p. 99).

It is still possible to recognise the hands of Keynes and Beveridge in the welfare state of today, although numerous legislative changes have eroded some of the original principles. As early as 1951, consumer charges for prescriptions were introduced into the health service, causing the resignation of the Minister, although the market made few other inroads until relatively recently. In the 1960s, insurance contributions became earnings related, as a response to the revenue limitations imposed by the flat rate system and the 1975 Social Security Act created the basis for a new pensions scheme, intended to achieve maturity by the end of the present century. In the same year, tax relief for dependent children was replaced by a flat rate and universal Child Benefit payment. A discussion of these and other recent changes, however, is more properly reserved for the remaining chapters of this book.

1.4 THE MAJOR THEMES OF THE BOOK

The next four chapters discuss efficiency aspects of cash benefits. Atkinson (Chapter 2) looks at technical problems in private insurance markets, a major result of which is to make risks like unemployment uninsurable. He goes on to set out what is, at least in part, an efficiency case for social insurance. Barr (Chapter 3) discusses the economics of pension provision. Here, too, an important uninsurable risk, inflation, gives an efficiency argument for state intervention. Whynes (Chapter 4) discusses how the need to contain the costs of poverty relief may (among other ill effects) create adverse incentives. Dustmann and Micklewright (Chapter 5) look in more detail at the incentive effects of cash benefits.

Chapters 6 and 7 discuss two key sets of equity issues. In Chapter 6, Piachaud explains the difficulties surrounding the definition and measurement of poverty and inequality. Jones and Posnett (Chapter 7) discuss attempts by economists to explain private charitable giving, a complementary transfer mechanism to government spending.

The remaining three chapters look specifically at benefits in kind. In Chapter 8, Culyer outlines a series of technical problems in the markets for health care and for medical insurance, and goes on to discuss attempts to introduce more competition into the National Health Service. Glennerster (Chapter 9) sets out the evolution of the economics of education since the mid-1950s and also assesses, *inter alia*, recent attempts to encourage more competition in the provision of education. MacLennan and Gibb (Chapter 10) review the economics of the housing market, examine the case for government intervention and appraise recent UK policy initiatives.

1.4.1 Common themes

A number of common threads run through the chapters. The overall analytical conclusion is the extent to which the issues raised by the welfare state fit very naturally into the conventional social welfare maximisation framework. Coherent policy formation is obliged to confront three sets of problems. *Imperfect information* may rule out the use of unrestricted private markets. *Problems of definition and measurement* can make it difficult or impossible to describe what is happening or to assess the effects of different policies. *Conflicting aims* mean that policy often has to be a compromise.

Imperfect information may give rise to either inefficiencies in existing markets or to missing markets. The latter arise particularly in respect of insurance against unemployment (Chapter 2), of inflation in the context of pensions (Chapter 3), and of important medical risks (Chapter 8). In other areas, imperfect information does not make private provision impossible, but inefficient. For instance, private insurers may be badly informed about the extent to which, if insurance pays the entire cost of medical treatment, doctors will prescribe more than the efficient quantity of treatment. This type of third-party payment problem is discussed in Chapter 8.

Problems of definition and measurement abound. How do we define a poverty line (objective 4, *supra*)? How large a drop in living standard is 'unacceptable' (objective 5)? The appropriate extent of vertical redistribution and a workable definition of horizontal equity (objectives 7 and 8) have been an ongoing debate between economists, and have plagued policy-makers for centuries. Even 'equality' is difficult to define unambiguously (Okun, 1975), especially in the context of benefits in kind like health care (Le Grand, 1982). These definitional problems are the principal concerns of Chapter 6.

Concepts like 'dignity', 'stigma' and 'social solidarity' (objectives 9 and 10) are hard to define and raise major measurement problems. Writers like Hayek (1976) argue in addition that the term 'social solidarity' is devoid of meaning, and that its pursuit is both pointless and dangerous.

Measurement problems arise in many ways. Efficiency objectives (1–3) have precise analytical definitions, but measurement problems such as the incidence of taxes, contributions and benefits, make it difficult to assess how far they are achieved. A key difficulty in assessing poverty is an inability to measure income flows *within* households. Benefit replacement rates (an important variable in assessing the incentive effects of benefits) are hard to measure (Chapter 5), not least because of the complexity of benefit formulae and the diversity of individual circumstance. Other data are not collected simply because of the expense of doing so (e.g. there are few longitudinal surveys of individuals).

Other difficulties make statistical estimation difficult. The presence of unobserved characteristics hinders estimation of the incentive effects of benefits (Chapter 5) and of models of charitable giving (Chapter 7). The screening problem (discussed in Chapter 9) arises because of the difficulty of establishing a causal link between post-primary education and individual productivity.

Many of the objectives of the welfare state are either potentially or inherently in conflict. The trade-off between efficiency and distributional objectives, and between horizontal equity and administrative simplicity are well known. Other objectives are almost inherently in conflict. Income smoothing implies that an individual with higher earnings should receive higher benefits, which is not easily compatible with the objective that benefits should be redistributive from rich to poor, and with the objective that benefits should contribute to social solidarity. On one interpretation of equity everyone should receive benefits related to their past contributions (e.g. actuarial pensions, as discussed in Chapter 4), but that, again, conflicts with the aim of redistribution to the less well off.

In practice there is an important trade off between targeting benefits tightly (in the pursuit of macro efficiency) on the one hand, and minimising labour-supply incentives, on the other. Thus greater selectivity, a major objective of government policy in the 1980s (see Chapter 3 section 3.5) and increased means testing (Chapter 4) go hand in hand, but conflict with other objectives. The choice of objectives and of priorities between them is one of the key normative issues in debates about the welfare state. Often a criticism of the welfare state is criticism not of the institution but of the chosen objectives.

1.4.2 Policy implications

Taken as a whole, the chapters suggest a number of overarching policy conclusions.

1. *Social insurance* is a widespread response to pervasive market failure (Chapters 2 and 3). By dealing with the gaps inherent in private insurance, it makes universal coverage possible.
2. *The role of incentives*: policy should go with rather than against the grain of incentives. This is particularly important in framing regulations. Rent control, for example, may give landlords incentives to reduce the quantity and/or quality of rented accommodation, thus defeating the object of the policy.
3. *The role of regulation*: a major justification for regulation is consumer protection in technically complex areas. Thus there is a major role for the state in regulating the conduct of private pension funds (Chapter 3) (similar arguments apply, more generally, to banking and other financial institutions). Regulation of medical training, and of the production and sale of medicines is justified for the same reason. Controls over medical spending are essential for a different reason – cost containment (Chapter 8). If well designed, such controls can combine universal coverage (i.e. horizontal equity) with cost containment (the macro efficiency objective).
4. *Taking a global view*: the range of technical problems, due largely to information problems, in the various parts of the welfare state requires a *strategy*, not just a collection of *ad hoc* policies. Successful strategies recognise the incentives faced by individuals and institutions, and use the government's power to

intervene if that is the most effective way of counteracting adverse incentives. Intervention can involve one or more of regulation, finance, public production or income transfers. The problem for policy design is to choose the right type of intervention, and to design the specific intervention so that it achieves its desired objective.

5. *The absence of any complete solution*: if there are no market failures, private markets *are* immensely efficient: they allow immense amounts of decentralised information to be processed at very little cost; the result, in certain, well-defined circumstances, is an efficient outcome. Precisely because markets can be so efficient, where market failures are serious, even the best-designed package of intervention has limitations. There is no such thing as a completely efficient system. As the discussions in Chapters 8 and 9 make clear, the greater the extent of market failure, the greater the problem for policy design.

2 Private and Social Insurance, and the Contributory Principle

A. B. ATKINSON*

2.1 INTRODUCTION

Social insurance has been widely regarded as the cornerstone of modern income maintenance policy. In most OECD countries social insurance accounts for the greater part of government spending on social security, and it is seen as fundamental to the prevention of poverty. Yet social insurance has come increasingly under attack.

Major attacks have come from two different directions. First, there are those concerned that the present system of income maintenance is failing to provide adequate support to those with low incomes. For example, in the case of the elderly, it is argued that the social insurance system makes generous provision for the pensioners of the twenty-first century but still leaves many of today's old people below the poverty line. What is needed, on this view, is to replace social insurance by a *basic income guarantee* which provides benefits which are linked to old age and not to previous contribution conditions. This line of argument is often linked to a desire to integrate the social security and income tax systems, with attention being drawn to the fact that tax expendi-

* This chapter first appeared as chapter 7 of A. B. Atkinson (1989) *Poverty and Social Security* (Hemel Hempstead: Harvester Wheatsheaf). Permission to republish is gratefully acknowledged.

tures (e.g. on higher tax allowances for the aged) perform a similar function to that of social security benefits and that the money could be more effectively allocated in a unified system.

The second, quite different, direction of attack is from those, like the British Conservative government from 1979, aiming to reduce state expenditure on income maintenance. If there is a constraint on total government spending, then, it is argued, *income-tested benefits* provide 'better value for money', targeting the payments to those most in need. Similarly, state expenditure could be reduced if social insurance were to be replaced by *private insurance*. Such a switch to private provision would, it is suggested, offer people greater choice and freedom, and provide benefits more efficiently. This is, therefore, a twin-pronged attack, with both income-testing and privatisation being advanced to replace social insurance.

In this chapter, I first describe the essential feature of the three methods of state income support: basic incomes, social insurance (and its relation to private insurance) and income-tested assistance. The next section of the chapter reviews the importance of these three methods in the development over this century of the income maintenance system in the UK. I then consider in section 2.4 the arguments which can be advanced for and against alternatives to social insurance, considering in turn private insurance, a return to income testing, and replacement of social insurance by a basic income scheme.

2.2 DEFINITIONS

2.2.1 Basic incomes

The definition of a basic income scheme is the simplest. Each person would receive a basic benefit which would be independent of income and differentiated according to only a small number of categories. The distinctions would include age, long-term disability and, possibly, householder status. They would *not* include employment status, the basic benefit being paid at the same rate to those out of work through unemployment or sickness as to those in work. It is typically envisaged that the introduction of the basic benefit scheme would be accompanied by the abolition of tax allowances. The basic benefits may indeed be seen as the 'cashing-out' of tax allowances, in just the way that Child Benefit in the UK replaced both an earlier Social Security Benefit and income tax allowances for children. All income apart from the basic benefits would then be subject to tax.

The relatively simple form of the basic benefit provides a bench-mark against which we can compare the two forms which have been used more extensively in practice: social insurance and income-tested assistance.

2.2.2 Social insurance

Social insurance benefits are similar to basic incomes in that they are not in general directly related to current income, but they differ in two significant respects. First, they are usually related to employment status, the purpose of the benefit being to replace (at least in part) lost earnings. Thus, the national insurance pension in the UK is a *retirement* pension and (for the first five years after the minimum retirement age) is conditional on retirement. The national insurance benefits for contingencies such as sickness and unemployment are *alternatives* to work income. The second difference is that payment of benefits is typically linked in some way to contributions paid (and may in this way be related to past income). Receipt of a national insurance pension is conditional on having contributed a minimum period during one's working life; eligibility for national insurance unemployment benefit depends on previous work history.

This contributory feature brings us to the question of the relationship between private and social insurance, a matter about which there is disagreement. There are those who argue that social insurance is simply private insurance run by the state, and that therefore it could be just as well, or better, run as private insurance (arguments which are discussed in section 2.4). Others claim that social insurance is a myth and that replacement by income-tested or basic benefits would make no difference.

That social insurance is different in fundamental respects from private insurance was clearly recognised by Beveridge, who said early in his report *Social Insurance and Allied Services* (UK, 1942, pp. 12–13) that:

while adjustment of premiums to risks is of the essence of voluntary insurance . . . this adjustment is not essential in insurance which is made compulsory by the power of the State . . . it is necessary in voluntary insurance to fund contributions . . . The State with its power of compelling successive generations of citizens to become insured and its powers of taxation is not under the necessity of accumulating reserves.

That is, social insurance does not necessarily provide an actuarily fair return to each person and there does not have to be funding. As Beveridge observed, the second issue is one 'of financial practice only', an insight which does not seem to be shared by the British Conservative government. (At the same time as it is worrying about the burden of state pensions to future generations, it is reducing the net worth of the public sector by selling public sector assets to finance tax cuts.)

The first distinction – the departure from actuarily fair individual insurance – has two aspects. First, social insurance does not involve a strict matching of contributions and benefits. It may, for example, embody a degree of redistribution *ex ante*, with lower paid workers obtaining a better deal than the higher paid. Secondly, the contract may be less tightly drawn. A private sector insurance policy specifies the contingencies and the benefits and these cannot in general be varied. A social insurance scheme has more flexibility. The government may vary the terms, eliminating or reducing benefits, or adding and improving them, particularly to cover needs which were not previously envisaged. Social insurance offers less certainty, but in recompense it offers the protection of what the French call 'solidarity', a term which was actually used in the government White Paper on Social Insurance: 'concrete expression is thus given to the solidarity and unity of the nation' (Minister of Reconstruction, 1944, p. 6). Or, as it was put by Beveridge, 'the term social insurance . . . implies both that it is compulsory and that men stand together with their fellows' (UK, 1942, p. 13).

2.2.3 Income-tested assistance

Income-tested benefits may, like social insurance, be related to employment status. Thus Income Support in Britain provides for those not in employment; and, conversely, Family Credit is only paid to families in work. But, unlike social insurance, eligibility for assistance, and the amount received, are dependent on current income. Income Support provides for those whose income would otherwise fall below a prescribed level, the payment being sufficient to bring people up to this level. Family Credit is reduced by 70p for each £1 increase in net income above a specified threshold, until entitlement is lost altogether. Housing benefit depends on the amount of housing costs and on family income.

Now it may be argued that this dependence on income is in fact no different from the combination of basic benefit and the taxation of income. Both present the individual or family with a budget constraint, and in principle any such budget constraint may be represented by a basic benefit (intercept) and a tax schedule. Formally, this is correct, but it ignores the differences in the way in which the schedule is affected and perceived – by both government and the citizen. From the standpoint of the government, the basic income scheme presents a clear set of choices with regard to the generosity of benefits on the one hand, and the tax structure on the other. In contrast, discussion of income-tested schemes typically confounds the two aspects (as where variations in the levels of benefit change the marginal tax rates of recipients) and separates the treatment of rich and poor (implicit marginal tax rates are enacted for the poor which would not be acceptable under the income tax).

From the standpoint of the recipient, an important feature of income-tested benefits is that they involve a separate and distinct administrative procedure. Under income-tested assistance, the person has to make a claim and has to provide proof of income; under the basic income neither step would be required. Such a separate administrative machinery may be a regrettable necessity. If many of the intended beneficiaries do not file income tax returns, then information about their incomes may not be available centrally; nor could the government agency identify potential claimants and inform them of their rights. On the other hand, some advocates of income testing see the separate administration as serving a positive function of deterring claimants, applying the principle of 'less eligibility'. These aspects are discussed in section 2.4.2.

2.3 THE UK EXPERIENCE

What role has been played at different times by these different types of benefit? An ILO report on the development of social security described a stylised model of its historical evolution:

> First was an era of paternalism: private charity and public poor relief provided for the poor, being often subject to harsh conditions which imposed stigma. Second was an era of social insurance : . . wider compulsory programmes were developed covering more and more occupations and more and more contingencies . . . In the third stage . . . the range of services is being extended with the aim of maintaining and enhancing the quality of life. (International Labour Office, 1984, p. 17)

How far does such a pattern of development describe the history of the UK? As was noted by Beveridge, 'since the beginning of the present century . . . there has been a strong movement against the form and spirit of the old poor law' (UK, 1942, p. 211). In part, this move took the form of replacing the Old Poor Law by more acceptable forms of income testing. The Old Age Pensions Act 1908 provided old age pensions which were means tested (and non-contributory) but destitution was not a condition. The Unemployment Act 1934 centralised the administration of assistance to the unemployed in the new Unemployment Assistance Board and the same body took over the payment of means-tested supplementary pensions under the Old Age and Widows' Pensions Act 1940.

But a major part of the change was the replacement of income-tested assistance by social insurance. The introduction of national insurance in the 1911 Act was the first step in Britain – long behind Bismarck's welfare system in Germany – towards replacing the Poor Law by contributory benefits. These covered unemployment (for certain trades) and sickness benefit administered by the approved friendly societies. The Contributory Pensions Act 1925 brought in contributory pensions of a non-means-tested kind and introduced widows' pensions.

As a result, the proportion of the benefit expenditure accounted for by social insurance increased over the first forty years of this century, as is shown in Figure 2.1, which is derived from the Beveridge report. In 1900, public assistance accounted for almost all of the expenditure (apart from workmen's compensation). By the end of the period, it accounted for just 10 per cent. If we add the 'new' income-tested benefits of unemployment assistance, non-contributory pensions and blind persons' assistance, then the total reaches 32.6 per cent. The picture is one of a growth of social insurance and a decline of income testing.

The intention of Beveridge was to take this further, extending the scope of national insurance and making its coverage universal. He stressed the 'strength of popular objection to any kind of means test' (UK, 1942, p. 12) and the aim of the plan was to reduce dependence on assistance. At the same time, Beveridge saw as a precondition for the success of his plan the introduction of a basic benefit for children – family allowances. So that for the first time, we had on a major scale a form of income support which was neither social insurance nor income-tested assistance (nor war-related).

The government did not accept the Beveridge proposals in full, but the broad thrust of a move to non-means-tested benefits was agreed. This is brought out in the table in the 1944 White Paper *Social Insurance* which shows the estimated effects in 1945 of the post-Beveridge proposals (1944, table V). The share of social insurance was to rise from 66.1 to 74.6 per cent, and the new family allowances would account for 11.9 per cent. As a result, means-tested benefits would fall from 33.9 to 13.5 per cent. Moreover, this fall was projected to continue to 1975, with social insurance accounting for 82 per cent in that year (1944, table VI).

The percentages in Figure 2.2 show what in fact happened. They are not fully comparable with those in Figure 2.1, nor with those just quoted, but they are sufficient to show that what transpired, even during the first twenty-five years up to 1969/70, was not entirely according to script. Basic benefits did indeed become sizeable at the outset, but fell over time as a percentage; this was due to the fact that family allowances failed to rise in line with other benefits (and to the reduced importance of war pensions,

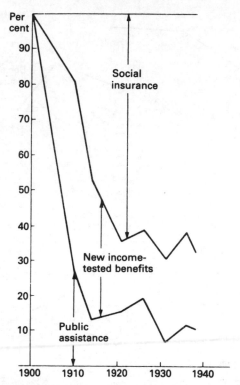

FIGURE 2.1 Share in social security spending 1900/1–1938/9

Source: UK (1942), p. 214.
Note: The figures do not include war pensions, which I have classified
as a basic benefit. These were at their highest after the First World
War, when they amounted to £105 million (Peacock and Wiseman,
1967, p. 168). Adding the figures for 1921 to those used in Fig. 2.1
would have shown war pensions as accounting for 46.9 per cent of the
total. By 1938, the expenditure had fallen to £39 million, and as a
fraction of the total it was 14.3 per cent.

included under this head, as time went on). There was some
expansion of social insurance, as more pensioners became eligible,
but the role of national assistance, the means-tested scheme, did
not die away. In 1949 there were 1.1 million payments being made
each week; in 1969/70 there were 2.7 million. As a percentage of the
total expenditure, national assistance increased, rather than fell.

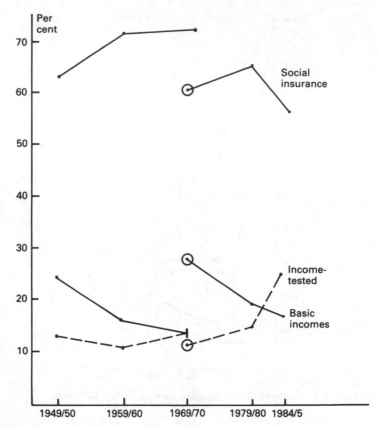

FIGURE 2.2   Share in total social security spending 1949/50–1984–5
Source: Department of Health and Social Security (1985a),
Background Papers. HMSO, Cmnd 9519, table 2.3, and own
calculations.

Notes:
a. There is a break between the figures for 1969/70 and 1979/80 on
   account of the introduction of Child Benefit, which replaced both
   family allowances (previously included) and child income tax
   allowances (not previously included). The alternative figures for
   1969/70 (circled) include estimates of the tax expenditure cost of child tax
   allowances based on that for 1968/9. Other changes in the benefit structure
   have not been allowed for, but are smaller in magnitude.
b. The figures do not include rate rebates. If these were included, then
   the percentages for 1984/5 and 1979/80 would become 55.3 per cent
   and 65.0 per cent for social insurance, 28.3 per cent and 15.7 per
   cent for income-tested benefits and 16.4 per cent and 19.3 per cent
   for basic incomes. Figures for earlier years would be little changed.

After 1969/70 several things happened. One was that the switch to Child Benefit made the figures no longer comparable, since a major part of the expenditure on the new Child Benefit was a cashing out of the tax expenditure on child tax allowances. The latter not being public expenditure was not included in the social security figures. For this reason I have made an approximate estimate of the figure for 1969/70 including the cost of the tax allowances; this is shown by the circled points. From this it is clear that it would be misleading to regard the figures as a continuous series. Taking the circled points and then those for 1979/80, we can see that the gradual upward trend in income-tested benefits became quite marked after 1979/80, when Mrs Thatcher took office. Basic benefits declined, despite the introduction in the 1970s of several new benefits for the disabled, such as the attendance allowance, the mobility allowance and the severe disablement allowance. What is more, after 1979/80 social insurance too began to decline, the rate of fall being quite steep.

What we are witnessing, therefore, is the reversal of the historical trend. The pattern of social security development in the UK is not moving on to a third stage, but is regressing to the first stage of income-tested assistance.

This regression has taken two main forms. The first is the introduction of new income-tested benefits. The family income supplement (now Family Credit) was a new income-tested benefit introduced in 1971. Rate rebates were brought in in 1966 and substantially extended in 1974. Rent rebates had been available to local authority tenants for many years, but were extended to other tenants in 1973, and the scheme made universal, so that the numbers in receipt increased very greatly. The second form of regression has been the greater reliance on existing income-tested benefits, notably Supplementary Benefit and Income Support, the successive renamings of national assistance. The restrictions on national insurance benefits, and the abolition of earnings-related supplements to unemployment and sickness benefits – together with the rise in unemployment – have meant that more families have had to rely on income-tested assistance.

This process was further accelerated by the changes in policy following the 1985 review of social security (Department of Health and Social Security, 1985a and b), which has set the course firmly in the direction of greater means testing. This affects people from cradle to grave. At birth, the universal maternity grant has been abolished and payments made only to low-income families via the Social Fund. For children, from 1988 the income-tested benefit has been extended and renamed Family Credit. The state earnings-related pension scheme, introduced in 1978 with the intention of reducing dependence on income-tested assistance in old age, has been scaled down: for example, the additional pension is calculated on 20 rather than 25 per cent of average earnings, and the average is to be taken over the whole of the lifetime rather than the best twenty years. Widows and widowers are to inherit only half of their spouse's pension. The universal death grant has been replaced by payments restricted to those with low incomes.

Finally, the government has also moved further in the direction of *private* as opposed to state pension provision. The scaling down of the state earnings-related pension scheme, for example, has been accompanied by fiscal and other incentives provided to encourage private provision. Similarly, there has been a transfer to employers of the obligation to pay sick pay for the first twenty-eight weeks of illness and to provide maternity pay.

2.4   ALTERNATIVES TO SOCIAL INSURANCE

2.4.1   Private insurance

This brings me to the first of the comparisons I want to make – that between social and private insurance. There are, of course, many more issues here than I can possibly cover in this chapter. Part of the message is indeed that the questions are more complex than they are sometimes portrayed. (For discussion of some of the issues not covered here, see, among others, Diamond, 1977; and Creedy and Disney, 1985.)

One of the sources of complexity is that the contingencies covered by social insurance are very varied. This should be borne in mind when considering the simple example chosen to illustrate the analysis. This is the case of sickness, where a worker has a probability p of being unable through illness to work and a probability $(1 - p)$ that he earns a wage w. In both cases he receives income from capital equal to k. We abstract from moral hazard considerations by assuming that malingering is not possible (this may involve administrative costs which I shall come to). Sickness insurance is represented as the person receiving $w(1 - \varrho) + k$ if well, where ϱ is the premium rate and $b + k$ if sick, where b is the benefit rate net of the premium. The purpose of taking this highly stylised example is to illustrate some of the issues involved; it is, however, evident that many important considerations are not captured by its assumptions.

We can plot the incomes in the two states ('work' and 'sickness') in a diagram (Figure 2.3). Starting from the no-insurance point (giving $w + k$ in work and k in sickness), if the insurance is actuarily fair, and there are no administrative costs, then $(1 - p)$ $\varrho w = pb$ and insurance allows the person to move along the dotted line with slope $- p / (1 - p)$. How much insurance people

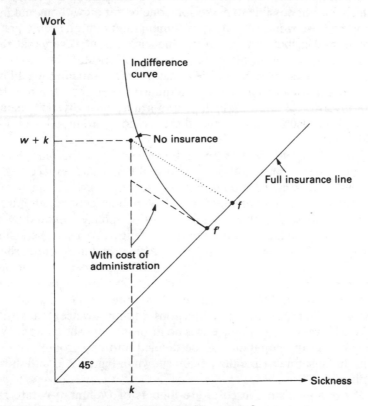

FIGURE 2.3 Insurance against sickness example

would buy depends on their preferences. Suppose that people are expected utility maximisers and that the utility of income is the same in both states: i.e. they maximise

$$(1 - p) \, U[w(1 - \varrho) + k] + p \, U[b + k]$$

If the person is risk-averse (i.e. U is strictly concave), then the point chosen will be f on the 45° line, giving full insurance, and this will be true regardless of the precise form of U (for all U the slope of the indifference curve is $- p \, / \, (1 - p)$ on the 45° line).

The basis for the argument in favour of privatisation of insurance has not always been made fully explicit, particularly the extent of its reliance on the theorems of welfare economics. If the latter are indeed the basis, then the argument is that market competition leads to a Pareto-efficient allocation, an allocation in which it is not possible to make someone better off without making someone else worse off, and government intervention is only justifiable on distributional grounds. One suspects, however, that the case for privatisation often has a less 'sophisticated' foundation, resting, for example, on the view that private companies would be better organised and have lower administrative costs. Or it may be the diversity of choice which is important, such diversity being valued in itself even where there is no gain in allocational efficiency.

The case in terms of administrative costs is important. Even though these considerations are usually ignored in economic analysis, they may be quantitatively as important as the dead-weight loss and other elements on which public economics tends to focus. Suppose that there is a fixed cost per policy, denoted by a, collected by deducting a/p from the benefit paid. Then the insurance cover offers the options shown in Figure 2.3 by the dashed line. Whether the full insurance option f' is superior to no insurance depends on the degree of aversion (or degree of curvature of the indifference curve). With the indifference curves shown in Figure 2.3, the person chooses full insurance, but with a less risk-averse set of preferences no insurance may be chosen. We may expect the population to be divided into two groups – those with full insurance (like the person shown in Figure 2.3) and those with none.

If the administrative costs are higher for (voluntary) state insurance, as is believed to be the case by those who suggest that employees of state organisations have less incentive to operate efficiently, then privatisation would offer both a saving of costs for those insured and the elimination of the distortion for those who are deterred from taking out insurance by the cost. On the other hand, state insurance may have the advantage over a multiplicity of private companies an account of economies of scale. Beveridge, for example, did an extensive analysis of the operating costs of private schemes, and noted that 'the markedly lower cost of administration in most forms of State insurance, as compared with most forms of voluntary insurance, arises essentially from the economies possible in the obtaining of premiums' (UK, 1942, p. 286). The obtaining of premiums includes, of course, not just the office costs but also those of selling the policies to customers. If state insurance is compulsory then these costs may well be lower and it is possible that – despite the compulsion – everyone would be better off. This is illustrated by the case where there are fixed administrative costs per policy, and there are two groups in the population, characterised by different attitudes towards risk. Suppose that the administrative cost of private insurance is such that the less risk-averse would prefer to opt out, but that the administrative costs of the state scheme are sufficiently lower that they would choose voluntarily to join the scheme. Social insurance could then raise the welfare of all.

The argument regarding diversity may take as its starting point the differences in preferences which we have noted. In our sickness example, suppose that people are identical in all respects except for their attitude towards risk (captured in the diagram by the shape of the indifference curves). They have the same asset income, and the same probability of sickness. Then if state sickness insurance is compulsory, involving full insurance for all, whereas private insurance allows people to opt out, then the latter would offer a freedom of choice which the state sector does not. The value of this extra choice depends on the extent of diversity of preferences, as has been pointed out in a different context by Weitzman (1977). If preferences are sufficiently concentrated that all prefer full insurance, then there will be no loss from compulsion.

Diversity may, however, refer to the number of suppliers from whom one can choose. Here it is typically taken for granted that a market system has the edge. This fails to consider whether perfect

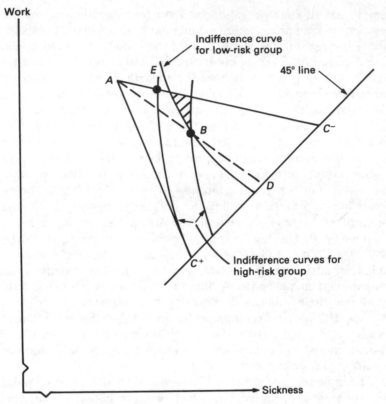

FIGURE 2.4 **Equilibrium in the perfectly competitive insurance market?**

competition is sustainable in the insurance market, an issue which has been addressed in the work of Rothschild and Stiglitz (1976), Riley (1975) and others (and which brings us back to the welfare economics theorems). To see the difficulties that may arise, suppose that people are identical in all respects except their risk of sickness, there being two classes of people with probabilities p^+ and p^- respectively, where $p^+ > p^-$. The indifference curves of the two types are shown in Figure 2.4. The absolute magnitude of the slope at any point is greater for the high-risk class, as is illustrated at the point B. This point lies on the dashed line AD which shows the locus of contracts which would break even if the whole population purchased insurance (the slope depends on the probabilities p^+ and p^- and on the proportion of the two groups in the population). The line AC^+ shows the locus of contracts which would break even if only the high-risk purchase insurance and AC^- those if only the low-risk purchase. (A 'contract' is a point in the diagram, offering a pair of incomes in the two states.)

The problem is that although individuals know to which group they belong, an insurance company cannot identify the riskiness of any individual customer. This imperfect information leads to problems of non-existence of competitive equilibrium, where an equilibrium is defined as a set of insurance contracts, such that no other contract exists which, if offered, would make a profit. Suppose in our example that the companies offer a contract if it makes a positive profit, and that they assume that their actions have no influence on the contracts offered by others. The equilibrium could consist of a state where all purchase the same contract, along AD. But at a point such as B, it is clear that a contract in the shaded area will attract the low-risk individuals (and not the high-risk individuals) and be profitable. A 'pooling equilibrium' cannot therefore be stable. The alternative is a 'separating equilibrium' with the high-risk group offered a contract along AC^+ and the low-risk along AC^-. But the latter contract must lie on the section AE, since otherwise the high-risk group would be attracted. This means that a contract along AD, such as that at B, would be attractive to the low-risk group, who would like to obtain more insurance than can be offered at E, and be profitable.

With this kind of adverse selection in the insurance market, a competitive equilibrium, in the sense defined, may not exist. It is possible to define alternative equilibrium concepts which ensure existence (see, for example, Wilson, 1977; Riley, 1979), but these do not seem a natural interpretation of what is involved in perfect competition. (It is also possible to consider an equilibrium in 'mixed strategies' – see Dasgupta and Maskin, 1986.) The central message is in fact that the market for insurance is unlikely to be perfectly competitive; and that one cannot make any straightforward statement about there being a large number of suppliers.

By the same token, there can be no simple appeal to the First Theorem of Welfare Economics; there is no guarantee that the market outcome will be Pareto-efficient. As is widely recognised by economic theorists, but less so by practitioners, the conditions for market competition to lead to a Pareto-efficient allocation are restrictive, including the existence of a full set of markets and perfect information. These are unlikely to be satisfied in reality, and their breakdown – in this case the absence of full information – brings into question the performance of the private alternative. (I have not discussed other problems, such as moral hazard, which affect the working of insurance markets – see Barr, 1987, chapter 5).

Before leaving the welfare economic argument, we should note that the model used here remains within the Arrow–Debreu framework in that it is concerned with *risk* rather than *uncertainty*, using the latter term in the sense of Knight (1921). The insurance is against a well-defined contingency, about which individuals can form probabilities. As suggested earlier, much of the function of social insurance is to provide for contingencies which are unforeseen and to allay fears about events which we cannot forecast. Looking backwards, it is hard to imagine that individuals could have taken out insurance to cover such events as the 1974 fuel price rise, the development of new surgical techniques, or the breakdown of the extended family. A looser form of contract, as with social insurance, may in this respect have significant advantages.

The case for privatisation whether in terms of administrative costs, diversity, or welfare economic efficiency, is therefore less straightforward than its proponents tend to suggest. Certainly it cannot be made simply by appeal to general principles. This does not, of course, mean that social insurance is necessarily preferable. What is needed is a careful evaluation of the relative performance of social and private insurance in particular contexts. This must be based on empirical evidence about such matters as the magnitude of administrative costs and the likely market structure. What is important is that this comparison should be even-handed, unlike the British government's analysis behind the *The Reform of Social Security* (Department of Health and Social Security, 1985a and b), which scrutinised the state pension system but failed to investigate in any systematic manner the shortcomings of private provision.

We should recognise that the economic arguments with regard to private insurance versus state income support are only part of the picture. The detailed weighing of the merits and demerits of the two systems may indeed be regarded as quite irrelevant by some, such as those who attach prior importance to the avoidance of individual coercion. As has been articulated by Nozick (1974), consideration of the end-states may have no role in the judgement; it is the means by which they are brought about that is the sole concern. Providing that individual rights have been acquired in a just manner, and are transferred according to just principles, then justifiable state intervention, according to Nozick, is limited to the prevention of violence, fraud and theft, and the enforcement of contracts. State compulsory insurance, on this view, is a violation of individual liberty, and as such unjustifiable. Social insurance would be rejected even if it could be shown to make everyone better off.

This is an example of the wider social and political factors which may dominate any decision. Although the British government's case for extending private pensions has been couched in terms of economic benefits and individual choice, it seems probable that a more basic political preference for private provision is the main factor underlying their policy.

2.4.2 Return to income testing

We turn now to the consideration of alternative forms of state income support. As we have seen in section 2.3, there was a historical pattern of development by which earlier means-tested programmes were supplanted by the introduction and expansion of social insurance, but that this has tended to be reversed in recent years in Britain.

The case for such a reversal of the historical trend is often made in terms of the 'target efficiency' of benefits in combating poverty, or the concentration of benefits on those with low income. The Institute for Fiscal Studies in presenting their proposed reform of social security argued that 'if our principal objective is to boost low incomes to an acceptable level, this could be done much more cheaply, and/or we could afford to be considerably more generous to the poor, if payments to those who do not strictly "need" the money were curtailed' (Dilnot, Kay and Morris, 1984, p. 55).

The issue concerns in part the shape of the budget constraint. The provision of a uniform benefit shifts the constraint in a parallel manner, leaving the marginal tax rate zero below the tax threshold. The introduction of income testing, with a rate of withdrawal t, tapers the benefit and makes the marginal tax rate t

up to the point where the benefit is totally withdrawn. In order to explore the implications in the context of the sickness example, let us suppose that there is no private insurance and simply a state benefit, at rate b, financed by a tax on those in work at rate ϱ. People are now assumed to be identical in all respects apart from their income from savings, denoted by k. Should the state benefit be income related, in the sense that the amount paid becomes $b - tk$, falling to zero if $b \leq tk$? If the government is assumed to maximise the integral of expected utilities subject to a revenue constraint, the revenue released by income testing being used to raise the level of benefit (the contribution rate ϱ is taken as fixed), then, not surprisingly, the introduction of income testing raises social welfare; and this continues until the withdrawal rate is set at 100 per cent, as with Income Support in Britain.

The argument against such a 100 per cent tax rate on benefits is obvious. We have taken no account of the disincentive to save which would be generated. In order to allow for this, we need to extend the model to incorporate the savings decision. The optimum choice of the rate of withdrawal then involves balancing the efficiency costs of the savings distortion against the gain from greater target efficiency. In general, the tax rate t will be strictly positive, so that in this sense income testing is desirable; and it could still be that a 100 per cent rate of withdrawal is optimal, even with a non-zero substitution elasticity for savings, since savings would be taxed at 100 per cent only in the state of the world where the person becomes sick.

It is in these terms that the public economics literature has tended to approach the issue of income testing, building on the literature on optimum taxation. For example, Kesselman and Garfinkel (1978) examine the choice between a negative income tax and a basic income scheme in terms of the desirability, or otherwise, of having a higher marginal rate of tax over the range where the person is a net beneficiary. However, our representation in terms of the shape of the budget constraint only comes to grips with the first element of income testing: that concerned with the tapering of benefit. The second feature of income testing – the fact that it is administered separately – must also be brought into the analysis. Although proposals have been made to administer income-tested benefits through the tax system, they typically require the provision of further information, or other actions, by those who wish to claim (as was the case with the Institute for Fiscal Studies scheme). This is important in view of the argument that this separate treatment is at best costly in time and at worst stigmatising. There are costs of time involved in informing oneself about the benefit, in claiming, in attending the relevant office, obtaining the necessary documentation, and in appealing against erroneous decisions.

The costs associated with the receipt of separate income-tested benefits mean that people do not always claim the assistance to which they are entitled. Where it is a matter of information and time, then modest amounts of benefit may not appear worth claiming. Others find the procedure demeaning and stigmatising, and refuse to claim even if the sums involved are sizeable. They may be fully informed of their rights but still not claim. The problem of incomplete take-up is a serious one. On several occasions, the effort has been made to improve the take-up rate of benefits, for example via extensive advertising. These have not in general achieved a lasting increase in take-up (see, for example, Atkinson, 1969).

For some people, the existence of such incomplete take-up is actually seen as desirable. Nichols and Zeckhauser (1982) argue in favour of 'ordeals', which is how they label the 'demeaning qualification tests and tedious administrative procedures'. They suggest that 'ordeals may enhance target efficiency' (ibid., p. 376), a view reminiscent of the New Poor Law Act of 1834. This, however, considers only one aspect of efficiency. As was pointed out by Weisbrod (1969), when he introduced the notion of target efficiency, it covers both accuracy in assisting *only* those in the target group and success in covering *all* of those in the group. A take-up rate below 100 per cent is as much evidence of failure as is the provision of benefits to those outside the target group.

In order to assess the case for income testing in place of social insurance, we have therefore to extend the model to incorporate the take-up decision. The most straightforward way in which this can be done is to introduce the time costs into a household production model. (The use of waiting time as a rationing device has been examined by Nichols *et al.*, 1971.) An income-tested benefit which involves H hours in claiming may be seen as providing a benefit equal to $b - \omega H$ in terms of 'full income', as defined by Becker (1965), where ω is the opportunity cost of time. It might, for example, be suggested that income testing is desirable since the poor have lower wage rates, and hence a lower opportunity cost of time, but this ignores the possibility that they are also 'time poor' (Vickrey, 1977) and constrained in their labour market choices. The problems in incorporating stigma are less tractable, although some interesting suggestions were made by Weisbrod (1970). One important consideration is that behaviour may be interdependent, as has been analysed by Cowell (1985). The probability that a person claims a given benefit may depend positively on the fraction of the population in receipt. If that is the case, then extension of means testing might make it more socially acceptable and raise the rate of take-up. Conversely, a more efficient targeting of benefits on the poor may reduce still further their rate of take-up.

Finally, it may again be the case that economic arguments are not decisive. Income testing may be rejected on account of a basic objection to policies which are inherently divisive: 'services specially designed for poor people . . . divide society, creating second class citizens who get second class treatment' (Donnison, 1982, p. 12). Or, more positively, primary importance may be attached to social integration and a sense of common identity: 'the principle that public services should provide a range of common experience that all citizens undergo' (Weale, 1983, p. 153). Solidarity may be an overriding goal just as much as liberty.

2.4.3 Basic incomes

Both basic incomes and social insurance are likely to be consistent with a goal of solidarity, but there are two major differences between them. First, there are the contribution conditions for social insurance, which raise a number of important issues, not least the way in which the programmes are perceived. Secondly, social insurance benefits are linked to work status. In my sickness example, the person receives under social insurance $w(1 - \varrho) + k$ if in work and $b + k$ if sick. Under a basic income scheme, the person would not receive any additional benefit for being sick; the amount would be, β say, in both states. So he receives $w(1 - t) + k(1 - t) + \beta$ if well and $k(1 - t) + \beta$ if sick.

There are two evident advantages to the basic income approach. First, there is no need to determine a person's employment status, with a consequent saving in administrative costs. The second advantage is that, by providing an adequate income regardless of employment circumstances, it deals with the problem to which social insurance as such has no answer – that of people who are low paid even though they are in work. This brings us to the important question of the relation between social security and the labour market. The Beveridge plan was based firmly on the assumption of the maintenance of full employment: 'it should be possible to make unemployment of any individual for more than 26 weeks continuously a rare thing in normal times' (UK, 1942, p. 164). This in itself would not have been enough, without some guarantee that the employment would be at a reasonable level of wages. Here Beveridge would no doubt have flinched at the thought of a minimum wage, but it is seen by many as the natural partner in the social insurance approach. The establishment of a minimum wage, at some premium over the benefit level, with guaranteed state employment at that rate, together with social insurance, would provide a coherent policy towards both the interruption of employment and low pay while at work. This is one possible 'vision' of the relationship between social security policy and the labour market.

Such a plan would, of course, represent a major change in labour market policy – at least as far as Britain is concerned – and it is scarcely surprising that income support policies which do not depend on full employment have been advocated. Here the basic income approach offers an alternative vision of the relationship. This starts from the right to a basic income, to which everyone is entitled, and to which earnings would be an addition, although they are all taxed, quite probably at a high rate, like 50 per cent. This approach allows diversity. If people choose not to work in the paid labour force, then they still receive the basic income. There would be no minimum wage, and the basic income scheme is consistent with the policy of the British Conservative government of seeking to create low-paid jobs. If employers wished to offer such jobs, then they could do so in the knowledge that those taking them would not be in poverty and that their income would be higher than if not at work.

What can economic analysis say about the choice between these schemes? If we consider first the design of the basic income scheme, we can see that the choice of β and the tax rate t is that which has been investigated in the literature on the optimum linear income tax. Suppose that in our sickness example people differ in their wage rate per hour, having identical preferences, and no income from capital ($k = 0$). There is assumed to be a perfectly elastic demand for any type of labour at the specified wage rate. Workers are assumed to choose their hours of work, utility being derived from net income and from leisure. There will be a critical wage rate, denoted by w_o, such that people with wages below this level choose not to work even if well, living from the basic income. The level of w_o is governed by β and t. The choice of t, and hence from the revenue constraint β, depends on the form of the social welfare function (see for example, Atkinson and Stiglitz, 1980, lecture 13), but the optimum solution involves one of two possibilities: either (type A) the critical wage w_o is below the lowest wage in the economy, denoted by w^-, which means that all choose to work, or (type B) $w_o > w^-$, in which the level of basic income is such that some people choose not to work.

Suppose that we have derived the optimum basic income scheme, balancing the benefits from a higher basic income against the costs of raising taxes (the balance depends of course on distributional judgements), and that we now consider the introduction of social insurance, paying an additional benefit b to the sick, who are correctly identified. (Diamond and Mirrlees, 1978, examine a theoretical model of social insurance where the government cannot distinguish between those unable to work and those who choose not to.) If the basic income optimum was of type A, then it can be shown that raising b marginally above zero (with offsetting adjustments) would raise social welfare where leisure is a normal good. This is because the sickness benefit, unlike β, is targeted to the lowest income group, and has no adverse income effect on labour supply. This result is parallel to the analysis of 'tagging' by Akerlof (1978). A categorical social insurance benefit can raise social welfare, providing that the extra administrative costs are not too great. (The same argument may apply to categorical income-tested schemes.)

This suggests that we have to balance the better targeting of social insurance against the cost of imposing the employment test. But we have not yet considered the minimum wage and the relation between benefit levels and net incomes in work. The optimum taxation models as developed to date are not very helpful in this regard, since the treatment of the labour market is insufficiently developed. In particular, they incorporate none of the elements which have been put forward to explain involuntary unemployment, such as implicit contracts, efficiency wages, or insider–outsider relations and trade unions. This is an area where further theoretical research is needed.

And again the welfare economic calculus may have to defer to wider considerations. There may be doubts about social arrangements which provide some people with no financial incentive to work. Ellwood and Summers refer to 'the value society places on self-reliance. We expect those who can to help themselves' (1986, p. 104). Gueron, writing about workfare in the US, refers to 'the now prevailing view that employable women – as well as men – have a responsibility to work and support their families' (1986, p. 2). It may therefore be imposed as a prior constraint that everyone should derive a financial gain from working. If this is the case, then solutions to the basic income design problem which are of type B will be ruled out. The basic income scheme may then be constrained to offer a level of β which on other grounds would be regarded as inadequate. The social insurance system can overcome this problem, providing that it can be accompanied by a minimum wage. However, this too may be rejected on ideological grounds.

2.5 CONCLUDING COMMENTS

One theme running through this chapter has been the need to recognise that economic arguments may only play a limited role in deciding such questions as the privatisation of social insurance or the return to means testing or the introduction of a basic income. Before the 1970s, the economic aspects of social insurance received little attention. In the 1970s and 1980s, this changed, not least because of the writing in the US which has stressed the impact of social insurance on the economy, such as the effect on incentives to work and save. In my view, there is a danger that too much weight may now be given to the economic arguments. The non-economic arguments – such as those concerned with liberty, solidarity, or divisiveness – require more attention. This is not to suggest that the economic arguments are unimportant. They can illustrate the advantages and disadvantages of different approaches, but they must be seen in perspective.

The second concluding reflection which is suggested by the analysis is that the determination of government policy has been considered in a classical public finance manner, without benefiting from the insights of the more recent public choice approach. In choosing the structure of income support, we have to consider the possibility that the government may follow its own objectives without regard for any notion of social welfare. The public choice theory has tended to emphasise the propensity of governments to expand state activity beyond the socially optimal level, but the reverse may also be true, with governments cutting back state provision. (For an analysis of the changing political forces determining the degree of redistribution, see Lindbeck, 1985.) Would income-tested benefits, being more focused, be more likely to escape the cuts made by right-wing governments? Or would these benefits, lacking a broad political base, be more easily cut, as would be suggested by Director's Law (Stigler, 1970)? Would a basic income, by linking taxes and benefits so directly, be more exposed to political forces? These are interesting and important questions.

3 Retirement Pensions

NICHOLAS BARR

3.1 THE BACKGROUND

3.1.1 The issues

Pensions raise major and controversial issues, not least because of their importance as an income source to large numbers of people and (related) because the combined expenditure on public and private pension schemes in Britain is currently of the order of 11 per cent of GDP (see Barr and Coulter, 1990, table 7.4 for historical data).

The potential list of issues is huge. Should pensions be actuarial, that is with benefits strictly related to past contributions (note that this rules out systematic redistribution from rich to poor)? What is the appropriate role for private pension schemes? What are the effects of pensions on aggregate labour supply, and on saving and output growth? To what extent do employer schemes affect individual decisions: for instance, pension design may reduce shirking (Lazear, 1986); vesting rules (which specify the length of service before a worker gains title to any pension benefits) reduce labour turnover (Wise, 1986); and benefit provisions can encourage older workers to retire early (Stock and Wise, 1988). Nor is concern limited to *retirement* pensions. Invalidity pensions raise other major issues. How strictly should entry be policed (countries with relaxed entry procedures have found that the number of invalidity pensioners can rise sharply during times of high unemployment, particularly for older workers)? Should an invalidity pension be awarded only if an individual is wholly unable to work, or should there be a graduated pension related to partial inability to work?

Should the size of the pension depend on cause (e.g. a higher pension in the case of industrial injury) or only on outcome?

After discussion in section 3.2 of different ways of organising pension finance, this chapter focuses on two issues: the demographic 'crisis' (section 3.3); and the differential retirement age for men and women (section 3.4). The concluding part of the chapter assesses pensions policy since the Second World War and ventures some brief predictions. The topics are chosen for two reasons: they are matters of current policy debate; and they raise very different sets of issues. The demographic issue is (more or less) a pure efficiency matter; the differential retirement age raises both equity and efficiency issues.

The demographic problem arises out of the twin peaks in the birth rate in 1948 and the mid-1960s, after which the birth rate declined rapidly. The same pattern is found in most industrialised countries. Currently, therefore, workers are plentiful and, since birth rates were low in the 1920s and 1930s, the number of pensioners is not excessive. But the 1948 cohort will retire in the years after 2008, with a second wave in 2025, when the mid-1960s cohort reaches retirement age. Since birth rates after the late 1960s were low, there will be few workers and large numbers of pensioners.

Table 3.1 shows that the effects are widespread and, in some countries, dramatic. On present trends, Germany and the Netherlands are projected to spend around 30 per cent of GDP on state pensions by 2040; averaged across OECD countries, pension spending is set to double from 10 to 20 per cent of GDP. In some countries rising labour force participation is a partial offset. In Germany[1] and Japan, however, the total contribution per head of the working age population is projected to rise by over 50 per cent, requiring substantial rates of economic growth if contribution rates are not to rise. These facts raise two major issues: how large is the problem; and what policies might alleviate matters?

The second issue arises out of the fact that the normal (and frequently mandatory) retirement age for women in the UK is 60, five years younger than for men, raising questions about how appropriately to define the relevant insurance pool, about labour supply and about whether such a rule is discriminatory.

TABLE 3.1 Demographic effects on the share of pension expenditure in GDP and financing burdens in various OECD countries, 1984–2040

	1984	2000	2020	2040
Australia				
Pensions as % GDP	6.0	6.7	9.1	12.4
Contribution/head, 15–64 group[a]		100	112	130
Canada				
Pensions as % GDP	6.1	7.7	11.6	15.2
Contribution/head, 15–64 group[a]		103	125	145
Germany				
Pensions as % GDP	13.7	16.4	21.6	31.1
Contributions/head, 15–64 group[a]		106	124	154
Japan				
Pensions as % GDP	6.0	9.4	14.0	15.7
Contributions/head, 15–64 group[a]		115	142	154
Netherlands				
Pensions as % GDP	12.1	13.4	19.6	28.5
Contributions/head, 15–64 group[a]		100	114	139
New Zealand				
Pensions as % GDP	8.9	9.3	13.0	20.3
Contributions/head, 15–64 group[a]		NA	NA	NA
Sweden				
Pensions as % GDP	12.9	12.1	15.9	18.0
Contributions/head, 15–64 group[a]		95	110	122
Switzerland				
Pensions as % GDP	8.8	10.6	16.9	21.1
Contributions/head, 15–64 group[a]		NA	NA	NA
United Kingdom				
Pensions as % GDP	7.7	7.5	8.6	11.2
Contributions/head, 15–64 group[a]		93	101	111
United States				
Pensions as % GDP	8.1	8.2	11.3	14.6
Contributions/head, 15–64 group[a]		96	117	131
OECD average as % GDP	10.3	11.4	15.1	20.2

[a] 1980 = 100.
Source: OECD (1988, 1989).

3.1.2 The objectives of pensions

The major objectives of the welfare state were discussed in Chapter 1. They are all relevant to pensions, but four stand out (for fuller discussion of this and other aspects of pension finance, see Barr, 1992).

1. Pensions should offer the elderly an adequate income in retirement (the poverty relief objective). The achievement of this objective usually requires redistribution from rich to poor.
2. Pensions should provide a mechanism which allows individuals to effect a redistribution to themselves over their life cycle (the income smoothing objective).
3. They should be affordable (the macroeconomic efficiency objective).
4. They should create minimal adverse incentives (the microeconomic efficiency objective).

3.2 DIFFERENT FORMS OF PENSION FINANCE

The purpose of pensions, from the viewpoint of the individual, is to make it possible to transfer consumption over time, i.e. to consume less than he/she produces during working life so that consumption can continue after retirement. In principle there are two (and *only* two) ways in which an individual can achieve this: by storing current production during working life; or by acquiring a claim on output produced after his/her retirement by the next generation of workers.

Storing current production is valid in limited circumstances. Many pensioners, for instance, will have paid off their mortgages during their working lives, enabling them, at least to some extent, to store housing services for their old age. As a general mechanism, however, this approach has at least three glaring deficiencies. First, it is *costly* both in terms of direct costs (e.g. keeping steak frozen for thirty years) and in terms of the opportunity cost of the return which could otherwise be made on such saving. Second is the issue of *uncertainty*, both about life expectancy after retirement and about tastes a long time in the future (e.g. medically mandated dietary restrictions). Third, whilst it is at least in principle possible to store goods, and also services deriving from physical capital, it is not possible to store *services deriving from human capital* such as (most important in old age) medical services.

Thus we are left with the second approach – building a claim on output produced by the next generation of workers after one's retirement. In principle, this can be achieved in two ways: through the acquisition of *financial assets*, which can be exchanged for goods after retirement; or through a *promise*, at a family level from one's children or at a national level from government, that one will be cared for in old age. The two pension mechanisms observed in practice, *funded* schemes and *Pay-As-You-Go* (PAYG) schemes follow precisely these two routes.

PAYG pensions – the usual form of state scheme – do not pay pensions out of an accumulated fund. Instead, the state taxes the current generation of workers (either through taxation generally, or in the form of national insurance contributions), and uses the proceeds to pay pensions to the retired generation. PAYG is thus a simple tax-transfer scheme.

Under a funded scheme (the usual mechanism in the private sector), an individual (and usually also his/her employer) pays contributions (usually a fraction of the wage) throughout working life into an account run by a pension fund, which can be a private, profit-maximising company or a non-profit occupational scheme. By the time the individual retires his/her past contributions plus the interest, dividends and capital gains they have earned over the years amount to a large lump sum. At its simplest, this is converted into an *annuity*, i.e. an annual income payment for life, with the property that the present value of the pension stream is equal to the lump sum for an individual with average life expectancy. Funded schemes thus combine saving (during working life) with insurance (the annuity). The annuity is essentially a bet between me and the insurance company. If I take out the annuity, thereby paying over my accumulated lump sum, and promptly drop dead, the insurance company wins the bet; if I live into my high nineties I win the bet, since the present value of the stream of pension payments I receive exceeds the lump sum. One way of thinking about an annuity is as insurance by the individual against living too long.

The previous paragraph described the generic funded scheme. Schemes in practice take many forms, of which two in particular should be distinguished. Under a *defined contribution* scheme, the contribution rate is fixed, so that the individual's pension, given his life expectancy, is determined *only* by the size of the lump sum accumulated during working life. The individual therefore bears two sorts of risk: that of unanticipated developments in the rate of return to pension assets during his working life; and that of unanticipated inflation after retirement. Insurance can protect the individual against the risks (described in the previous paragraph) associated with longevity; however, the individual bears the entire risk associated with different real rates of return to pension assets.

Under a *defined benefit* scheme, almost invariably run at a firm or industry level, the firm promises to pay an annuity at retirement; the size of the annuity depends on the employee's wage in his/her final year (or few years) of work and upon length of service; a typical formula is one-eightieth of final salary per year of service, up to a maximum of forty years. Thus the annuity is, in effect, wage indexed until retirement, though as we shall see, not typically indexed thereafter. The employee contribution is generally a fraction of his/her salary. In consequence, the employer's contribution becomes the endogenous variable. In a defined benefit scheme, it is the firm or industry which bears the risk in the face of unanticipated changes in the real rate of return to pension assets.

3.3 THE DEMOGRAPHIC PROBLEM

3.3.1 The naive argument

The essence of the demographic problem described earlier is that it leads to an increase in the *gerontic dependency ratio*, i.e. the ratio of pensioners to workers. Under PAYG the problem is obvious: if there are more pensioners per worker, a given contribution by each worker results in a lower real pension for each pensioner. Funding, it is argued, avoids this problem. This section discusses the pitfalls of that argument. Such a view should not be interpreted as an attack on the funding principle, but on expecting funded schemes to do more than they are capable of doing.

The naive funding argument points out that if there is a large generation of workers, as currently, it will build up a large stock of savings; when they retire, after 2008, and are followed by a smaller workforce, there is no problem since pensioners can live off their accumulated saving. The argument, in essence, is that each pensioner supports himself through his own previous savings; thus there is no problem if there is a large number of pensioners.

The problem with the argument is that it is based on what Samuelson calls the *fallacy of composition*, that is the assumption that because something is true for an individual, it will be true for large numbers of individuals. It is, of course, true that an *individual* can finance retirement by exchanging previously accumulated money for goods. But if *everyone* tries to do so, no goods will be produced and the system collapses. At a macroeconomic level, the effect of the demographic problem is that the dissaving of a large pensioner generation out of their large accumulation of pensions funds, will exceed the saving (in the form of pension contributions) of the smaller succeeding workforce. At a given level of output, the resulting fall in saving creates inflationary pressures, reducing the purchasing power of pensions. The result, through a different mechanism is broadly the same as under PAYG (for fuller discussion, see Barr, 1987, chapter 9). Since funding and PAYG are simply methods of organising claims by workers on future output, the similarity of outcome should not be surprising.

3.3.2 Insurance arguments

Microeconomic theory leads to the same conclusion. Chapter 2 set out the sort of market failures which make private insurance inefficient or impossible in the face of adverse selection and moral hazard. These are not the only problems insurance markets face. In particular, private insurance requires in addition (i) that the insurable risk is known or estimable, and (ii) that individual risks are independent. Neither is a problem for the probability distribution of age-at-death: statistics on life expectancy are well developed; and the probability that I will die at a given age is, by and large, independent of anyone else's age-at-death.

The objective of income smoothing, however, requires that individuals can make plans about consumption after retirement. Thus they need to know about their *real* pension, and hence require information about price levels after retirement, i.e. about the probability distribution of future levels of inflation. Herein lies the problem: it is not possible for a private insurance company to predict the probability distribution of inflation, say, thirty years hence. Moreover, if any one member of a funded pension scheme faces a given rate of inflation, so do they all, so that the inflation risk is most emphatically *not* independent across individuals. Put another way, the mechanism of private insurance can offer protection against an *individual* shock, but not against a *common* shock like a decline in the workforce.

If pensioners cannot insure each other, could they obtain protection in some other way? The answer would be yes only if real rates of return to pension assets were independent of inflation. As an empirical matter, this is not the case. The dependence is partly the result of distortions elsewhere (e.g. non-indexed tax systems) which could in principle be corrected. However, where an inflationary shock represents other adverse movements in the economy, no private agency can offer a complete hedge against inflation. Bodie (1989) argues that short-term deposit accounts are the least bad hedge, since short-term interest rates are revised frequently; Zeckhauser and Patel (1987) find that buying futures contracts on government bonds eliminates only about one-third of the risk of unanticipated inflation.

Thus inflation is an uninsurable risk; and private-sector hedges offer incomplete protection. Though there is controversy as to why no private-sector financial instruments offer a risk-free real return, the empirical conclusion is clear. Bodie's survey points out that 'virtually no private pension plans in the US offer automatic inflation protection after retirement' (Bodie, 1990, p. 36). Gordon, in her cross-national survey, concludes that 'indexing of pension benefits after retirement . . . presents serious difficulties in funded employer pension plans. . . .' (Gordon, 1988, p. 169).

In sum, a defined benefit scheme, can offer the individual protection against unanticipated inflation during his/her contribution years. Neither type of scheme, however, deals well with post-retirement inflation.

3.3.3 The economic growth argument

A different line of defence argues that funding leads (i) to an increase in savings, hence (ii) to increased investment, and hence (iii) to higher output growth than PAYG, and thereby makes it easier to finance pensions in the face of demographic change. Each of the three links requires qualification.

On the first link, it is, in any case, only while a fund is building up that saving might be higher; in steady state, saving by workers is matched by dissaving by pensioners. Furthermore, opinion is divided as to whether funding increases saving even during the build-up phase. The debate is both theoretical and empirical. A key question is whether increased pension saving (e.g. through a funded scheme) does or does not offset other saving. The answer depends on the broader determinants of saving, and in particular on the extent to which people save only or mainly to finance retirement, or whether they save also to make bequests.

To understand the roots of the debate it is necessary to go back to a famous paper by Feldstein (1974). He argued that PAYG financing tends to reduce saving; but that if pensions induce earlier retirement, savings would increase to pay for a longer retirement after a shorter working life. He therefore concluded that the issue is theoretically indeterminate.

Aaron (1982) surveys three theoretical models of the determinants of saving: the life-cycle model (which rules out bequests); the multigenerational model (which allows bequests); and the short-horizon model (which relaxes the assumption that individuals make rational lifetime plans based on, more or less, full information). Feldstein's use of the life-cycle model was criticised *inter alia* on the grounds that with a life-cycle model an increase in PAYG benefits *must* reduce savings; with a multigenerational model, in contrast, increased benefits could instead increase bequests (and hence not reduce savings). Aaron summarises the theoretical debate by observing

> that a person determined to find a respected theoretical argument to support a preconception will find one, and that a person without preconceptions will find a bewildering diversity of answers in economic theory about whether social security [i.e. pensions] is more likely to raise or to lower consumption or labor supply . . . To get by this theoretical impasse, one turns with hope to the empirical research . . . As will become clear, most of these hopes remain unfulfilled. (Ibid., p. 28)

Feldstein's empirical work, based on time-series data, concluded that the US social security scheme (which is PAYG) reduced personal saving by about 50 per cent and the capital stock by 38 per cent below what it would have been in the absence of the social security system. There were several lines of criticism: additional variables such as the unemployment rate or a measure of permanent income tended to reduce the effect on saving, and to destroy its statistical significance; and the results were highly sensitive to the time-period over which the relation was estimated. The results were finally discredited by Leimer and Lesnoy (1982) who found an important error in some of Feldstein's data. They also pointed out that the results are very sensitive to the way in which people are assumed to form expectations.

Aaron (1982, p. 45) concluded that 'it would be pointless to continue the . . . debate, even if better data should become available'. Subsequent work (Auerbach *et al.*, 1989; Auerbach and Kotlikoff, 1990) uses a 75-period life-cycle general equilibrium model to simulate the effects of demographic change under different pension regimes. The results highlight the key role of expectations and their impact on retirement behaviour. Since the formation of expectations is unmeasurable, the issue remains unresolved.

So far as the second link is concerned, increased saving does not necessarily lead to more investment; pension savings could instead be used to buy old masters. On the third link, the objective is to channel resources into their most productive investment use. But it cannot just be *assumed* that pension managers make more efficient choices than other agents. Nor do state funded schemes necessarily fare better. Experience in Sweden and Japan, where the state earnings related pensions are funded, suggests that such schemes 'offer powerful evidence that this option may only invite squandering capital funds in wasteful, low-yield investments [which] should give pause to anyone proposing similar accumulations elsewhere' (Rosa, 1982, p. 212).

3.3.4 Policies to cope with demographic change

What policies, then, might government adopt? In principle there are only three solutions. Either demand could be reduced by paying lower pensions (reducing pensioner demand) or by maintaining real pensions financed out of higher contributions (thus reducing worker demand). Alternatively, and the only complete solution, output could be increased sufficiently so that a constant contribution rate can finance an unchanged real pension. This can be done in only two generic ways: by increasing output per worker; and/or by increasing the number of workers. The first can be achieved through improvements in the quantity and quality of capital equipment, and in the quality of labour. Relevant policies are:

(a) increased investment in physical capital, such as machinery and factories;
(b) increased research and development expenditure (i.e. not only more, but better machines);
(c) increased investment in human capital, producing a better educated and trained workforce.

Policies to increase the number of workers include:

(d) reducing the rate of unemployment;
(e) encouraging married women to rejoin the labour force, for instance through adequate child care facilities;
(f) raising the age at which retirement pensions are paid, or giving people an incentive to defer retirement;
(g) importing labour (generous immigration policies, 'guest-workers'): obvious solutions under this head would be to award UK passports to Hong Kong citizens; and West Germany is absorbing workers from the (younger) East German population.

The previous paragraph is not controversial (see, for instance, Holzmann 1988; Falkingham, 1989). What *is* controversial is whether or not funding leads to higher output growth than PAYG. Funding has no bearing on policies (c)–(g). It is true that pensions affect labour supply; but to the extent that that is relevant, what matters is the *level* of the pension not its *source*. Any effect must be through the first two policies. This brings us back to earlier arguments which suggested scepticism about the likely size of the effect of funding on saving and investment. The conclusion is that policy should be concerned with all of policies (a)–(g), rather than focusing too sharply on funding, which (i) is only an indirect method of attack, and (ii) relates only to the first two policies.

3.4   THE AGE OF RETIREMENT

3.4.1   Facts and implications

Britain is unusual, though not alone, in having a lower mandatory retirement age for women; it is five years younger than for men also in Australia, and three years younger in Japan. That fact, combined with women's greater longevity, has major implications.

The standard retirement age for men in the UK is 65, at which age male life expectancy is 77 years. For women, the standard retirement age is 60, with a life expectancy of 80 years. The typical man is thus retired for twelve years, the typical woman for twenty; put another way, on average it costs 20/12 times as much to pay a given pension to a woman as to a man. Thus if men and women pay the same contributions and receive the same benefits, women receive 20/12 times as much pension as men per pound of contribution. The problem is not a result only of the retirement age differential. If the age of retirement were equalised (a topic to which we return below), the typical British woman would be retired for fifteen years, and the cost differential would be reduced, but not eliminated.

It should be noted that there is a genuine ambiguity over how to define equality in the context of pensions.

- Equality could be defined in terms of the *weekly pension*. In that case, a man and a woman with an identical earnings stream would pay identical contributions and receive an identical weekly pension; but the woman, on average, would receive her pension for longer. Thus the man pays more than the woman per pound of weekly pension.
- Alternatively, equality could be defined in terms of the *present value* of the pension stream: a man and woman with an identical earnings record would accumulate identical lump sums, which would finance identical pension streams over their expected lifetime; under this arrangement, however, the woman would receive a lower weekly pension.

3.4.2 Arguments for equalisation of pensions and normal retirement ages

Three issues require discussion: (i) whether equality for pensions should be defined in terms of the weekly pension or the lifetime pension stream; (ii) whether the age of retirement should be the same for men and women; (iii) and, if so, whether the equalised retirement age should be 60 or 65.

One argument is favour of the equal-weekly-pension definition is a simple equity one. The case can be strengthened by observing that such a rule has only minimal efficiency costs. The standard argument for charging actuarial premiums (i.e. premiums related to individual risk) is that to do otherwise would cause inefficiency. Thus, to avoid adverse labour supply incentives, it is correctly argued that individuals should be allowed to retire early only on the basis of an actuarially reduced pension. But incentive issues arise only where individuals have *choice*. In the present context, however, people cannot choose whether to be a man or a woman, nor to choose their longevity. Thus there is no efficiency loss in making it mandatory for pension schemes to put men and women into a common risk pool.

Such a policy, however, must be mandatory. Otherwise pension schemes consisting mainly of men would be able to pay higher pensions, and there would be an incentive to try to exclude women. A strict regulatory regime is therefore necessary to avoid discrimination. Overt discrimination is covered under existing legislation. Implicit discrimination, however, is more difficult to police (e.g. a pension scheme open only to current and former rugby players).

A separate issue is whether there should be a common retirement age for men and women. Here the argument for equalisation is even stronger. The present arrangement is discriminatory in two ways. It discriminates against those women who want to work longer than 60. There have already been several cases brought against the UK government in the European Courts on precisely this issue. Second, it can discriminate against men. Under the present system, if a man and a woman have an indentical lifetime earnings profile and both retire at 65,[2] the woman will have a pension 37.5 per cent higher than the man's, because the national insurance pension is raised by 7.5 per cent for each year by which retirement is deferred beyond normal retirement age. On both grounds, the differential retirement age is indefensible.

Finally, should the retirement age be equalised at 60 or 65? Here, again, the answer is unambiguous. Given the demographic prospects, the common retirement age should be 65, or perhaps even older.

3.5 POST-WAR PENSIONS POLICY IN THE UNITED KINGDOM

3.5.1 The past

In the light of previous discussion it is possible to shed some light on the shape of post-war pensions policy.

The original Beveridge scheme embodied in the 1946 National Insurance Act was in many ways actuarial. Individuals bought a weekly stamp, that is a flat-rate contribution, for which they received flat-rate benefits. The premium did not reflect differences in individual risk; but since membership was compulsory it did reflect the *average* risk. In contrast with later arrangements, the weekly stamp can be regarded not as a lump sum (and hence regressive) tax, but as a compulsory insurance premium.

The introduction of graduated pensions: the flat-rate contribution in the 1946 Act was a heavier imposition for individuals with lower incomes, leading to political pressures to keep it small. It followed that benefits had to be small, a source of increasing dissatisfaction over the 1950s. From 1961, therefore, a compulsory additional earnings-related contribution was levied above a certain level of earnings, which gave entitlement to an earnings-related pension in addition to the flat-rate pension. The additional pension bore a strict actuarial relation to additional contributions. Each £7.50 of graduated contribution entitled a man to an extra 2½ pence of weekly pension; for women, because of their greater average longevity, the extra 2½ pence per week cost an additional £9 of contributions.

Clearly the major aim was income smoothing. A subsidiary objective was horizontal equity: there had always been state assistance for earnings-related pensions through tax relief for occupational pensions; but these went mainly to salary earners. One view of graduated pensions is that they reduced inequality between salary earners and wage earners.

The 1974 Labour government pursued the objective of poverty relief by increasing the basic pension as soon as it gained office. Later that year, it published a White Paper (UK, 1974), which kept the previous flat-rate arrangements, on which was superimposed a state earnings-related pension scheme (SERPS). The explicit aims of the White Paper were:

- to avoid means testing (*inter alia* to avoid its stigmatising effect);
- to pay benefits which were indexed to changes in prices or earnings (income smoothing);
- to pay earnings-related benefits (income smoothing);
- to redistribute towards the less well off (vertical equity);
- to offer equality for women (horizontal equity).

Since most of these objectives are hard to achieve in a private scheme, it was almost inevitable that the White Paper should advocate the state earnings-related scheme implemented in the 1975 Social Security Pensions Act.

There was an increase in the basic pension in 1974, which reflected greater weight on poverty relief; on the face of it, so too did the emphasis on indexation, which ensured that the poverty line was not eroded by inflation. In many ways, however, the change was more form than substance. The 1946 National Insurance Act made no mention of uprating benefits in line with inflation, and benefits in the early years were uprated only infrequently.[3] Under the 1975 Social Security Act and Social Security Pensions Act, the level of SERPS and various other benefits was to be reviewed annually and uprated in line with prices or, in the case of the basic pension, with earnings or prices, whichever was the larger.[4] The requirement to review benefits annually, it can be argued, made little difference. Benefits between 1948 and 1975 had in practice remained a constant fraction of average pre-tax earnings so exactly that it is clear that successive governments had an unwritten behavioural rule to maintain the relativity (Barr, 1981).[5]

The 1985 review: the results of 'the most fundamental examination of our social security system since the Second World War'

(UK, 1985a, Preface) were published as a Green Paper and in a White Paper later in the same year (UK, 1985b). Notwithstanding the claim to be a fundamental review, the bulk of the proposed changes were little more than housekeeping improvements (e.g. measures to reduce the likelihood of poor families losing more in benefit than they gained in extra earnings).

Nevertheless, the Green and White Papers gave a valuable insight into the government's objectives:

- '[T]he social security system must be capable of meeting genuine need' (UK, 1985a, para. 1.12), i.e. the objective of poverty relief.
- [T]he social security system must be consistent with the Government's overall objectives for the economy' (ibid.) (the macroeconomic efficiency objective).
- [T]he social security system must be simple to understand and easy to administer' (ibid.).

These objectives are consistent with private, non-redistributive, actuarial provision of the earnings-related pension. It is therefore not surprising that the Green Paper (UK, 1985a) proposed the abolition of SERPS and its replacement, for the most part, by occupational (i.e private, funded) pensions. The proposal was hotly opposed, not least by the pensions industry, worried that it might be expected to offer pensions not only to salaried professionals in stable jobs but also to the less well off. The White Paper (UK, 1985b) was more circumspect, retaining SERPS but reducing benefits in later years. Specifically, under the 1975 Social Security Pensions Act, the state earnings-related pension scheme (SERPS) pays a pension of one-quarter of the excess of an individual's average earnings above a threshold. Thus an individual with twice the earnings – and hence twice the contributions – will receive less than twice the total pension (basic pension plus SERPS). These arrangements, which still apply at present, will be changed in three major ways, starting in 2000. From 2010 the pension will be one-fifth rather than one-quarter of the relevant amount, the reduction having been phased in over the previous ten years. Second, average earnings will be measured not over an individual's best twenty years, as hitherto, but over his/her full working life. Third, the surviving spouse will inherit up to half, rather than all, of his/her spouse's earnings-related pension. These changes increase the importance of the basic, flat-rate pension, and hence increase the redistributive tilt in the state pension scheme.

Alongside the 1985 reforms, further incentives were given to individuals to contract out of SERPS to join defined benefit occupational schemes. Another key part of the legislation allowed individuals, subject to certain regulations, to opt out of both SERPS *and* occupational provision and make their own pension arrangements either through an insurance company or, even more individually, by building up a portfolio of assets of their own choosing. Such individual pensions have two effects: because they are defined contribution schemes, they face the individual with the risk of unanticipated inflation during contributions years; and, because they are based strictly on individual contributions, they also imply that a woman will receive a lower weekly pension than a man with an indentical contributions record. Individual pensions thus greatly extend the actuarial element in earnings-related pensions.

The Green Paper proposal to abolish SERPS was an attempt to shift earnings-related pensions from the non-actuarial stance of the 1975 legislation back to stricter actuarial principles. In the end, because of widespread concern at the proposed abolition of SERPS, the White Paper represented a much smaller move in an actuarial direction. The changes after 2000 reduce the weight put on equity objectives. For instance, the calculation of benefits over a whole working life rather than over the best twenty years works to the disadvantage of individuals with fluctuating incomes, particularly those individuals (mainly women) who have spells in and out of the labour force.

However, though the redistributive element in the state scheme was reduced, the move towards actuarial principles was only partial. Whether such a move is good or bad depends on the answers to two questions: first, and ideological, is whether one believes that pensions should be redistributive; second, and largely technical, is whether or not a move towards funding is an effective response to demographic prospects. On the latter issue, earlier discussion focused on two issues: whether or not the demographic problem is serious; and what policies might improve matters. The Green Paper's response was largely to duck the problem by advocating that earnings-related provision should be mainly a private sector activity; the White Paper, as we have seen, retained SERPS but reduced benefits in later years.

It can be argued that the White Paper policy is the right one. Either the SERPS promise of 1975, with hindsight, was too generous or it was not. If output grows sufficiently to allow the original promise to be kept, pensions can be raised in future years (with PAYG it is easy to increase pensions, but politically difficult to lower them). If, on the other hand, the original promise was too generous, then the strategy of making the promise less generous has much to commend it in comparison with the Green Paper alternative of scrapping SERPS. The 1975 Social Security Pensions Act was based on nearly two decades of debate, with considerable all party support for the final outcome. Little has changed since 1975, save that the scheme has perhaps turned out to be unrealistically generous, given likely demographic trends and their effect on output. The proposed changes should reduce the most acute cost (i.e. demand-side pressures), particularly if buttressed by the supply-side policies discussed in section 3.4. In the USA similar changes, in the form of future increases in contribution rates and in the retirement age, have already been announced.

3.5.2 The future

Policies in the face of demographic change discussed earlier imply the following trends over the next one to two decades. There will be increased mechanisation to raise the productivity of individual workers. At risk of indulging in wishful thinking, there might also be increased investment in labour, through raised staying-on rates at school, higher age participation rates in higher education and greater emphasis on training both prior to entering the labour force, and on a continuing basis.

A second set of policies would increase labour-force participation. Child-care facilities, often run by firms to attract married women, will improve dramatically. Even if immigration policies remain tight, the European Community will relax entry conditions for 'guestworkers'. The age of retirement for women will be raised to that for men; and both men and women will be offered incentives to defer retirement even further.

4 The Poverty Trap

DAVID WHYNES

4.1 INTRODUCTION

The economy of the United Kingdom is, and for a long time has been, market capitalist. The principal allocation and distribution mechanism in the market economy is the exchange of commodities owned privately by individual economic agents. The incomes received by these agents are therefore functions of their relative successes in making exchanges with others. The poor in such an economy – those in receipt of the lowest incomes – are either those who happen to possess few exchangeable assets or those whose available assets command little exchange value. Unless one can make particularly strong assumptions about the distribution of assets amongst agents, the existence of income inequality within any market economy at any given time must be taken as axiomatic.

The existence of a class of persons with non-existent or low market incomes has long been recognised in the United Kingdom. Significantly, it has also been recognised as constituting a social problem, requiring a statutory response. The earliest remedies involved income redistribution from rich to poor, initially at the parish level but coming to lie eventually within the orbit of local government. The principal contribution of the twentieth century was to parallel income redistribution between individuals with an intertemporal transfer system of social insurance, with the responsibility for the administration of the bulk of poverty relief falling on central government. The change in policy structure over time was accompanied by a change in scale. In the mid-1880s, the statutory allocation of national resources to the relief of the poor was approximately £8 million, amounting to perhaps one-hundredth of 1 per cent of gross national product (Mitchell and Deane, 1962). In the mid-1980s, the government's annual social security budget for the UK amounted to approximately £45 billion, approaching 12 per cent of national product, and this figure does not include additional welfare benefits to the poor paid in kind e.g. health care, public housing and education (Barr, 1987).

The fundamental question to be asked of any policies directed against poverty is – do they result in the poor becoming less poor? Attempting to answer this question, an empirical study by Beckerman and Clark (1982) concluded that the number of people living in conditions of poverty in the UK would have been seven times higher had not a social security system of the type then prevailing been in operation. O'Higgins (1985a) estimated that the poorest 20 per cent of UK households earned only 0.6 per cent of market income in 1982, yet received 11.3 per cent of national disposable income, as a result of income redistribution. Survey data for 1986 reveal that the average annual final income of the poorest 20 per cent of UK households was raised from £130 to £4130 (from 1 to 47 per cent of the national average) as a result of the receipt of state welfare benefits, both in cash and in kind. This increase was financed, in part, from net transfers from richer households. The final income of the average household amongst the richest 20 per cent amounted to 70 per cent of its market income (CSO, 1990, p. 94). It is therefore impossible to escape the conclusions that a considerable quantity of resources is being redistributed, and that the lower income groups are the net recipients.

An apparently minor rewording of the original question, however, prevents us from drawing such straightforward conclusions. In asking whether poverty policy enables a poor household to become less poor we enter an area of contemporary debate which forms the principal subject of the present chapter. The proposition to be considered is that, whilst the prevailing system grants poor households more net income than they would otherwise receive as a result of market forces, it does not enable them to escape from the circumstances which created their poverty in the first place; indeed, it might well serve to perpetuate it. Poor households might become trapped in their poverty.

4.2 THE POVERTY PLATEAU

The broad structure of income redistribution instruments in the United Kingdom can be outlined very simply. There are four components:

1. For earned incomes above a statutory tax payment threshold, a proportion of the difference between the earned income and the tax threshold is paid into the Consolidated Fund, the government's main revenue and expenditure account. For example, were the tax rate to be 0.25, the tax threshold £3000 and the individual's income £7000, then £1000 would be payable to the fund as income tax.
2. All employees and employers make obligatory contributions to the National Insurance Fund. This fund then makes disbursements to employees in the event of their withdrawal from the labour market, arising from unemployment, long-term sickness or old age (most sick pay in the short-term is the responsibility of the employer). Contributions are earnings related, up to a maximum contribution level, and all the benefits are liable for taxation.
3. The Consolidated Fund finances a class of non-contributory, means-tested benefits. Principal amongst such benefits are, first, *Income Support*, paid to any individual whose nominal income falls below a statutorily defined level. The level of benefit available is the difference between the individual's nominal income and the defined level. Second, *Family Credit* is available to low-income families with breadwinners in full-time employment. Again, an income threshold level for eligibility is defined, and the maximum credit available to a given family is determined by family size. If family income is less than the threshold level the maximum credit is paid. If family income exceeds the defined level, the family receives the maximum reduced by a proportion of the excess of income over the threshold. Assume, for example, that the defined eligibility level is £50 per week and the maximum credit available is £40. A family with a weekly income of £30 would thus receive the maximum, giving a gross income of £70 per week. Assuming that the proportionate reduction, or 'taper', for incomes in excess of the threshold is 50 per cent, a family earning £60 per

week would be entitled to £[40–0.5(60–50)], i.e. £35 in Family
Credit, giving a gross weekly income of £95. Finally, *Housing
Benefit*, administered by local authorities to assist those on low
incomes to meet accommodation expenses, has broadly similar
operational characteristics (including a taper) to Family Credit.
4. There exists a class of tax-financed, non-means-tested benefits,
   the receipt of which are contingent solely upon applicant circumstances. Examples include the flat-rate Child Benefit (available to all those responsible for the upkeep of children) and
   mobility allowances (for the severely disabled).

In addition, certain of these benefits, such as Income Support, are
'passport' benefits. Being in receipt of such benefits entitles the
individual or household to receive additional services free of
charge, for example, medical prescriptions, dental treatment and
school meals for children. It is important to appreciate that, despite frequent changes in nomenclature and operating criteria, 'the
system we have today is essentially the same as that introduced in
1934' (Atkinson, 1989, p. 91).

Beyond the simplicity of the broad structure, however, matters
become mind-bogglingly complex, especially with respect to the
precise specification of tax liability, benefit eligibility rules (estimation of household nominal incomes) and payment levels. The
Child Poverty Action Group publish annual claimants' guides to
obtaining benefits, and their volumes for 1988/9 contain 630 dense-
ly packed pages which deal only with the major benefits (CPAG,
1988; 1989). It is only by consulting compendia of this nature that
one can fully understand the system's operation, assuming that
one possesses the necessary legalistic mind. Income tax rates have
gradually fallen over the past decade and benefit levels are reviewed regularly, the majority being revised each year. Amendments to social welfare legislation have been enacted on almost an
annual basis. Most importantly, the rate of flow of the supplementary regulations issued by government to agencies responsible for the day-to-day administration of the system has been
even higher.

As explained earlier, a household's disposable income after
redistribution depends both upon taxes and insurance contributions paid and upon benefits received. Both, moreover, depend in
some degree upon the level of 'nominal' household income. In

general, as nominal income rises, tax and contribution liabilities increase whilst benefit entitlements decline. Depending upon the regulations in force and upon precise family circumstances, it is possible for a household to discover that its net disposable does not vary substantially over a range of nominal incomes. Piachaud (1971) was one of the first to examine this phenomenon, and he provided the following example. In 1971, a four-child family earning £20 per week had a tax/insurance liability of £2.20. At this income school meals would be provided free of charge. Including benefits from Family Allowance (a forerunner of Family Credit), net disposable income for the household amounted to £19.70. However, a nominal earned income of £23 per week incurred a tax/insurance liability of £3.25, and this higher income disqualified the family from receiving free school meals (weekly cost £1.75). In consequence, net disposable income amounted to £19.90, from which it can be concluded that a 15 per cent increase in nominal income generated only a 1 per cent increase in disposable income. As Piachaud noted, the effect is equivalent to the payment of a 93 per cent 'marginal tax rate' on the extra earned income. Bradshaw and Wakeman (1972) were able to provide similar instances – a two-child family, for example, received only a 14 per cent increase in disposable income from a nominal income rise of 71 per cent (£14 to £24 per week), implying a 'marginal tax rate' of 80 per cent.

The phenomenon which these examples are illustrating is termed the 'poverty plateau'. Its manifestation is a flat distribution of disposable incomes over a range of increasing nominal incomes, and it occurs as a result of gains in nominal income made by a household being substantially eroded by increases in liabilities or losses of benefit. A general model of the effect is impossible to construct owing to the regular revisions which have been made to the social security system. The following idealised example, however, illustrates the essential points.

Assume that the household's nominal weekly income is Y, the combined income tax/national insurance contribution threshold is Y_I, and the combined tax/insurance contribution rate is r. Additional household income is available under a system of income support analogous to Family Credit. The weekly income threshold for eligibility for the maximum amount of income support (C) is Y_F (assumed $> Y_I$), and the taper on amounts above the threshold is t. Family support is a passport to additional benefits of value P, and the family also receives non-means-tested benefits to the value N. It accordingly follows that, for nominal incomes between zero and Y_I, household disposable income (Y_D) may be represented as:

$$Y_D = Y + C + P + N$$

and $dY_D/dY = 1$. For incomes greater than Y_I but less than Y_F:

$$Y_D = Y - r(Y - Y_I) + C + P + N$$

implying a rate of change of disposable income with respect to nominal income of $(1 - r)$. Beyond Y_F, the taper on income support operates, with the result that:

$$Y_D = Y - r(Y - Y_I) + C - t(Y - Y_F) + P + N$$

up to the nominal income, Y_S, where benefits tend to zero ($Y_S = Y_F + C/t$). In this range, $dY_D/dY = (1 - r - t)$, which must be smaller than $(1 - r)$ as long as the taper is positive. Indeed, a combined tax rate and support taper approaching unity will necessarily produce a very low rate of increase of disposable income for increases in nominal income within the range ($Y_F < Y < Y_S$). At Y_S, the taper ceases to operate but benefits of the absolute value P are thereafter lost. Beyond Y_S no further benefits are available and dY_D/dY reverts to $(1 - r)$. These effects are represented diagrammatically in Figure 4.1 and the 'plateau' effect is immediately evident. Also evident is the significant consequence of the loss of benefits P when the household is no longer eligible for the 'passport' family support. As may be seen, the effective marginal tax rate on income levels immediately above Y_S exceeds 100 per cent owing to the loss of this benefit.

Since the identification of the poverty plateau, a considerable amount of effort has been directed towards estimating its precise magnitude. For the early 1980s, Parker (1982) notes that, in the case of a single person, a full-time job at £1.75 per hour could generate approximately the same disposable weekly income as a half-time job, owing to tax increase and benefit decrease effects. The net disposable income for a lone mother with two children varied only between £48 and £56 per week for nominal earned incomes in the range zero to £100 per week. CPAG (1982) estimated the implications of nominal income changes for the net disposable income of a family containing three children as follows. At £50 per week, an earner was responsible for income tax and insurance contributions of approximately 39 pence in the pound, although assistance with rent, rates and the Family Income Supplement (FIS – analogous to the modern Family Credit) brought disposable income to approximately £90 per week. As nominal income increased, however, all such assistance decreased, FIS at a taper of 50 pence for every extra pound of nominal income, and rent and rate allowances by smaller rates. In consequence, disposable income for a nominal income of £100 was actually £2 per week lower than for £50. At a nominal income of £101 eligibility for FIS ceased and, with it, eligibility for free school meals. In consequence, disposable income at £101 was estimated to be £6 *lower* than for £100, implying a marginal tax rate well in excess of 100 per cent. In fact, disposable income did not exceed that obtained from a nominal income of £50 until weekly earnings of £123 were exceeded. These calculations mirror closely the theoretical portrayal in Figure 4.1.

The 1986 Social Security Act was instrumental in ameliorating some of the extremes of the poverty plateau, by requiring that family credit and housing benefit eligibility be assessed with respect to post-tax, as opposed to pre-tax, income. The effect was to ensure that benefit gains were less likely to be more than offset by tax losses. This having been said, the issue of the poverty plateau remains, and our original model can easily be modified to demonstrate the point. Revising the earlier equation for the relevant range, $Y_F < Y < Y_S$, we obtain:

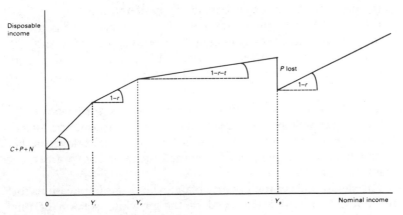

FIGURE 4.1   The poverty plateau

$$Y_D = Y - r(Y - Y_I) + C - t[Y - r(Y - Y_I) - Y_F] + P + N$$

and $dY_D/dY) = (1 - r - t + rt) = (1 - r)(1 - t)$. The plateau in this range accordingly becomes less flat than the one portrayed in Figure 4.1; for example, with $r = 0.25$ and $t = 0.7$, the marginal increase in disposable income with respect to changes in nominal income is 0.05 according to the original formulation, but 0.23 in the revised version. However, this should be compared to the situation of richer households well above the plateau who can expect a marginal increase of £0.75 from every pound of earned income. Hill (1990) elegantly expresses the practical implications of the present system as follows:

> Consider the example of a low-paid worker who is entitled to both family credit and housing benefit. What happens when that worker receives a pay rise of £1 per week? First, that additional pound may be reduced by 25 pence income tax and by social security contributions which may be as much as nine pence in the pound. If these are taken into account, therefore, the actual gain from that pound increase in income will already have been reduced by 34 pence. Then, the remaining 66 per cent affects the individual's entitlement to family credit which has a 70 per cent taper. That means that family credit will be reduced by 70 per cent of that 66 pence, leaving the individual with no more than a 20 pence gain. However, that is not the end of the story. Even this small residual gain will affect the individual's claim to housing benefit. The housing benefit taper, if the individual is entitled to both rent and community charge rebate, is 80 pence in the pound. Thus, the remaining 20 pence will be reduced by 80 per cent of it, giving an eventual net gain from that pound increase in gross income of only 4 pence. (Ibid., p. 106)

From Hill's figures, it would still appear possible for a poor individual to face a 96 per cent marginal tax rate. It should be added that working pensioners at present face a 100 per cent taper on the National Insurance pension, for earned incomes above a certain amount.

The significance of the poverty plateau lies in its implications for the question raised at the end of the previous section of this chapter – does poverty policy enable the poor to become richer? It is quite clear, given the existence of the plateau, that households within the relevant income range will find that attempts to increase their nominal incomes result, at best, in only minor improvements in their disposable incomes. In this sense they can be truly said to be trapped in poverty. It is also possible to argue, on intuitive grounds, that higher marginal tax rates for the poor hardly constitutes a fair criterion for income redistribution. Atkinson (1989) has estimated that, for 1980, the majority of UK households (approximately 75 per cent) faced marginal tax rates of 37 per cent, which represented at that time the standard income tax and National Insurance contributions. However, 8 per cent faced the higher effective marginal tax rates of the poverty plateau, brought about by the tax/benefit interaction described above. Parker (1989) suggests that 40 per cent of the UK population were eligible for withdrawable benefits in 1986 – pensioners, families in which the earner was unemployed or sick, large families with low earned incomes. The incomes of all these families would thus be vulnerable to the plateau effect in some degree.

4.3 ELIMINATING THE POVERTY PLATEAU

The poverty plateau described in section 4.2 results from the interaction of the income tax liabilities, National Insurance contributions and means-tested benefits. The specific problem is relatively recent in origin, arising because of changes in the constituent elements.

Since the Second World War, 'fiscal drag' has persisted, arising from the reluctance of successive Chancellors of the Exchequer to increase the tax threshold in line with increases in earnings. The tax base – that amount of income available to the government for taxation – has been gradually eroded by the increasing generosity of tax relief on such outgoings as mortgage interest and private pension contributions. In an attempt to generate sufficient revenue over time, therefore, the government has required more and more lower-income families to pay income tax. In the case of a childless couple, the tax break-even point (the income at which tax liability begins after deduction of allowances) shifted from two-thirds to one-third of average earnings between 1950 and 1983. For a married couple with two children the point was approximately one-third *above* average male manual earnings in 1950, but one-third *below* in 1985 (Parker, 1989).

Between 1975 and 1984, National Insurance contributions rose from 6 to 9 per cent of nominal income, partly because of reduced government transfers to the fund and partly because of increased demands (higher unemployment and the reform of the state pension scheme). The final contribution to the creation of the poverty plateau was the range of means-tested benefits – Family Income Supplement, rent allowances and rate rebates – introduced by the Conservative government between 1970 and 1974. These were intended to reflect the party's commitment to greater selectivity in the scope of welfare provision and have passed unchanged in principle into the present social security structure (Deacon and Bradshaw, 1983).

One further, and longer-term, change in economic structure has also contributed to the creation of the modern poverty plateau. The relief of poverty in the nineteenth century was founded upon a very fundamental principle relating to conditions of entitlement, the 1834 Poor Law Commissioners asserting that: 'The first and most essential of all conditions is that the situation of the individual relieved should not be made really or apparently so eligible as the situation of the independent labourer of the lowest class' (quoted by Brown, 1990, p. 3) The incomes of those on state benefits, in other words, ought to be less than the lowest incomes prevailing in the labour market. Nowadays this principle can be observed not to hold – it is quite possible for households to receive weekly benefits well in excess of that which could be earned as a result of the sale of labour. Two factors account for this, the first being the institution of National Insurance. Whilst labour market incomes may be within the theoretical range zero to infinity, depending upon conditions of supply and demand, insurance benefits will be positive, as determined by the household's contribution record and the weekly level of pay-out as set by the government. Second, the gradual political enfranchisement of the bulk of the population, which occurred between the 1832 Reform Act and the 1969 lowering of the voting age to 18 years, required government actions to reflect more accurately matters of popular concern. Given that modern UK electorates include pensioners, the unemployed, the sick, and families on low incomes, it is hardly surprising that increases in benefits over the past century have occurred. The poor command a great many votes, which will be used, one assumes, to further their own interests. Modern market incomes, however, are determined as they always have been, with reference to impersonal forces as opposed to political will.

Compressing the range of nominal incomes along the poverty plateau, or increasing its gradient, by statutory means, necessitates reversing the trends mentioned above. Returning to the equations derived earlier, it is evident that raising the tax threshold (Y_t), lowering the rate of income tax/insurance contributions (r) and the taper (t) on means-tested benefits, changing the eligibility criteria for additional benefits (P) obtained via 'passport', and increasing non-means-tested benefits (N) will all have the effect of increasing the amount of disposable income for any given nominal income. Lowering the taper (t) on means-tested benefits would make far more households eligible for means-tested benefits (Y_s increases). The 'passport' problem, which produces the abrupt fall in disposable income after eligibility for means-tested benefits ceases, would be resolved only by a change in the way in which these benefits were operated. The introduction of some degree of taper into these benefits, or the provision of the relevant services to all at zero price (e.g. abolishing prescription charges), represent two such possibilities. Of all the non-means-tested benefits which ease the situations of households along the poverty plateau, Child Benefit appears to be the most significant. This is because the arrival of children in a low-income household can be an important contributor towards pushing the family into poverty, as a result of the combination of additional costs of child care and the loss of income owing to one parent ceasing paid employment. The incomes of the poorest 25 per cent of households with children is presently very much lower than the incomes of childless households. Oppenheim (1990) suggests that the average income in a childless household amongst the poorest 25 per cent is 25 per cent higher than the income of a two-child household, and more than double the income of a four-child household. As Deacon and Bradshaw (1983, p. 172) note: 'Child benefit increases are a better focussed method of reducing the poverty trap because virtually only families with children are caught in it.'

One important caveat must be applied to the whole of the preceding analysis. The assumption has been made throughout that households will be claiming their full benefit entitlement, yet evidence suggests that this is not the case. Because of the recent reforms of the social security system an accurate assessment of take-up of present benefits is impossible, although official estimates for the mid-1980s suggested that the take-up for Supplementary Benefit (Income Support) was 76 per cent and for Family Income Supplement (Family Credit) 54 per cent (Hill, 1990). Research into the reasons for non-take-up of benefits suggest that a number of factors are relevant. First, households may be ignorant of the benefits to which they are entitled. Second, they may find the administrative procedures too complex and too difficult to handle. Third, claiming benefits – 'living off the state' – has always had associated with it a degree of social stigma. Fourth, claimants may be deterred if they are reluctant to allow officials to probe into their personal circumstances (means-tested benefits are granted only after detailed enquiries into household means). Finally, for some households, the amount of benefit available will be insignificant and thus not worth claiming. It is officially recognised that 'take-up tends to be higher as the amount of entitlement increases' (Hansard, in Atkinson, 1989, p. 192). The clear implication is that there exists a sizeable minority of households who, strictly speaking, are poorer than they need to be. One of the virtues claimed for Child Benefit is that its take-up rate is particularly high, on the grounds that (i) it is well understood and easy to obtain, (ii) no means-test enquiries are involved, (iii) for poor households, the value of the benefit is substantial, and (iv) being available to all, no negative social stigma is attached to its receipt.

Over the past two decades, a number of modifications to the prevailing structure of social security have been suggested, with the intention of eliminating the worst effects of the poverty plateau. During the late 1960s and early 1970s, the United States, which had been encountering very similar problems to those of the United Kingdom, was the scene of a number of practical experiments involving 'Negative Income Taxes' (NIT). Comprehensive trials were conducted in New Jersey (Pechman and Timane, 1975) and in Denver and Seattle (Robins *et al.*, 1980). Households in this latter experiment were guaranteed a minimum disposable income or support level, determined by household size. Increases in nominal income resulting from earnings were reduced by a taper (t) up to a threshold point; thereafter, household incomes were reduced by the income tax rate (r). Figure 4.2 illustrates the

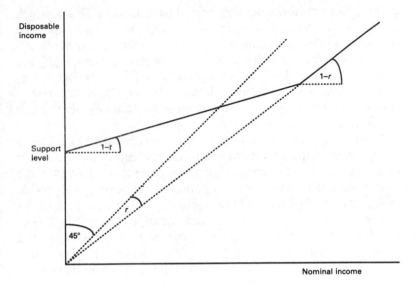

FIGURE 4.2 Negative income tax

system. As is evident, the poverty plateau of the form portrayed in Figure 4.1 does not exist and, in this respect, the system succeeds in defeating the problem posed. However, the Denver/Seattle experiment produced an additional and very significant conclusion, namely, that the rates of marital dissolution and family breakdown tend to increase dramatically as a result of guaranteed support. Indeed, this result was predicted by the experimenters, on the grounds that the benefit penalties incurred as a result from leaving the family fall considerably under the NIT model. Single persons simply become households in their own right and are therefore eligible for their own support income.

More recently, Parker (1989) has advocated a range of 'Basic Income Guarantee' (BIG) schemes as a solution to the poverty plateau. The precise details of these schemes are complex, although the broad principles are extremely simple. Substantial administrative reform is envisaged, including the abolition of tax reliefs and virtually all of the present welfare benefits, plus the integration of income tax payments and insurance contributions into the 'basic income contribution' (BIC). All individuals are entitled to a statutorily defined 'partial basic income' (PBI), which can be supplemented in specific circumstances, e.g. expectant mothers, children, pensioners, disabled persons, lone parents. All incomes derived from, for example, earnings or savings (Y) are subject to tax, or BIC, at a standard rate (r). In consequence, disposable income, Y_D, equals $[PBI + (1 - r)Y]$. A linear relationship between nominal and disposable incomes accordingly exists, and the poverty plateau disappears.

There is, of course, one other very obvious method of increasing the gradient of the poverty plateau, namely, reducing support for those on the lowest incomes. For the moment, we shall presume that making the very poor even poorer is not seen as a desirable policy option. However, *all* the alternatives above (excluding this one) entail some net cost to the Exchequer. The simple raising of Child Benefit by £1, for example, means total costs of several hundred million pounds per year. The US negative tax experiment, a more extreme case, was estimated to imply additional costs of $30 billion (1974 prices!) for national implementation. Assuming the government's budgetary stance is to be maintained, these costs will have to be recouped from revenues gained elsewhere in the tax system, for example, via the introduction of higher rates of tax for richer households (the BIG schemes are self-financing under the assumption of higher rates of income tax than those presently prevailing). The implications of funding poverty relief will concern us in a later section.

4.4 POVERTY AS A CLOSED SYSTEM

Judged in the theoretical terms of Figure 4.1, a household is confined to the poverty plateau unless it is capable of obtaining a nominal weekly income of a level beyond that at which the benefit tapers operate. This approach to the problem of poverty entrapment is not invalid but, being concerned solely with present income, it is clearly unidimensional. Moreover, it does not address the fundamental question of how the household becomes poor in the first place.

A reasonably clear causal explanation of poverty exists in the case of the elderly. Provision for old age takes the form of deductions from current earned income, as contributions to National

Insurance and private pensions or savings schemes. Individuals sufficiently well paid during their period of employment will be in a position, other things being equal, to transfer sizeable sums to finance their future retirements. Individuals in low-wage employment, however, will have proportionately less current income available for forward transfer. Historically, reliance on the state pension alone has made such households amongst the poorest in the country, for the state pension has yielded a weekly income of between 16 and 20 per cent of average earnings for the past two decades (Oppenheim, 1990). As the household's income position having ceased work is completely determined by its consumption and savings decisions during work, low-earnings households are constrained to become low-pension households. Put the other way around, a presently poor pensioner household is either one which had insufficient resources or opportunities in the past to supplement its state pension, or one in which resources and opportunities or resources were used to gratify current as opposed to future needs. In either case, resources from the past are unavailable to ameliorate conditions in the present.

'Lone parenting' is another circumstance where the explanation of poverty is relatively straightforward. Unless the circumstances of the household prior to marital breakdown are such that the child-carer can be adequately supported by the ex-partner, divorce or separation obliges the carer to choose between the labour market and state benefits in order to obtain a livelihood. The labour market option, however, even assuming that employment is available, requires the generation of a sufficiently high income to cover the costs of child care whilst the parent is working. In 1985, more than half of lone parents were dependent upon state benefits (Parker, 1989).

Turning to more complex cases, the socio-economic characteristics of the poor have been the subject of detailed research in the recent past. The important 'Black Report' (Townsend and Davidson, 1982), for example, identified a strong association between occupational class (i.e. household income levels) and the incidence of poor health. The prevalence of long-standing illness amongst unskilled manual workers has been found to be around three times that amongst professionals. A contemporary reappraisal of the report (Davy-Smith *et al.*, 1990) concludes that, not only do the associations still hold, but the health imbalance between rich and poor has increased. Brown and Madge (1982) observed a correlation between the probability of unemployment and the occupational class of the employee (workers with lower levels of skill were more likely to become unemployed), and an association between low income and poor housing conditions. Most significantly, they also identified the possibility of 'multiple deprivation'. Several manifestations of poverty, in other words, such as job instability, disability, poor health and substandard housing might well all coexist within a single household. 'All the evidence suggests that although many deprived families suffer only from a single form of adversity, there is, at the same time, a tendency for a variety of problems to become concentrated in certain families' (ibid., p. 150). Deprivation 'is quite commonly compounded by overlap to become multiple deprivation, and it may sometimes be followed by similar patterns in the next generation' (ibid., p. 178).

By way of illustration of the implications of such findings, consider the following scenario, based on a model developed by Jackson (1972). Assume a household in which the principal earner has a low level of educational attainment (a low stock of human capital). This will constrain him or her to holding an unskilled manual job, which will typically generate below-average earnings. Low income will oblige the family to seek accommodation at low rent, and the quality of such accommodation is correspondingly likely to be poor. Poor housing conditions – damp, inadequate heating and overcrowding – exercise detrimental effects upon health status. As technical change in the economy advances, the unskilled worker's position in the competitive labour market deteriorates, a process exacerbated by declining health. The likelihood of unemployment for this worker therefore increases and, with it, the likelihood of the family becoming dependent upon state welfare benefits. With unemployment, this household reaches the poverty plateau, at which point further forces may come into play. An even lower household income might require the search for even cheaper housing, with increased health risks. A prolonged period of unemployment may further weaken the worker's competitive position in the labour market, and reduce the likelihood of a job in the future. Long-term unemployment will, moreover, tend to erode any accumulated savings which the family may possess, owing to the requirements of daily living. The poverty of the present generation might well have implications for that of the future, because the children of this family would face a strong financial incentive to seek remunerative employment as soon as possible, in order either to support the family or to escape from it. However, this short-term income is purchased at the expense of obtaining educational qualifications which would have secured more favourable earning opportunities in the future. Indeed, poverty may constrain the children to follow exactly in their parents' footsteps. (An interesting test of this latter hypothesis is provided by the follow-up of Rowntree's 1901 study of York – Atkinson, Maynard and Trinder, 1983.)

The household in the above scenario has clearly become trapped in poverty. Both the psychological and the economic consequences of such a trap can be profound, as Oppenheim (1990) notes. These consequences include the sense of the family continually 'going short', spending less on foodstuffs, clothing and essential services than the average. They also include a sense of isolation from social activities owing to lack of finance, the creation of a sense of dependency on others, stress and anxiety, and the feeling of being involved in a constant battle with the authorities in order to claim benefits. Empirical sociological studies, such as those included in Allen *et al.* (1986), further highlight the adverse effects of poverty on family and race relations, including crime and homelessness. Poverty also induces debt, as families struggle to cope with household expenses. Berthoud and Kempson (1990) have demonstrated a strong negative association between household income and the likelihood of a household having outstanding debt – 28 per cent of households with weekly incomes below £100 appear to have outstanding debts, compared with 15 per cent of 'average income' households and 3 per cent of the richest households. The majority of the debt problems of low income families appear to be associated with the purchase of housing, heating and other essential services. Debt has an immediate short-term consequence on poverty, because the state is empowered to enforce deductions from benefits to cover arrears in tax, power and public sector rent. However, the long-term effect of debt accumulation is to further the entrapment of the household into poverty, owing to escalating debt service requirements.

As was discussed in the previous section of this chapter, increasing welfare benefits can do much to alleviate the predicament of individuals and households trapped in these forms of structural poverty. Indeed, in the case of pensioners, an increase in the statutory level of benefit probably represents the only solution. For many other poor people, however, alternative means of escape may be available. One possible solution to poverty induced by low wages, for example, is the institution of a national minimum wage within the labour market, although such an institution has little to commend it. From the theoretical point of view, raising wages entails raising firms' costs, with the predicted effects of (i) price inflation, (ii) reduced competitiveness, and (iii) reduced demand for labour, i.e. unemployment. Another possibility appears more attractive.

Unemployment is a major cause of poverty, and the unemployment level in the United Kingdom has been of the order of 10 per cent for the past decade. A reduction in the rate of unemployment would clearly have beneficial effects in terms of poverty reduction, as the following simple model demonstrates. Suppose the economy consists of ninety employed persons, each receiving a weekly wage of £1000. These people pay a 1 per cent income tax to support ten unemployed persons, and each of the latter therefore receives £90 per week. Now suppose that five of these unemployed obtain work, also at £1000 per week. With ninety-five earners each paying a 1 per cent tax, this economy can afford a more than doubled unemployment benefit of £190 per person. Alternatively, a benefit of £133 per unemployed person (still almost 50 per cent higher than in the original position) can be afforded with a reduced tax rate of 0.7 per cent. Were unemployment in this model economy to increase to 15 per cent, however, a 1 per cent tax rate would only produce an unemployment benefit of £57 per unemployed person, making the unemployed very much poorer than before. In fact, a tax rate of approximately 1.5 per cent on each employed person would be necessary to maintain the benefit at £90. By these calculations, transforming welfare claimants into taxpayers produces potential gains for all concerned.

Increases in employment within the economy should therefore improve the fortunes of both the formerly unemployed and those remaining unemployed. Economic theory suggests that employment increases result from the stimulation of aggregate demand, although there has been considerable debate throughout the 1980s over where the responsibility for such stimulation lies. Traditional Keynesians see the responsibility lying with the government, and would recommend expansionary fiscal and monetary policies to generate employment increases. The governments of the 1980s, in contrast, have been much more sceptical of their own powers to control events and have expressed more faith in the expansionary potential of private economic agents. For their part, their macroeconomic management over the past decade has been, in the main, contractionary (high interest rates and net reductions in public spending).

Given an expansion of aggregate demand, the acquisition of skills offers an unemployed person an increased probability of obtaining a job and thereby moving out of poverty. Indeed, the Denver–Seattle NIT experiments included training incentives as an element of their support packages, and it was concluded that 'subsidies clearly induced people to take additional schooling' (Robins *et al.*, 1980, p. 278). It has, nevertheless, become commonplace to remark that the United Kingdom has a very poor record in this respect, with far fewer young people 'staying on' after school than in comparable industrial economies. Ainley and Corney (1990) argue that this is because training has never been seen as a principal force in economic development in the United Kingdom, despite attempts by the now-downgraded Manpower Services Commission to signal its significance during the 1970s and 1980s. Reliance has always been placed on the capacity of industry to train labour very much on a *laissez-faire* basis; the German system, by contrast, is employer-led and employer-financed but is highly organised.

4.5 HOW MUCH IS POVERTY RELIEF WORTH?

In the preceding sections we have examined a variety of ways in which households can become trapped in poverty and suggested a variety of remedies to facilitate their escape. All these remedies, however, have one thing in common – they all require net income transfers from relatively rich taxpayers in the short term. This is true whether one conceives of poverty relief as the eradication of the poverty plateau or as investment in the poor, enabling them to escape by improving their earning opportunities. Poverty, it seems, is the one social problem which *can* be resolved by 'throwing money at it', but the question remains – how much should be thrown? The answer to this question depends crucially on the assumptions one makes with respect to the motivations of tax-payers in a market capitalist economy, and there are three alternatives. Unfortunately, as we shall see, it is quite possible to deduce that, from the point of view of the taxpayer, the poverty plateau is *not* a problem.

First, allocating resources to a poverty relief policy might be seen as reflecting private concern for one's own immediate circumstances. It is not irrational for a presently rich individual, fearing poverty in the future, to contribute towards the collective provision of a safety net to cushion a possible fall from affluence, so long as the expected benefits exceed the expected costs. Such a safety net, whilst preserving the given individual from destitution, would also preserve others in similar situations. Suppose, for example, society consists of 100 individuals, ninety of whom will be working at any one time (at an income of £1000 per month), and ten of whom will be unemployed (zero income). Assuming that each individual faces the same chances of unemployment, he or she is faced with a 90 per cent chance of receiving £1000 and a 10 per cent chance of total destitution. Providing welfare benefits to each of the ten paupers of £200 per month would entail deducting £22.2 per month from each income-earner, confronting each with a 90 per cent chance of earning £978.8 and a 10 per cent chance of receiving £200. Although each individual's expected income under the two scenarios is identical (£900), the welfare benefit alternative offers a guarantee of income even under adverse circumstances. Sacrificing income at the top end for security at the bottom might well be interpreted as the prudent strategy. It is this insurance logic, of course, which underlay the Beveridge welfare proposals of the 1940s.

The evidence considered earlier, however, suggests that individuals do not face equal probabilities of unemployment, the jobs of more skilled individuals being both more remunerative and more secure. Accordingly, consider a society comprising sixty rich individuals earning £1000, each facing a probability of unemployment of 0.1, and forty poor individuals earning £500, each facing a probability of unemployment of 0.5. Again, the proposed level of unemployment benefit is £200 per week. As there will be twenty-six individuals unemployed at any one time (six rich and twenty poor), the required total benefit is £5200. Total earned income is

£(54 000 + 10 000), as generated by rich and poor, implying a necessary contribution rate of 8.12 per cent. This contribution rate is quite acceptable to the poor; without the unemployment benefit system they face an expected income of $0.5(500) + 0.5(0) = £250$, whilst, with it, they face an expected income of $0.5(459.4) + 0.5(200) = £329.7$. The rich, on the other hand, will find this rate quite unacceptable. With no benefit guarantee for unemployment they face an expected income of $0.9(1000) + 0.1(0) = £900$ whilst, with it, their expected income will be $0.9(918.8) + 0.1(200) = £846.9$. Assuming that this society is democratically constructed, the poverty relief proposal will defeated by fifty-four votes to forty-six (the latter comprising the forty poor who would have gained, plus the six formerly rich but now unemployed). No provision for the poor will be made in this society, because the majority are not willing to pay for it. On the basis of empirical studies of income distribution during the 1980s, for example, O'Higgins (1985b) and Hills (1990), this model might well be appropriate to the prevailing situation in the United Kingdom.

Second, poverty policy might be seen as a response to an externality effect within the market economy. Although conducting their affairs in the market, individuals might express a concern over the equity of outcome as it applies to other people. Richer people might therefore be concerned about the welfare of the poor and would thus willing to transfer resources towards them. James Buchanan (1968) has argued that the existence of poverty within a community does not, in itself, pose any external diseconomy on remaining members, although its manifestations do. It is the fact that a family 'lives in a dilapidated house and dresses its children in rags that imposes on our sensibilities' (ibid., p. 189). Economists such as Culyer (1980) have gone on to argue that caring for others in specific areas related to poverty is an empirical fact:

> Were caring not in large part specific, we would be hard put to explain the existence of the Welfare State, and familiar arguments for subsidies, vouchers, etc., would have no economic rationale . . . The very *existence* of the Welfare State is evidence *for* the proposition that specific caring exists, for if individuals did not care for one another then no externality would exist and there would be little reason for collectivist action. (Ibid., p. 65).

According to this motivational assumption, poverty relief in the market economy is essentially charity, and it is up to the donors to determine the form in which charity is given.

Finally, poverty policy might be interpreted as an instrument of social control. This issue of control arises from the evident capacity of the market economy to generate extremes in both income and wealth, and thus to produce a class of gainers – the rich – and a class of losers – the poor. The appreciation of this state of affairs leads directly to the Hobbesian question, namely, why should those evidently disadvantaged by a social system continue to permit its existence? Adam Smith, in his *Lectures on Jurisprudence* delivered in the 1760s, found the following answer: 'Laws and government may be considered in . . . every case, as a combination of the rich to oppress the poor, and preserve to themselves the inequality of goods, which would otherwise be soon destroyed by the attacks of the poor, who, if not hindered by government, would soon reduce the others to an equality with themselves by open violence' (quoted by Winch, 1978, p. 58). This theme was taken up again in the *Wealth of Nations*: 'For one very rich man, there must be at least five hundred poor . . . The affluence of the rich excites the indignation of the poor, who are often both driven by want, and prompted by envy to invade his possessions . . . It is only under the shelter of the civil magistrate, that the owner of that valuable property . . . can sleep a single night in security' (Smith, 1873, p. 297).

In Smith's world, where poverty relief was rudimentary, political and legal repression appeared the only answers to the control of the poor, although the institution of collectivised social security opens up new possibilities. First, the escalation of the level of poverty relief such as has occurred during the twentieth century should have the effect, *ceteris paribus*, of diminishing the revolutionary or criminal tendencies of the poor, as the perceived benefits accruing to the losers in the system increase. Indeed, it is rational for the richer members of society to be willing to transfer some of their incomes to the poor if, as a result of so doing, the risks of the expropriation of the remainder are more than proportionately reduced. Contrary to Buchanan's assertion cited above, there *can* exist additional externalities from poverty, namely, the risks of the rich losing their properties by theft or violence. Second, the modern contributory mechanism of poverty relief, financed by virtually all adult workers and a substantial number of the unemployed, incorporates all such individuals into a 'club'. In that all pay membership fees, all have an incentive to ensure the retention of the integrity of the club in order to obtain benefits. Finally, the provision of a very comprehensive range of benefits such as presently exists in the UK implies that the more one's position in the market economy's income distribution deteriorates then the more one becomes reliant upon state welfare benefits which are themselves generated by the market economy. Put crudely, the worse the system treats you then the more you come to rely on it. Taken together, these factors act as a powerful adjunct to Smith's political and legal repression as the mechanism for the retention of the integrity of market capitalism. The prevailing mechanism of poverty relief will require reform only when it proves destructive to the social fabric.

In answering the question – how much is poverty relief worth? – we conclude (i) possibly very little, if the self-interested taxpayer does not consider future poverty a likely state of the world for him or her to occupy, (ii) as much as the individual in capitalist society is willing to pay for the gratification of the relief of distress in others, or (iii) the minimum necessary to maintain the social fabric from which the taxpayer benefits. Moreover, with respect to this last point, there is no reason to expect the taxpayers to interpret the solution as assisting the poor in obtaining economic independence. They might well find it cheaper simply to maintain the poor on welfare benefits.

4.6 SUMMARY

This chapter has considered the notion of the poverty trap, in the sense of households being disabled from alleviating their own poverty. The poverty plateau represents such a trap, and comes about due to the interaction of the benefits and the tax/contributions systems. The consequence is to generate high effective marginal tax rates for an extended range of low nominal incomes. However, households can also be trapped in poverty due to the coincidence of a number of factors, such as unemployment, poor health, large families, and so forth. A variety of measures to eliminate these poverty traps have been discussed, ranging from 'negative income taxes' and 'guaranteed basic incomes' to demand management and the provision of training. All such measures, however, require a redistribution of income and there exist good economic reasons to believe that, in a democratic market capitalist economy, such redistribution has a low likelihood of occurring.

5 Benefits, Incentives and Uncertainty

CHRISTIAN DUSTMANN and
JOHN MICKLEWRIGHT*

5.1 INTRODUCTION

The effects of cash benefit programmes on individual behaviour in market economies has been the subject of enormous – and continuing – attention in the literature. This alone provides sufficient motivation for periodic reviews. At the present time, a most important additional motivation is the economic transformation of Eastern European economies – a 'current issue' not just in welfare economics but in every other aspect of economic analysis. What will be the effect of existing benefit programmes in Eastern Europe in the changed economic climate, for example the relatively generous family allowance programmes? What will be the effect of new programmes, most notably unemployment compensation schemes (not previously present due to the official absence of open unemployment in command economies and the incentives for enterprise managers to hoard labour)?

We do not attempt answers to these questions. Nor do we provide a comprehensive review of the huge body of theoretical and empirical evidence from Western market economies on the incentive effects of cash benefits. This would take far more space than we have and, moreover, there are available extensive recent reviews, for example, Atkinson (1987), Hurd (1990), Atkinson

* John Micklewright would like to acknowledge the debt to joint work with A. B. Atkinson, who is thanked for his comments.

and Micklewright (1990), Moffit (1992) and Barr (1992). Important current issues in the literature identified by these reviews cover a variety of areas. These include (i) the need to consider the impact of the full set of institutional details of a particular benefit programme (there is much more to be considered than simply the level of benefit), (ii) the implication for behaviour of the difference in operation between social insurance benefit and means-tested assistance benefit, and (iii) the difficulties involved in practice in separating the pure effect of benefit schemes on behaviour from unobserved characteristics which both affect behaviour and benefit entitlement.[1]

In this chapter we highlight one aspect of the literature which we feel deserves more analysis: the treatment of uncertainty. Uncertainty with respect to benefit entitlements and labour market prospects can be expected to be present in both established market economies and the transitional former command economies. In section 5.2 we consider the impact of uncertainty surrounding entitlement to benefit. This is not allowed for in the great majority of analyses of disincentive effects of benefits. Although uncertainty is at the root of several models of the labour market that have been used to consider benefit effects – for example the job search model – the benefits themselves are typically viewed as certain. In reality, entitlement to benefit may not be known in advance with any precision, as anyone who has claimed any but the most simple cash benefit knows. The details of real world benefit schemes are typically very complex and it is often the case that the potential claimant cannot be sure about his or her entitlement. There may be uncertainty about the rules and/or uncertainty about the way the rules are applied by the authorities responsible for the administration of benefits. This can be expected to affect individuals' behaviour. Section 5.2 draws on the small literature in this area to show that the picture of disincentive effects obtained from standard textbook analysis with certain benefit entitlements can be quite misleading.

In section 5.3 we consider the situation where benefit entitlement is certain but labour market prospects are uncertain; this also contrasts with the standard labour–leisure choice analysis. In this section we consider the impact of a given benefit system on the behaviour of the individual attempting to optimise in the presence of labour market uncertainty. This behaviour contrasts with that which one would find under certainty. In section 5.4 we present an analysis in which uncertainty is again about labour market prospects rather than the operation of benefit schemes, but where we focus on *family* decisions. We consider the impact of benefit schemes where entitlement depends on the income of a claimant's family, that is a 'means-tested' benefit. This is an important institutional feature of many benefit schemes but the implications of this means test for the labour supply of other family members has received relatively little attention. Our analysis extends a recent small literature on this issue which has been based on a static analysis. We show how the picture changes when intertemporal aspects in the presence of uncertainty are considered.

5.2 UNCERTAINTY OF ENTITLEMENT AND INDIVIDUAL BEHAVIOUR

The absence of uncertainty about benefit entitlement in much analysis of the impact of benefits on work incentives may be illustrated considering the job search model.[2] In the standard model an unemployed individual is seen as searching for work across a known distribution of wage offers. Uncertainty is at the root of the model. The distribution of wages is assumed to be known but the searcher is assumed not to know *a priori* the level of the wage in any given offer from this distribution; it is uncertain (hence the 'search'). Furthermore, the model allows for the receipt of a job offer (at any wage level) in a given period to be uncertain. In some extensions of the basic model the duration of a job which is accepted is additionally assumed to be uncertain (e.g. Hey and Mavromaras, 1981). The model defines a 'reservation wage', the wage at which the individual is indifferent between accepting a job and continuing search. The level of the reservation wage determines whether the individual accepts a particular job offer and this level is influenced by all the uncertainty just described.

However, the uncertainty applies only to *jobs and wages* and, in contrast, the entitlement to the unemployment *benefits* in the model (which also determine the reservation wage) is almost invariably considered to be known. The searcher is assumed to know with certainty the future stream of unemployment benefits.

The treatment of unemployment benefits in the job search model is representative in that the vast bulk of literature on the

disincentive effects of cash-benefit schemes assumes that claimants
know their benefit entitlements with certainty. There is good
reason to believe that in practice some considerable uncertainty
may surround benefit income.

As far as unemployment benefit is concerned this uncertainty
may arise for a number of reasons. First, when an individual
makes an initial claim for benefit it may take some time to assess
entitlement; about one in ten of all persons in the registered
unemployed stock in Britain in 1988 were waiting for their unemployment insurance entitlement to be determined, with the figure
very much higher in short durations (Micklewright, 1990). Secondly, in most unemployment compensation schemes there exists the
possibility that refusal of a job offer may result in disqualification
from benefit; the individual will be uncertain whether this sanction
will apply in his particular case or not. Thirdly, the duration of
benefit entitlement is finite in the typical unemployment insurance
programme and in some countries' schemes the entitlement cannot
be predicted with certainty at the start of the unemployment spell.
For example, the period of entitlement to unemployment insurance in the US is extended if the state unemployment rate rises
above a certain threshold. This extension applies both to new
claimants and to those whose spell of unemployment is already in
progress; the latter group could not be expected to have foreseen
such an extension with certainty. Even in countries where the
entitlement period is fixed, and where claimants are fully informed
about this period, there may be considerable uncertainty surrounding the entitlement to any means-tested benefits which may
follow unemployment insurance (means-tested benefit being more
complex).

The evidence just given on uncertainty of unemployment benefit
entitlement related to Western economies. Nagy (1991) provides
an example of uncertainty surrounding this type of benefit in
transitional economies. He finds that there was a considerable lack
of information and an existence of administrative error in the
operation of a new Hungarian unemployment benefit scheme during 1989. Evidence of uncertainty surrounding entitlement to
other types of benefit may be seen. The divergence between actual
and anticipated state pension benefits in the United States is
described by Bernheim (1987). (Mitchell, 1988, finds ignorance of
private pension entitlement to be widespread.) The receipt of

means-tested benefit is particularly subject to uncertainty. This may arise for a number of reasons. Claimants may be uncertain of getting an accurate assessment according to the rules of what may be a complex benefit; in the United Kingdom in 1975, an investigation showed that 17 per cent of a sample of Supplementary Benefit claims contained some kind of administrative error (Supplementary Benefits Commission, 1976, p. 184). Furthermore, entitlement to means-tested benefits may be strongly influenced by the decisions of officials administrating benefit programmes who can have considerable discretion over awards made.

All this suggests the need for the introduction of entitlement uncertainty into models of the disincentive effects of benefits. We illustrate the impact of benefit uncertainty on the analysis of incentives in a static model. This will show how the standard labour–leisure choice analysis can be very misleading. We take two examples from the small literature which has relaxed the assumption of certain entitlement.

5.2.1 Transition from unemployment

The uncertainty surrounding benefits which may be received by unemployed family men forms the focus of the analysis by Jenkins and Millar (1989). The uncertainty considered does not relate to the benefit receipt when unemployed which Jenkins and Millar argue 'in the near future is relatively certain' (ibid., p. 138). Rather, there is assumed to be uncertainty about the means-tested benefits which may be received on return to work. In Britain, the country motivating their analysis, employed family heads on low income may apply for means-tested benefits and

> on return to work, total family income can come from earnings, child benefit, family credit, and housing benefit, and at the time of the participation decision, the amount to be received from these various sources is relatively uncertain, primarily because the transition into work implies reassessment for means-tested benefits. (Ibid.)

The authors go on to point out that although the out-of-work benefits may be just as complex, the change in status by moving into work implies that in-work income is more uncertain.

The implications of this source of uncertainty is analysed by Jenkins and Millar in a static model. Individuals choose between certain income when unemployed and an uncertain in-work income. The latter is made up of three parts: (i) earnings which are assumed to be known, (ii) benefits received with certainty, and (iii) means-tested benefits received with uncertainty. Uncertainty surrounding means-tested in-work benefits is simplified so that there are only two possibilities, a relatively high benefit, F_1, and a relatively low one, F_2 $(= F_1 - d)$, where d is simply the difference between benefits received in the favourable and unfavourable cases. The relatively lower benefit F_2 is received with probability p and F_1 with probability $1 - p$, these being the probabilities which the individual perceives (i.e. subjective probabilities). Gross earned income in work is given by W times H where these refer to the wage and hours of work, respectively. When this form of income exceeds a tax-free allowance, A, it is assumed to be subject to a single marginal tax rate, t. A universal child benefit of B per child is paid in work and not included in the means test for the in-work benefit described above, but is assumed to be means tested away when out of work. Income when out of work is given by C_0. Assuming $W \cdot H > A$, income in work for a person with n children is given by

$$C_1 = (1 - t)W \cdot H + t \cdot A + n \cdot B + F_1, \qquad \text{with}$$
$$\text{probability } 1 - p \quad (5.1)$$

and by

$$C_2 = C_1 - d \qquad \text{with probability } p. \quad (5.2)$$

If individuals maximise expected utility, the individual will work if

$$(1 - p) \cdot U[C_1, L_e] + p \cdot U[C_2, L_e] > U[C_0, L_U] \quad (5.3)$$

where L_e and L_U are leisure when employed and unemployed respectively and where the utility function $U[. .]$ is assumed to display risk aversion.

This framework is used to derive a number of results concerning the effects of different policy parameters on the decision to work. For example, the authors compare the effect on the participation decision of measures designed to reduce the degree of uncertainty surrounding means testing via a reduction in d, with those measures increasing certain income out of work via Child Benefit, B, or subsidies to the wage, W. Jerkins and Millar stress that their analysis of policy options is 'speculative rather than conclusive'. However, their model does show the richer view of disincentive effects that can be obtained by considering income risk related to benefit entitlement.

5.2.2 Disability insurance and leaving the labour force

When an individual with a disability applies for a disability pension the receipt of that pension is not certain: it depends on a medical assessment of the degree of disability. Why should this uncertainty be of any behavioural significance? One possibility is the stigma or 'hassle' associated with the process of application, this resulting in a failure to apply for benefit. In the model presented by Halpern and Hausman (1984, 1986), the impact of uncertainty surrounding entitlement stems from the fact that workers must quit work before they can apply for benefit. This requirement is present in the disability insurance system in the United States which motivated Halpern and Hausman's model. In 1980, only 22 per cent of applications for disability benefit were immediately granted (although the figure rose as a result of appeals against the initial decision), indicating a substantial degree of uncertainty concerning the outcome of an application (Halpern and Hausman, 1986, table 14.1).

Halpern and Hausman assume that if the claim is unsuccessful the wage that the individual may then command in the labour market is less than if no application for benefit had taken place. In other words, the applicant cannot return to a job at the previous wage. The authors argue that this assumption may be justified on a number of grounds: human capital may erode during the wait for the application to be processed; the employer may believe that the disability that led to the benefit claim will result in a further quit in the near future.

The problem for the claimant in a single period framework is illustrated in Figure 5.1. Let Y equal non-labour income and D a means-tested disability benefit; W is the wage in the job occupied at the time the decision to apply is taken and W^* the wage that will be on offer if a claim for benefit is made and is rejected. The probability of a claim being accepted is p. The individual must therefore choose between facing on the one hand budget constraint OYA at wage W with certainty, and on the other ODB with probability p and OYC at wage W^* with probability $(1 - p)$.

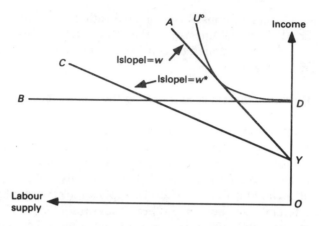

FIGURE 5.1   Labour supply and disability benefit

In order to illustrate the argument we have represented preferences in the diagram (indifference curve U^0) such that the individual would be indifferent between continuing in work and
applying for benefit *if* the latter were certain. The individual has,
however, to take into account the possibility that a claim for
benefit will be rejected which would result in him facing a lower
wage rate than before. If the individual in the diagram believes
that there is any uncertainty about the outcome of his application
($p < 1$) then no claim will be made.

In general, an individual will chose to apply for disability benefit
if

$$p \cdot U[D] + (1 - p) \cdot V[W^*, Y] > V[W, Y]. \qquad (5.4)$$

$U[D]$ is the value of the direct utility function at zero hours of
work in the event of a successful claim and $V[. .]$ is the indirect
utility function evaluated at the relevant wages and unearned
income if the individual does not claim, or claims and is refused.
Uncertainty implies that an individual cannot make a simple
choice between two certain alternatives and the standard labour–
leisure analysis would be misleading, as we have described above.

5.2.3 Empirical analysis

So far we have considered the disincentive effects of benefits when entitlement uncertainty is introduced into theoretical analysis. However, this type of uncertainty should also be considered in empirical analysis. Again, in general this is not done. For example, empirical analysis of unemployment duration which specifies the probabilities of leaving unemployment in a given week typically defines this probability as a function of the ratio of current out-of-work income to that which would be received in work; the latter includes entitlement to means-tested benefits assumed to be received with certainty, see for example Nickell (1979), Atkinson *et al.* (1984).

That uncertainty about benefit entitlement *does* appear to effect behaviour in practice is suggested by the empirical work on unemployment duration by Katz and Meyer (1990). This research used microdata from administrative records on individual spells of unemployment from the USA. The authors model the individual's probability of leaving unemployment in a given week as a function of not only his current unemployment insurance (*UI*) benefit level but also the remaining weeks of a finite entitlement period to *UI*. The sample was drawn during a time of rising unemployment and under federal law this led to an extension of *UI* entitlement being triggered for some individuals present in the data, this happening after they had entered unemployment. The impact of real-world uncertainty is suggested by the coefficient of a dummy variable taking the value one in the week when *UI* entitlement would have ended were it not to have been extended. The probability of leaving unemployment is estimated to be sharply higher in this week suggesting that the subjective probability attached to an extension of entitlement was low; the extension was not seen as certain by the individuals (or by their former employers).[3]

Halpern and Hausman (1984; 1986) empiricise their theoretical model of uncertainty and disability benefit entitlement which was outlined above by assuming an explicit functional form for the labour supply equation. They then recover the corresponding indirect and then direct utility functions ($V[. .]$ and $U[. .]$ in equation (5.4) via Roy's Indentity (see Hausman, 1981). The sample survey used to estimate the model includes both claimants and non-claimants for disability benefit and contains information on the outcome of claims and on wages (W, and W^* in the case of an unsuccessful claim). A binary model of the probability of a claim being successful is used to calculate predicted values of p; the information on post-claim wages for unsuccessful applicants provides the basis for predicting W^* for all individuals. These predictions are then used in the estimation of the empirical version of equation (5.4) above explaining the probability of applying for benefit.

The results of Halpern and Hausman's empirical model enable them to assess the effect of a change in p on the decision to apply for benefit. This effect varies with the degree of risk aversion assumed in the utility function; the greater the risk aversity the greater is the effect of changes in the probability of claim acceptance. The authors conclude that changes in this probability do have an important effect but note that since the data do not appear consistent with much risk aversion, the effect of changes in disability benefit level (D in equation (5.4)) are probably more important.

5.3   UNCERTAIN LABOUR MARKET PROSPECTS

The type of uncertainty considered in the last section was exclusively related to benefit prospects, but not to wages or employment opportunities. We now turn to an analysis of the problem from another viewpoint: how do incentive effects of a given benefit scheme change if wages and employment prospects are uncertain? We restrict our attention to a static model of labour–leisure choice.

The issue was investigated in detail by Cowell (1981). He distinguishes between two types of wage uncertainty. First, uncertainty with respect to the wage rate itself. For a given supply of labour H, the individual will obtain an uncertain return W, but he will be employed with certainty. Secondly, for a given wage of level W and desired hours H, it is uncertain whether he will be employed. Cowell investigates the impact of different tax and benefit schemes on the optimal supply of labour.

In his basic model the combined tax and income maintenance system has the following form:

$$T = (t \cdot W \cdot \mathrm{H}) - B; \tag{5.5}$$

t is a uniform marginal tax rate levied on all earned income, W is the wage rate, H is the amount of time offered to the market. B are benefits which in the basic model are assumed to be universal, depending neither on the individual's choices nor on the outcome of any uncertain event (an example of such a benefit would be Child Benefit in the UK). T may be positive or negative, depending on whether the individual pays more tax than he receives in benefit or vice versa. In contrast to the standard labour–leisure choice analysis, the wage W is a stochastic variable, depending on the state of nature. To keep the model simple, there are only two states of the world: a favourable one in which $W = W^1$, with probability $(1 - p)$, and an unfavourable one, in which $W = W^2$, with probability p. If $W^2 = 0$ this generalises the analysis to the second type of uncertainty mentioned above. Disposable income is then given by $W \cdot H - T$.

The individual maximises a specific form of utility function with leisure and consumption as its arguments; this function exhibits decreasing absolute risk aversion. Maximisation is subject to the stochastic budget constraint described above. Cowell now investigates separately the impact of changes in the transfer B or the marginal tax rate t on the supply of labour under the assumption that the disutility of work is equal to the disutility of involuntary unemployment. He first confirms that if there is *no* uncertainty ($p = 0$), both an increase in B for constant t and an increase in t for constant B will decrease the supply of labour (assuming leisure is a normal good). These are the conventional results: both policies are found to provide a disincentive effect.

However, in the case of uncertainty, the impact of both policies on labour supply is ambiguous. An increase in the lump sum transfer B or the marginal tax rate t may *increase* labour supply for certain values of p and of the elasticity of utility with respect to consumption. These effects are due to the uncertainty reducing role of the tax and income maintenance scheme. An increase in the tax rate t reduces the dispersion of possible returns from the supply of labour to the market. An increase in the transfer B increases the guaranteed income of the individual. Cowell points out that standard portfolio theory would suggest that either policy would encourage risk-taking, in this case supplying labour in return for the uncertain W.

When undertaking policy reform, governments may change

both taxes and benefits at the same time. They are also interested in defining particular target groups. Thus for policy purposes, two questions arise: first, is it possible to increase the progressivity of the tax and income maintenance scheme and to raise work incentives without changing expected *ex-post* consumption or expected tax liabilities? Secondly, is it possible to identify the segment of the population for which the positive incentive effect is likely to occur? Cowell confirms that the first of these questions can be answered in the affirmative, the occurrence of the incentive-increasing effect depending on the degree of risk aversion, probabilities of the state of the world p, and on the ratio of transfer income to net earnings. Regarding the second question, he identifies the segment of the population for which the incentive-increasing effects are most likely to occur as being characterised 'by relatively high risk aversion, significant but not enormous wage risk, and not too high a ratio of non-employment income to earnings' (ibid., p. 702). People with these characteristics may be fairly poor with little income other than earnings, high income variability and with quite strong risk aversion. Cowell's analysis shows that the introduction of uncertainty with respect to labour market prospects may change the perception of an optimal tax and benefit scheme.

5.4   MEANS-TESTED BENEFIT AND INTERTEMPORAL UNCERTAINTY

To this point we have considered the decisions of *individuals* in the presence of uncertainty. In this section we introduce uncertainty into the analysis of the effect of benefits on *family* labour supply. We do this by considering the impact of a benefit in which entitlement depends on family income, in other words, there is a family means test. We look at the impact of the means test not on the benefit claimant's behaviour but on the labour supply of other members of the claimant's family.[4] This serves two purposes. First, we highlight an area of the literature on disincentives which we believe deserves more attention; there has been surprisingly little recognition of the need to look at the effect of means testing the benefit of one person in the family on the labour supply of other members whose income is included in this means test. Secondly, we show how the presence of uncertainty can rationalise empirical facts that are inconsistent with the predictions of the few studies of this issue to date; these are based on a static model with no uncertainty. The uncertainty we are concerned with in this section relates to job prospects, as in section 5.3; we assume that the operation of the means test and the administration of benefit is itself certain.

Discussion of the distinction between the impact on the labour market of insurance and means-tested unemployment benefit often neglects the fact that the latter imposes a high marginal rate of tax on family income. Consider the situation of an unemployed man receiving means-tested benefit with maximum entitlement (if no other family income is present) of b. If his wife works, her earnings reduce her husband's benefit pound for pound, once they exceed a disregarded level k. In other words, family income is subjected to an implicit 100 per cent marginal rate of tax when her earnings are in the range $[k, b + k]$; the upper threshold applies since the husband's benefit entitlement expires at this point. This system is essentially that which applies in the UK benefit Income Support, received by some two-thirds of men in the registered unemployed stock; the system also describes the essentials of the German Unemployment Assistance benefit (Arbeitslosenhilfe).

The resulting budget constraint in a static labour–leisure choice diagram is shown in Figure 5.2. We assume that the family has no sources of income other than the means-tested unemployment benefit and the wife's earnings, earned at the wage rate W^w (we ignore explicit income taxes). The budget constraint in Figure 5.2 is flat along the segment AB. With conventional preferences, no woman should locate along this part of the budget constraint in a simple labour–leisure choice model.

The impact of the means test in practice has been investigated in Britain by Garcia (1985; 1989) and Kell and Wright (1990). Both estimate econometric models of female labour supply in which the current period labour supply of women married to unemployed men is related to their current period budget constraint of the type shown in Figure 5.2. The results of both studies suggest that the Income Support means test has a significant impact on the behaviour of married women.

However, it remains the case that, in defiance of the prediction of the simplest theoretical model, some women married to unemployed men in Britain *are* observed to be supplying hours at a level

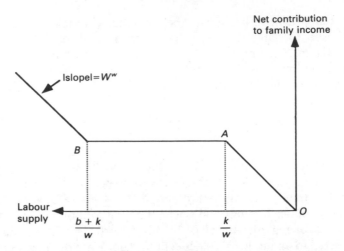

FIGURE 5.2   Budget constraint for wife with husband unemployed

which suggest that they are located along the flat segment in Figure 5.2 (Dilnot and Kell, 1987). This may be because work itself yields utility or because constraints placed by employers on hours worked rule out location at the kink point A. But in our view an important possible explanation involves the introduction of uncertainty into the analysis as we show in the rest of this section.

A static framework in which wife's current labour supply is modelled as a function of the current budget constraint neglects the fact that the disincentive from means testing is only *temporary*, lasting just as long as the husband is unemployed. What difference should the recognition of the temporary nature of the budget constraint make to the analysis? If the wife was not working prior to the husband's unemployment then no changes are needed. But if the wife does have a job when her husband enters unemployment then she needs to consider whether quitting to avoid a temporary disincentive is the right long-run strategy – she may want her job back when the husband leaves unemployment and the disincentive from means testing is removed.

In what follows we set up a simple two-period model assuming that the husband is unemployed in the first period but may or may not be in the second period. The wife has to decide whether to quit in the first period in the face of the means test applied to her

earnings as part of her husband's unemployment benefit assessment. If she does quit we assume that her job prospects in the
second period are uncertain; if she stays in her job in the first
period we assume that she can retain it with certainty in the second
period. This is the key assumption of the model; uncertainty about
her future job prospects reduce the wife's propensity to quit in the
first period (the uncertainty about the husband's employment
prospects is not in fact important to the main result).

This feature is similar to an important aspect of the Halpern and
Hausman model of disability benefit and participation which was
discussed in section 5:2. Just as we assume that quitting reduces
future employment prospects, Halpern and Hausman assumed
that quitting and making an application for disability benefit would
reduce the wage the individual could command in the labour
market if the application were to be rejected. (Note that Halpern
and Hausman collapse their model onto one period but the same
intertemporal considerations are implicitly present.)

In period one the husband is unemployed with *potential* benefit
entitlement b; the actual benefit amount received depends on the
operation of the means test. In the second period the husband will
be offered with probability, p, a job paying E^H, where $E^H > b$.
The wife, who prior to the husband's unemployment has been
working, must decide in the first period whether to quit or to carry
on in her job. Her working results in a level of earnings, E^W; if she
works in the second period she also receives this level of earnings
since we assume that the wage rate is the same in both periods and
that constraints on the demand side of the labour market are such
that hours are not variable (a single hours–wage package is all that
is available). She cannot make marginal changes to her hours in
period one (or period two) – she simply has to decide whether to
work, and receive E^W, or to quit, in which case we assume she
receives c, the equivalent of the opportunity costs of her employment; these may comprise travel-to-work costs and child-care expenses, and where $c < E^W$. (We assume that she receives no
unemployment benefit herself, being disqualified from receipt for
voluntarily leaving her job). If she quits in the first period she
receives a job offer in the second period with probability q.

The wife's earnings are disregarded for the purpose of the
benefit means test up to a level k. We assume that if she works her
earnings exceed this disregarded level ($E^W > k$). Between k and

$[k + b]$ her earnings result in an implicit 100 per cent marginal rate of tax on her husband's benefit. Accordingly, if the husband is unemployed and the wife employed, the net contribution of her work to family income in that period is equal to s, where

$$s = k \qquad\qquad \text{if } E^W < b + k \qquad\qquad (5.6)$$
$$= k + E^W - (b + k) \text{ otherwise.}$$

The opportunity costs of the wife working are assumed to exceed the income she can contribute if the husband is unemployed ($c > s$).

To derive results we need to specify how the couple takes decisions and what yields them utility. We assume that neither husband nor wife derives utility from leisure; if the wife quits work in the first period it is because she wishes to gain c and not because she enjoys leisure. For simplicity we assume that the couple operate as a unit and are risk-neutral. This implies that their aim is simply to maximise their total joint two-period income (we ignore discounting).[5] Given those assumptions we have made already, this specific optimising behaviour has two implications for the couple's labour supply decisions. First, the husband will always accept a job offer in period two. Secondly, if her husband is employed in period two, the wife will work if she can in that period but she will not if he is still unemployed.

The only decision variable in the model is the wife's decision as to whether to quit or not in the first period. If she does, total two-period income is given by the following expression:

$$I^1 = b + c + E^H + E^w \qquad \text{with probability } p{\cdot}q.$$
$$I^2 = b + 2{\cdot}c + E^H \qquad \text{with probability } p{\cdot}(1 - q)$$
$$I^3 = 2{\cdot}[b + c] \qquad\qquad \text{with probability } (1 - p);$$

and by the following if she does not quit:

$$I^4 = b + s + E^H + E^W \qquad \text{with probability } p$$
$$I^5 = 2{\cdot}b + s + c \qquad\qquad \text{with probability } (1 - p).$$

The wife will quit in period one if expected two-period income stemming from this decision exceeds that if she continues to work despite the means test. She will quit if:

$$[p{\cdot}q{\cdot}I^1 + p{\cdot}(1 - q){\cdot}I^2 + (1 - p){\cdot}I^3] > [p{\cdot}I^4 + (1 - p){\cdot}I^5] \quad (5.7)$$

Equation (5.7) can be used to show that the decision to quit in the first period depends positively on the opportunity cost of her working, c, her second period probability of a job offer if she quits in the first period, q, and her husband's benefit, b. The decision depends negatively on her earning power E^w, the lower threshold for the means test, k (in the case that $E^w > [b + k]$), and on the husband's second period probability of a job, p.

This simple model has several undesirable features, including the absence of any utility derived from leisure. Nevertheless, we feel that even the risk-neutral version described above offers useful insights into the potential effect of a common form of benefit system and gives a richer view of its implications for incentives to work in the family-decision-making context than would be obtained from a static model. The richer view stems from the introduction of uncertainty about the wife's future job prospects. As with the introduction of entitlement uncertainty in the models reviewed in section 5.2, we believe that this adds a realism to the analysis of the disincentive effects of benefit systems which has been too often missing in much of the literature.

5.5 SUMMARY

In this chapter we have argued for more attention to be paid to certain forms of uncertainty in the analysis of the disincentive effects of benefits. In section 5.2 we reviewed research which has allowed for the important real world feature of uncertainty surrounding entitlement to benefits. As the awareness of the complexity of benefit schemes increases among those doing research on incentives, so should the need to consider entitlement uncertainty. This uncertainty is present in well-established benefit programmes in Western economies; it seems not unreasonable to suppose that it is even more prevalent in certain benefit programmes in the transition economies of Eastern Europe, notably those which are entirely new such as unemployment benefit. Uncertainty of this form implies that the standard analysis of incentive effects which assumes certain benefit entitlement may lead to misleading results. It may also imply that incentives could be improved in some cases by simply reducing uncertainty, although in others the opposite may be true.

In section 5.3 we considered the impact of a given benefit system if uncertainty about labour market prospects is introduced in a simple static model. The paper which we reviewed showed that conclusions under uncertainty could be rather different from those when labour market prospects are certain. Section 5.4 also focused on uncertainty of labour market prospects but in the context of family rather than individual labour supply. Looking at couples where the husband is unemployed, we analysed the effect on the wife's labour supply of including her income in a means test for her husband's benefit. We used a simple two-period model of family behaviour. When the future probability of a job is considered, we showed how a static model's prediction that a married woman would quit in the face of a 100 per cent implicit marginal tax rate on her earnings is too simple a representation of the situation. This again shows how consideration of uncertainty modifies one's conclusions about benefit effects. We hope that research of the type we have considered in this chapter will feature prominently in the literature on incentives in the future.

6 The Definition and Measurement of Poverty and Inequality

DAVID PIACHAUD

6.1 INTRODUCTION

Economics has conventionally been concerned with efficiency and equity, with far more attention to the former. Yet economics is not just about the aggregate level of production, it is also about how resources are shared and how widely prosperity is distributed – with the degree of inequity. The ultimate test of equity is the extent of poverty. This is a crucial test of an economy and is obvious when comparing, for example, India and Europe; it is also true when considering the distribution of welfare within any one country.

In the next section some evidence on poverty and inequality is presented. In part this is to set the scene in a British context but also it serves as a reference point for the subsequent discussion. Then the measure of income is discussed in section 6.3, followed by consideration of concepts of poverty in section 6.4. Finally, issues of measurement are considered in section 6.5. Most attention is given here to the definition of poverty about which there have been considerable controversies. The reason for this is worth considering at the outset. Poverty is not a politically neutral concept: it is a bad thing. In most people's minds there is a moral imperative attached to poverty in that, while it may be a description of the situation, it also implies that something ought to be done about it. By contrast other descriptions of the economy – for

TABLE 6.1   Distribution of incomes, 1977 and 1988

		Percentage shares of quintile groups				
		Bottom	2nd	3rd	4th	Top
Equivalised original income						
	1977	3.6	10	18	26	43
	1988	1.9	7	16	25	50
Equivalised disposable income						
	1977	9.7	14	18	23	36
	1987	7.6	11	16	23	42

Source: 'The Effects of Taxes and Benefits on Household Income, 1988', *Economic Trends*, March 1991, table N.

example the proportion of workers employed in the service sector – carry no obvious policy imperatives. The political sensitivity of poverty has inevitably meant that there have been controversies about its extent, and whether it is increasing or decreasing. These controversies have been fuelled by academic disagreements which this chapter will attempt to elucidate rather than resolve.

6.2   EVIDENCE ON INEQUALITY AND POVERTY

The distribution of incomes is shown in Table 6.1. Two concepts of income are used. First, original income which comprises earnings from employment and self-employment, occupational pensions and income from capital. Second, disposable income which is original income plus cash benefits less direct taxes. In each case income is equivalised or adjusted for household size, as discussed in section 6.3.2 below. The table shows the degree of inequality that exists and how it increased between 1977 and 1988.

The extent of poverty is illustrated in Table 6.2, taking half average income level as the poverty line. As can be seen, the extent of poverty differs greatly between different family types and depending on economic status. In total, poverty more than doubled between 1979 and 1987.

These, then, are some of the facts about Britain. Yet these facts are all based on particular definitions, measures and services; it is these with which this chapter is primarily concerned. It should not be forgotten, however, than concern about poverty and inequality does not arise primarily because it raises interesting academic issues, but because of their social and personal consequences and the political and moral challenge they raise.

6.3 INCOME

On questions of tackling poverty and inequality the most common conceptual framework is that laid down by Robin Hood – taking from the rich and giving to the poor. This has the virtue of simplicity and it is a widely shared framework but it is somewhat lacking in sophistication. If we are to define who is rich and who is poor some method of defining income levels is necessary. No doubt at the extremes income levels may be self evident – the Sheriff was rich and Friar Tuck was poor. Yet if economic analysis is to clarify policy choices concerning poverty and inequality, appropriate measures of income are essential. The concept of income is rarely given much attention in economic literature. Income is defined as command over resources over time or as the level of consumption that can be afforded while retaining capital intact. Yet in relation to the measurement of income inequality and poverty the concept of income is extremely important and raises many problems.

In this section the focus will be on four aspects of measuring income: the income unit to be used; the adjustment for size of income unit; the measurement of income; and the time period over which income is measured.

6.3.1 The income unit

The analysis of income levels is greatly complicated by the fact that people have always, and will no doubt continue to be, congregated in 'clumps' – usually known as family or income units. Yet these clumps are not clear cut. For example, is a student on a meagre grant with affluent parents part of an impoverished term-time unit or a prosperous vacation unit?

108   *The Definition and Measurement of Poverty and Inequality*

TABLE 6.2   Extent of poverty, 1979 and 1987

	Percentage of individuals with income below half of the average	
	1979	1987
Family type		
Married pensioners	18	27
Single pensioners	9	23
Married with children	9	20
Married without children	4	20
Single with children	29	47
Single without children	6	15
Economic status		
Pensioners	14	25
Full-time workers	3	8
Sick or disabled	32	32
Lone parents	44	58
Unemployed	47	59
All	9.4	19.4
Number ('000s)	4930	10 500

Note: Income is equivalised household disposable income after housing costs.
Source: *Households Below Average Income*, Department of Social Security, 1990.

These clumps vary over time and may be related to income level. For example, take an elderly woman living apart from her prosperous daughter; this constitutes two income units. If the income of the elderly person falls drastically, for example due to a stock market crash, then one of the units has moved down the income distribution. If, then, the prosperous daughter asks her pauperised mother to live with her there is now only one income unit which now has a satisfactory overall income. Similarly, young people returning to the parental home may reduce the number of low-income units, even though young people may feel that their overall welfare has worsened by not having an independent existence.

The appropriate income unit is usually assumed to be a unit in which economic decisions about paid and unpaid work and about consumption are made jointly and in which resources are pooled. In reality, of course, families vary from those in which there is total harmony and, perhaps, a total loss of identity to those in which individuals while sharing the same roof have virtually no economic relationships with each other. For purposes of measuring income levels, this diversity is highly problematical.

Beveridge in his report on social security assumed, and the means-tested elements of the social security system continue to this day to assume, that in households comprising a man and woman who are married or 'living as man and wife' there is pooling of resources and that each is to be expected to take financial responsibility for the other. Yet such an approach conflicts with any notion of independent treatment, such as many people wish to see for the income tax system, and it conflicts with the reality of many households. To enforce this notion of joint responsibility and to avoid treating unmarried couples more favourably than married couples, the income support system has developed elaborate and often intrusive cohabitation rules. These rules may arouse hostility in part because of the nature of the investigations used to apply them (so called 'sex snoopers') but the more fundamental issue is about the definition of the appropriate income unit. Many individuals assert that they have a right to certain minimum income for themselves, regardless of other individuals with whom they choose to associate or live.

A related policy question is whether benefits for children should be payable to mothers or fathers? This was hotly contested following the government recommendation in the 1980s (subsequently abandoned) that Family Credits should be paid through the pay packet to fathers. This would have had no apparent 'differential' effect if the income unit considered is the family; however, if the income unit considered is the individual switching benefits to the father from the mother has very different results.

Clearly there are a great many problems in analysing the individual distribution of incomes since the command over resources of many individuals is directly affected by the resources of whoever they live with. Nevertheless, the Beveridge framework based on the family unit is liable in important respects to reinforce the dependence of women and conflicts with the goal of individual treatment.

It is hard to see that there can be absolutely right or wrong definition of the appropriate unit but it must be recognised that the definition determines how much inequality of income is revealed and it determines the impact of particular policies on that distribution. Broadly speaking, the larger the units considered the less is the apparent low income. For example, the government figures on households below average income indicate less relative poverty than similar figures based on families. The assumption that there is generally income pooling across households remains untested.

6.3.2   Adjustment for size of income unit

Any useful comparison between nations of income levels must take account of the size of nations. Similarly, an income of, say, £100 per week can imply very different standards of living: for a single person it may be adequate whereas for a couple with three children it may represent dire poverty. There is, therefore, good reason to adjust income according to the size of income unit. One method of doing this is to treat all members equally and calculate income per capita. On this basis the three-child family on £100 has an income of only £20 per capita – one-fifth of that of the single person.

There are reasons why income per capita is not a good indicator of income level. The three-child family on £500 per week has the same per capita income as the single person on £100 yet most would think that the family was substantially better off. Two factors are relevant to the comparison. First, there are economies of scale. Most obviously, in relation to housing, two people in the same household need one dwelling, not two. Similarly, heating, a washing machine, a motor car, a television and a telephone can all be shared. Food and clothing cannot be shared at the time of use but in different ways there can be economies of scale: food purchased in bulk often costs less per helping than single helpings; clothing three children does not cost three times as much as clothing one child since many clothes can be passed on. Second, individual needs differ. This is the most obvious in relation to small children; their consumption of food is less than that of adults and their consumption of many items such as alcohol and tobacco should be zero.

In order to take account of economies of scale and variations in needs, attempts have been made to construct equivalence scales with which to adjust – or in the new, less than felicitous, terminology to 'equivalise' – incomes. The scale in use by the government in producing figures such as those in Table 6.1 treats a couple with no dependents as the reference point with a value of 1.00; other households have values as follows (for income after housing costs):

1st adult	0.55
2nd or 3rd adult	0.45
Each subsequent adult	0.40
Each dependent aged 0–1	0.07
Each dependent aged 2–4	0.18
Each dependent aged 5–7	0.21
Each dependent aged 8–10	0.23
Each dependent aged 11–12	0.26
Each dependent aged 13–15	0.28
Each dependent aged 16 or over	0.38

A couple with three children aged 4, 6 and 8 would therefore have an equivalence scale of 1.62 – that is 0.55 + 0.45 + 0.18 + 0.21 + 0.23 – or three-fifths more than a couple alone. This contrasts with a per capita basis which implies 150 per cent more for the five person over the two-person household. The adjusted or 'equivalised' income is obtained by dividing the household income by its equivalence scale. The implication is that a three-child family on £162 is at the same equivalised income as a couple on £100, or a single person on £55.

The question of how the equivalence scale should be constructed is a controversial matter. Several approaches have been used. One is to start from an assessment of needs; this is discussed in section 6.4.2 below. Second, expenditure may be analysed in relation to income for different sizes of household in order to determine income levels at which the same proportion (or same absolute amount) is spent on certain necessities (e.g. food) or on certain luxuries (e.g. beer or entertainment). Such analyses become highly complex and their interpretation is contentious. It is very doubtful if any objective, non-judgemental scale can ever exist. For example, some may argue that the decision to have a child with consequent increased food expenditure and decreased beer expenditure is purely a matter of choice so that a child should count for zero. Yet it is evident that levels of living do depend on the size of the income unit so that using some equivalence scale is necessary.

6.3.3 The measure of income

In studies of personal income distribution, the usual basis for comparing incomes of families or individuals is net money income. This measure is convenient for many purposes and fairly readily accessible. But such a measure does leave a number of problems which have important policy implications.

There may be substantial costs associated with employment – for travel to work, for clothing or other special equipment for work – and it is even possible to argue that certain types of employment such as coal mining necessitate substantial expenditure on special nutrients such as beer. For many the largest costs of employment are for child care. The returns from employment in gross and net post-expenses terms are very different. Comparisons of those in employment with those who are retired or unemployed can be problematic. To treat an employed individual with £100 net income as being at the same point in the income distribution as a retired person with £100 net income may represent a serious distortion. On the other hand, there may be important benefits of employment such as providing a heated work place, thereby saving on heating of the home, and a variety of fringe benefits, mainly enjoyed by the better paid workers, such as the use of a telephone, a car or medical insurance.

The net money income measure takes no account of the value of home production. The most common form of home production is preparation of unprepared foods, which are far cheaper than factory prepared or take away foods. Thus again those in employment may be disadvantaged in that they lack the time to engage in these home production activities. On the other hand, the assumption that the unemployed are able to boost their command over resources through extensive home production – working on an allotment, home decorating and repairing cars – may in many cases be misconceived since the psychological debilitation of unemployment may be severe.

Another problem with the use of net money income is that it fails to discriminate between those who may choose to take a low income and enjoy more leisure (either for sleeping or for home production) from those who may get more income but enjoy less leisure. For example, someone with £50 per week for twenty hours work may be judged at the bottom of the income distribution and below the poverty level, whereas somebody receiving £100 for sixty hours work might not be regarded as poor. If these two people were engaged in the same type of employment and could choose their hours of work, then clearly this measure of net money income is an inadequate indication of their relative economic circumstances. What this points to is the need to treat both money and time in an integrated way and to consider not only those who are 'money poor' but also those who are 'time poor'. We would like to know opportunities – we only know outcomes. Those who are really poor are those whose opportunities, or choice-sets, are most severely constrained.

The concept of income is of a flow over time. Clearly command over resources over a time period needs to take account of the returns from capital assets but simply looking at the returns to capital may for some purposes be inadequate. For example, the imputed income of owner-occupied housing may be included in the measure of income, but this does not take account of the capital asset. Elderly people who own their own houses could in theory remortgage them and purchase annuities which would give them substantially increased incomes. Not many elderly people do this in part because of the practical problems and fears of inflation but more fundamentally because they choose to retain their capital intact and bequeath it to their heirs. It may be argued that they regard the benefit to them of making such a bequest as at least equivalent to the potential extra income from an annuity. The fact that a capital sum is potentially available to many elderly people which could be converted into income again poses a problem in comparing the circumstances of the elderly with those of other groups in society – and in turn is important in considering the priority to be given to the provision of social security to elderly owner occupiers.

6.3.4 The time period

Should incomes be assessed on a weekly, monthly, annual or lifetime basis? Many live on a week-to-week, even daily, basis, more and more are paid monthly, the tax system operates on an annual basis, and economists would ideally like to know lifetime incomes – although this is hard to measure until someone has died. Again, there is no right answer; different periods are relevant for different questions. The social security system has for the most part been based on a weekly form of assessment and payment. In the past this reflected the payment system to the great majority of those in employment and it also accorded with the budgeting period over which most people operated. It is clearly useless to argue to claimants of income support that for most of their life, or even most of the previous year, they have had plenty of income with which to make provision for rainy days if, when they present themselves, they have no money left. Some claimants – as with a few on very high incomes – find it extremely difficult to manage between one weekly payment and the next. In order to cut the costs of administration there is pressure to move social security to a longer time-period and this will mean that fewer people may be assessed as being in need of benefits. But for those who find budgeting over a weekly period a severe problem, a longer time-period will impose even more strains.

One feature of the income support system that has been changed by the recent reforms does relate to the time-period of assessment. In the past Supplementary Benefit recipients were eligible for single payments for clothing or bedding in certain circumstances; these were in effect an 'extra' on top of the scale rates. It was argued by the government that this was arbitrary and unfair since the scale rates were intended in normal circumstances to provide for such items and some claimants managed to put money aside to buy new shoes and replace household goods – others did not. The basis for the single payments was essentially that in the case of those faced with pressing, emergency needs, bygones should be bygones. The consequence of treating bygones as bygones is, of course, that those who have set money aside in the past find that their thrift is unrewarded. The new system replaces most single payments with a system of loans operated by the Social Fund. This has effectively meant that people are forced to budget over longer time-periods. But it also means that when the loans are being recovered people receive less than the full-scale rates and the problem of managing on very low income is thereby exacerbated.

The longer the time period used to assess income levels, the more transient fluctuations are smoothed out. It may be reassuring for a student to know that his or her lifetime income may be high, and a bank manager knowing this may allow an overdraft so that consumption can exceed current income. A sick or unemployed person may be less secure and have no alternative but to meet this week's income and bills out of this week's income. The lower the income level and the capital resources which can be drawn on, the more difficult it is to transfer resources over time and the more pressing are present circumstances. Taking a long view is a luxury of the affluent.

6.4 CONCEPTS OF POVERTY

6.4.1 The definition of needs

At the simplest level people may be said to be poor if their income is less than their needs. To operationalise such a definition it is necessary to measure income and to define needs. What could be simpler? As the previous section showed, measuring income is not as simple as it might seem. What of defining needs?

The first question is whether poverty can be defined in *absolute* terms or must be considered in *relative* terms. An absolute definition of needs implies a standard that is fixed and unchanging over time. If the price level changes then of course the amount of money needed to meet a certain set of needs will increase, but with an absolute standard the set of needs will remain the same in perpetuity. An absolute standard may be extremely low – for example what is necessary to ensure survival – alternatively an absolute standard may be quite high allowing for decent clothing, for transportation and for entertainment. But it is intrinsic in an absolute standard that it does not change over time. This is very important since if, with economic growth, some of the increased prosperity trickles down to the poorest then, over a period of time, absolute poverty is likely to diminish.

Most recent writers on poverty have rejected the idea that there can be an absolute definition of poverty. Instead they have argued that poverty is a relative concept and must be so defined. People's needs are determined by the society in which they live. This is not a new idea; as Adam Smith (1776) put it:

> By necessaries, I understand not only the commodities which are indispensably necessary for the support of life but whatever

the custom of the country renders it indecent for creditable
people, even of the lowest order, to be without. A linen shirt,
for example, is strictly speaking not a necessity of life. The
Greeks and Romans lived, I suppose, very comfortably though
they had no linen. But in the present time . . . a creditable
day-labourer would be ashamed to appear in public without a
linen shirt, the want of which would be supposed to denote that
disgraceful state of poverty.

As standards of living in society have improved then minimum
needs have also increased. A century ago nobody had a television;
now many would regard a television as a necessity and someone
who could not afford a television as being in poverty. A century
ago poor people would not have expected to have a newspaper;
now a newspaper may be regarded as a necessity (if only to find
out what is on the television). A relative standard is essential if the
poverty level is to be based on prevailing standards in the society.

Using an absolute standard and applying it uniformly around the
world, one might conclude that there were virtually no poor people in Britain if one used a standard appropriate for India. If,
however, poverty is seen in relation to standards of the particular
society, then it is quite possible for there to be poverty in Britain at
the same time that there is poverty in India. As Townsend (1979)
wrote in his important work *Poverty in the UK:* 'Individuals . . .
can be said to be in poverty when they lack the resources to obtain
the types of diet, participate in the activities and have the living
conditions and amenities which are customary, or at least widely
encouraged or approved, in the societies to which they belong.'

Both concepts – of absolute and of relative poverty – present
considerable problems. In terms of absolute poverty, what is
necessary for survival? Is a roof over one's head a requirement or
is a cardboard box sufficient? In terms of relative poverty is someone poor if they are below half-average income levels, or one-
tenth of the average, or 90 percent of the average? Some suggest
relative poverty is merely another term to describe inequality. Yet
while there will always be a bottom-tenth of the income distribution, it is not inevitable that any one must fall below, say, half
average income levels. Thus, relative poverty can be abolished.
What distinguishes relative poverty from inequality is that the
focus is on the bottom end of the income distribution and the

distribution of income at the top end is not relevant, except in so far as the behaviour of the rich sets standards that may become customary.

Many researchers have tried to find some objective basis for determining appropriate poverty levels. Whether they have succeeded is open to question. In the next sections the three main types of approaches are described and discussed, drawing heavily on Piachaud (1987).

6.4.2 Budget standard methods

The first approach consists in determining how much needs to be spent on different types of expenditure. Basically, experts make professional judgement as to what needs to be spent for food, for clothing, for housing, for heating and so on.

This is the approach that was adopted by Rowntree's (1901) pioneering study of poverty in York in 1899. Rowntree drew on nutritional studies that had attempted to assess the dietary requirements for the maintenance of physical efficiency and costed the 'necessary nutrients at the lowest cost possible with a certain amount of variety'. This diet, containing large quantities of bread, porridge, dumplings and dripping, was not one that would have been appetising then or now. But it was based on a professional judgement about nutritional adequacy and thus had a certain scientific objectivity. Rowntree's definition of what was needed in terms of clothing, housing and heating relied much more on prevailing custom among the poor of York than on any professional judgement. For example, there were no heating standards laid down in 1899; even now the heating standards that exist reflect judgements about comfort rather than any objective assessment of what is necessary for survival.

Many attempts have been made to define the cost of minimum requirements using a budget standard approach. For example, one study attempted to estimate the cost of a child in modern Britain using the latest nutritional standards, assessments of the durability and cost of clothing, costs of heating and other items and including components for the cost of a holiday and for pocket money (Piachaud, 1979). These last two items are clearly not necessary for the survival of a child, but reflect the fact that for participation in normal social life these have become 'necessary'. The potential of budget standard methods has been usefully discussed by Brad-shaw *et al.* (1987).

The budget standard approach to defining a set of needs and costing them has much to commend it. If it is suggested that a particular poverty level or social security benefit level is adequate to provide the minimum, then it is important to try to assess whether this is the case. There are, however, a number of serious difficulties with this approach.

Budget standard approaches revolve very substantially around the cost of food using nutritional standards to determine an adequate diet. In the United States, for example, the official poverty standard is set at three times the cost of the nutritional requirements for households of different sizes; this reflects the fact that when the standards were set in the 1960s food expenditure represented approximately one-third of the expenditure of poor households. The nutritional foundation of many poverty levels probably reflects a reverence for the natural science of the nutritionist on the part of the mere social scientist. Yet on closer examination the scientific basis for minimum nutritional requirements is, in many cases, rather flimsy. Individual requirements are highly variable, reflecting differences in body weight, physical activity and metabolic efficiency. Thus some average minimum requirement may be inadequate for some and excessive for others. Even the food component in budget standard studies is less than clear cut or objective.

Everybody needs food; what else is necessary is much more problematic. Who is to define what is to be included? For some groups, such as children, there may be a reasonable degree of social consensus; few would argue that children in Britain should have toys, school outings and a holiday. For adults, however, there is much less consensus. Tobacco and alcohol may not be necessary for survival – indeed they may be positive threats to it – but many people regard them as requirements in daily life. Should such items be included in a budget standard and, if so, to what extent?

Some would argue that smoking and tobacco are clearly unnecessary and should not be included as necessities. Such a stern approach does not, however, eliminate the problem. If, for example, the cost of the 'approved necessities' is £50 per week, ensuring that everyone has £50 per week would not be sufficient to ensure that everyone had all the approved necessities. Many would spend a considerable proportion of their £50 on smoking and drinking, leaving less than £50 for the approved necessities – which would be an inadequate budget for them. Thus judgement and moralising assessments of what people need and how they ought to spend their money are futile if they do not take account of what people actually do. If one poses the question – how much money do people need so that *everyone* spends an adequate amount on food? – then there is probably no answer at all. Some people given an income of £500 or £5000 per week may chose to spend all of it on gambling or dangerous drugs and fail to provide an adequate diet for themselves or their children. Individual variations in behaviour present a major problem in defining a poverty standard which can be applied to the population as a whole.

A final problem with the budget standard approach lies in the costing of particular items. Suppose a certain quantity of potatoes is defined as being a necessary and a relatively cheap component of an adequate diet: how are these potatoes to be costed? Potatoes can be purchased in many forms, ranging from raw potatoes encrusted in mud to oven-ready chips; the unit price of these potatoes varies by a factor of five or more. The higher price of oven-ready chips is in effect a payment for the processing of the potatoes up to the point at which only a minimum of preparation time is necessary. There is a trade off between the consumer's time and the cost of the product. The same consideration could be applied to clothing where one can, with adequate skills and time, make one's own clothes, as used to be much more common in the past, or one can purchase ready made clothes. The problem is that the definition of the physical quantities of food or clothing that are required leaves open the question of the time inputs that the user should be expected to make; yet these time inputs make a crucial difference to the cost and how much needs to be provided in a budget for each item.

These then are all problems associated with using a budget standard approach to define poverty levels. Nevertheless, budget standard studies have illuminated the literature on poverty. It is only by trying to spell out the consequences of particular requirements in financial terms – or alternatively spelling out what a particular amount of money will purchase – that one can get a solid impression of what the particular standard represents.

6.4.3 Social consensus approaches

A second approach is to find out what people think should be the poverty level. Perhaps the most attractive feature of the social consensus approach is that it seeks to cast aside self-opinionated experts, and let the people decide. As Mack and Lansley (1985) claimed: 'For the first time ever, the poor in Britain have been identified as those who fall below the minimum standard of living laid down by society.'

A major study, in which large samples from many countries were asked what they thought was the minimum income on which somebody in their circumstances could manage, was carried out by van Praag and associates (1982) funded by the European Community. As an indicator of cross-national variations in perspectives on poverty such research is interesting but there is a number of problems with it. The way 'minimum income' is interpreted by respondents may differ: does it include the income of other household members, secondary earnings, and state benefits and what account was taken of differences in housing costs? There are also inescapable conceptual problems with research of this type. Respondents' answers must inevitably be influenced by their notions of the purpose of the study. The results represent a majority view of what minimum is needed but this is, in effect, a prescription for others which may differ from the views of those living on low incomes or from the level that taxpayers are willing to provide.

Mack and Lansley in their *Breadline Britain* surveys asked their sample which of a long list of items they regarded as necessities, and asked which items they lacked because they could not afford them. Answers for some of the items are shown in Table 6.3. They defined as poor those that lacked three or more of these items that most regarded as necessities; on this basis one-fifth of the population was poor. As a survey both of public opinion about poverty and of numbers lacking certain items this research is extremely interesting. Since it has been repeated in 1983 and 1990 it allows a comparison of how standards have changed; the results make clear that expectations have risen with general living standards and that most people think that the poor should share in rising prosperity.

There are, however, problems in using this type of research to define a poverty level. A general problem with this approach is that the 'experts' and their judgements are not easily disposed of in

TABLE 6.3 'Necessary' items, 1990

	Proportion deeming items to be necessary	Proportion lacking each item because they could not afford it
A damp free home	98	2
Three meals a day for children	90	–
Washing machine	73	4
Presents for friends or family once a year	69	5
New, not secondhand, clothes	65	4
A television	58	1
A car	26	18
Pack of cigarettes every other day	18	5
A video	13	10

Source: J. Mack and S. Lansley, *Breadline Britain, 1990s*, HarperCollins, 1991.

the search for public opinion: in defining what is the minimum standard of living laid down by society, someone must define the questions.

One problem arises in trying to convert the items judged to be necessary into levels of consumption, expenditure, or income. Some of the items, such as three meals a day for children or a damp free home, could cost widely varying amounts; there is no unambiguous way of getting from the necessary items to a poverty level.

A second problem is that many of those who lacked 'necessities' did not lack 'non-necessities'. In Mack and Lansley's (1985) first study only 14 per cent of their sample thought that a packet of cigarettes every other day was a necessity; but 42 per cent of the sample, no doubt including many of those who were poor, had a packet of cigarettes every other day. Is a household poor that cannot afford necessities but affords non-necessities? Ashton (1984), puts this criticism as follows:

The lack of three or more items has to be because the household cannot afford them in order for it to be counted among those in poverty. But the reason for lacking them is self-assessed. Many people who say they cannot afford an essential may have, or may have had, the resources to purchase it but allocate their resources instead for an apparent non-essential. To give an example, a household might lack the items 'carpets in the living room and bedroom' because they claim they cannot afford them, but may possess, say, an expensive hi-fi stereo unit. We are asked to accept that when someone says they cannot afford a particular item, they have not chosen instead to spend their money on something else that they regard as more essential (or desirable), but which does not appear on LWT's list.

Without some judgement about what margin, if any, is to be allowed for non-necessities, it is hard to see how any social consensus approach can move from a list of necessities to a determination of the income necessary to provide theses necessities.

Turning to the level which people are prepared to pay for, or a financeable poverty level, Ashton (ibid.) argues:

What the LWT Breadline Britain research has shown, judged by the amount of money people were prepared to be taxed to provide it, is that we are not willing to set the standard much above the current state minima. This suggests that 100 per cent of the basic SB levels is much nearer a 'society-approved' definition of poverty than any other one yet devised.

In short, the social consensus approach still requires expert involvement in defining questions and interpreting answers. It fails to resolve the problem when the practices of the poor do not correspond with priorities prescribed by the majority, and it does not necessarily produce a poverty level which taxpayers will pay for. (Other approaches are just as vulnerable on this last point but the social consensus approach is the only one which seeks to define what has majority support.) Finally, and perhaps most importantly, there may be no real social consensus – the opinions of those who are poor, of the majority, of taxpayers, and of those who are rich may be at odds; which opinions prevail depends on the distribution of power in society.

6.4.4 Behavioural approach

The behavioural approach has been most compellingly proposed by Townsend (1979). He endeavoured to 'define the style of living which is generally shared or approved in each society, and find whether there is . . . a point in the scale of the distribution of resources below which, as resources diminish, families find it particularly difficult to share in the customs, activities and diets comprising their society's style of living'. He attempted 'to provide an estimate of objective poverty on the basis of a level of deprivation disproportionate to resources'. This approach seeks, by examining behaviour in relation to income, to identify a poverty level on the basis of a change in social behaviour. Below a certain poverty level or threshold, it is argued, the loss of each pound of income increases deprivation sharply whereas above this level deprivation declines more slowly.

Townsend compiled a list of sixty indicators of 'style of living' covering diet, clothing, fuel and light, home amenities, housing, recreation, education, health and social relations. These indicators were expressed as indicators of deprivation and a 'score' for different forms of deprivation was added up, based on twelve selected characteristics. Taking the mean deprivation index for different income groups, Townsend found a clear relationship with income.

The indication that a threshold may exist was based by Townsend on the following steps. First, incomes were adjusted for household size by expressing them as proportions of the Supplementary Benefit scale rate for that household. Second, he grouped households by this adjusted income level, and estimated the most common value of the deprivation index for each group, the 'modal value'. Third, he plotted this modal value against the income level (expressed in logarithmic form). From this he concluded: 'As income diminishes from the highest levels, so deprivation steadily increases, but below 150 per cent of the supplementary benefit standard, deprivation begins to increase swiftly.'

What is not in doubt is that the poor have less choice and are more constrained than those better off or that there is genuine and severe poverty. What has been questioned are the choice of indicators used – do they indicate choices or constraints? – second, the existence of a threshold – is there a marked changed in deprivation below a certain level or is there a continuum? – and, third, the attainability of the goal of an objective, scientific measurement of poverty (Piachaud, 1981).

The absence of satisfactory evidence of a poverty threshold should not occasion any surprise since the relative nature of poverty and the fact that there is diversity in styles of living mean that a clear-cut threshold between the poor and the rest of society is extremely improbable. Subsequent attempts to establish a threshold have been unconvincing and it remains unproven that a threshold exists at which a clear shift in behaviour occurs. In behavioural terms, to find a threshold has not, in this writer's judgement, been successful.

This work and other work in this tradition does serve an extremely important function: it identifies those social and personal activities from which those in poverty (however defined) tend generally, but not invariably, to be excluded. Whether they are excluded due to lack of income is another question, but if social scientists can at least measure the extent of exclusion of the poor then they have done something that is worthwhile.

6.4.5   Can needs be defined?

Having discussed three illuminating approaches to defining a poverty level and suggested that each of them has limitations, what conclusion can be drawn? While each approach has been criticised, none has been rejected totally. Each in effect addresses a different question. Each has something important to contribute.

The budget standard approach allows those components which can usefully be defined by experts to be costed. The social consensus approach provides a social definition of necessities. The behavioural approach enables the relationship between income levels and patterns of expenditure and consumption to be analysed. Further, behavioural studies can be used to examine other effects, such as restrictions on participation in social activities, associated with living in or close to poverty.

None of the approaches discussed, nor any combination of them, can provide a unique scientific and objective measure of poverty. As Atkinson (1985) has written: 'It would patently be preferable to specify a single poverty standard and hence obtain a clearcut measure of the extent of poverty. This would however present an "all or nothing" approach, since those who disagree with the standard are likely to reject the findings out of hand.'

In discussions of poverty many different concepts and definitions are used. Not all can be discussed here but it may be useful to clarify some of the differences.

Poverty has been defined on the basis of income – a flow concept. Many in talking about the poor think primarily in terms of those with very little or no wealth – with no stock of capital. There is no doubt that one might question the poverty of someone with zero income if they were sitting on a million pounds capital reserve in the bank. By contrast, someone with an income a little above the poverty level who lacked any financial reserves might be particularly vulnerable to sickness or unemployment. What is perhaps most crucial is the liquidity of the wealth. Should an elderly person with a very valuable painting on the wall which yields no money income, although it may yield aesthetic pleasure, be expected to realise this asset and convert it into income. This may seem a rather abstract question but it is precisely the issue that arises in determining eligibility for Income Support, where the means test is primarily based on income but also takes account of capital in the form of financial assets, but not of other physical assets.

A second, somewhat related problem is associated with the cost of housing. If housing operated in a manner akin to the market for food, one could say that £25 per week would purchase a certain quality and quantity of housing throughout the country. This sum will, however, purchase very different amounts of housing depending on the type and history of tenancy, the location and the associated amenities. For Income Support purposes, the Department of Social Security in effect adds on actual housing costs (subject to certain limits) rather than allow some average amount. This is in contrast to the provision for all other forms of expenditure for which a total is provided which the recipient can then allocate according to his or her preferences. The underlying assumption that poor individuals have little control over their housing circumstances may reflect the imperfections of the housing market and a desire not to force those fallen on hard times to migrate to cheaper housing areas, loosing contact with their community, family and friends, but this treatment of housing costs itself adds to the imperfections of the housing market.

The measurement of income in relation to needs as a means of assessing poverty does provide a measure of command over resources. It is often, however, not the aggregate command over resources that is a matter of concern but the consumption of particular items. An obvious reason for concern about poverty may be inadequate consumption of food. Again, in recent years there has been increasing concern about 'fuel poverty' – those who, because of low incomes or high heating requirements or low efficiency of heating systems, may be unable to keep themselves warm in winter. In the USA there has long been concern about the 'medically indigent' – those who even with quite high incomes may be unable to afford the medical bills that arise as a result of their medical condition. In each of these cases the concern is about inadequate consumption of a particular item rather than about the overall level of income.

Other approaches to poverty may be more concerned with 'outcomes' rather than 'incomes'. Measures of deprivation and disadvantage may focus on rates of unemployment, overcrowding, mortality and other social indicators all of which may be associated with poverty defined in the more limited sense used here. Discussion of such indicators would extend beyond the scope of this chapter.

6.5   THE MEASUREMENT OF POVERTY AND INEQUALITY

In this section the statistics used to describe poverty will be discussed, and then the problems of collecting empirical data on poverty will be assessed.

6.5.1   Poverty measures

The most obvious measure of poverty is the number of people living below the poverty line – a head count. If this increases poverty has got worse and if it decreases, there is less poverty. Such a conclusion would, however, be hasty and possibly quite wrong. If the poverty line is £50 per week then raising someone from £49 to £51 would take them out of poverty and reduce the number by one. On the other hand, raising somebody from an income of £40 to £49 would leave them still in poverty and not reduce the total at all. To measure poverty more accurately than a head count allows, it is necessary to look at how far different individuals fell below the poverty line. Individual shortfalls can be aggregated to estimate an overall 'poverty gap' (Beckerman and Clark, 1982). This represents the extra income needed to bring all those below the poverty line just up to it.

A particular problem arises if the poverty level used is associated with or close to the levels of social security that the government provides. When British government estimates of low-income families were based on a benchmark of the Supplementary Benefit scale (the pre-cursor to Income Support), the effect of raising the Supplementary Benefit scale and making most of the poorest better off was to increase the apparent extent of poverty. For obvious reasons the government felt that doing more for the poor should not have the effect of producing more apparent poverty. Even with the new form of statistics that estimate numbers below different proportions of average income levels, it is possible for a fairly small change in social security benefits to produce big changes in numbers below particular levels.

The measurement of income inequality has been the subject of substantial literature (summarised in Atkinson, 1983a). Virtually all statistical measures of inequality have been applied at some time or other to the distribution of incomes – the coefficient of variation, the variance of the logarithm of income, mean deviation, interquartile and interdecile deviation and many more. The most commonly used summary measure is the Gini coefficient which measures the extent to which the distribution of incomes (be it gross or net, actual or equivalised income) differs from a state of total equality. However, as Atkinson points out: 'Measures such as the Gini coefficient are not purely "statistical" and they embody implicit judgements about the weight to be attached to the inequality of different points on the income scale.' Atkinson (1970) has proposed a measure of inequality in which distributional objectives are explicitly built in by in effect weighting the concern with inequality; thus society may be altogether indifferent to who is unequal – inequality at the top being treated on a par with inequality at the bottom – or, at the other extreme, it may only be concerned with the circumstances of the very poorest.

6.5.2   Sources of data

The studies mentioned above, of Rowntree, of Townsend, and of Mack and Lansley, were explicit studies designed to investigate poverty. Such studies have been immensely valuable but they were also extremely costly; and only a television company could afford recent data collection specifically on poverty. Now most analyses of poverty rely on secondary analysis of government surveys such as the Family Expenditure Survey and the General Household Survey. These surveys have now become extremely technically sophisticated with questions on income running to twenty or more pages. They have samples of around 7000 and 10 000 households respectively and achieve a response rate of about 70 per cent. Their cost runs into millions of pounds. In many respects they provide a wealth of data which is readily available for reanalysis. Compared to twenty years ago data on poverty and inequality has expanded greatly. There are, however, a number of problems, mostly intractable.

Even with large sample surveys the numbers in the poverty sample or with very high incomes can be quite small, particularly when the sample is broken down by family size or other distinguishing characteristics. Thus the question of whether poverty or inequality is increasing or decreasing among a particular subgroup is often hard to resolve. The coverage of these surveys is also a matter for concern: non-respondents may be disproportionately distributed and those not living in a household at all – for example, homeless people – are excluded.

There is one respect, though, in which little progress has been made, in part because the conceptual and practical problems are very severe. The income of families or households can be measured with some precision. The income, or command over resources, of individuals *within* families is very hard to measure. How much of joint food expenditure does each family member consume? Do all get equal benefits from a washing machine, car or yacht? How far can answers to questions about inequality within households be relied on?

A final problem that warrants mention is that most survey data are snapshots of circumstances. In order to understand changes over time and separate the ephemeral from the longer term it is necessary to obtain longitudinal data. This is time-consuming, difficult and expensive. Such data has been collected in the USA, in the Michigan Panel Study, but it is only just beginning to be collected in Britain in the Essex Longitudinal Study.

6.6 CONCLUSION

Measuring poverty and inequality is not easy. Yet as long as there is concern about equity in society there will be a need to try to measure. Better measures are preferable to worse measures and it is for economists and social statisticians to refine them so that they represent reality as well as possible, while recognising that what is real differs between observers. If the term 'poverty' carries with it the implication and moral imperative that something should be done about it, then the study of poverty is only ultimately justifiable if it influences individual and social attitudes and actions. This must be borne in mind constantly if discussion on the definition of poverty is to avoid becoming an academic debate worthy of Nero – a semantic and statistical squabble that is parasitic, voyeuristic and utterly unconstructive and which treats 'the poor' as passive objects for attention, whether benign or malevolent – a discussion that is part of the problem rather than part of the solution.

7 The Economics of Charity

ANDREW M. JONES and JOHN W. POSNETT

7.1 INTRODUCTION

In 1985/6 the net income of the approximately 140 000 charities registered in England and Wales was of the order of £12.65 billion, or 4.1 per cent of Gross National Product (Posnett, 1987). One of the most challenging and apparently paradoxical aspects of individual behaviour is the observation that individuals are willing, voluntarily, to transfer their own income for the benefit of others; either directly (from donor to recipient), or indirectly through a charitable intermediary. This type of behaviour appears to run counter to the basic tenets of economics, which sees individuals as essentially selfish, utility-maximisers.

The first part of this chapter reviews some of the attempts made by economists to resolve this paradox, and to produce a consistent theoretical model of giving behaviour. The second section reviews the wide range of empirical studies designed to explore the determinants of giving and, in particular, to test the effectiveness of tax concessions to charitable contributions. As yet, no consensus has been reached on either of these important issues.

7.2 MODELS OF GIVING

7.2.1 The public good theory of philanthropy

Early attempts to explain charitable giving are based on the existence of an externality relationship between donor and recipient

(Hochman and Rodgers, 1969; Becker, 1974; Arrow, 1981). The donor is assumed to maximise a utility function of the form:

$$u_i = u_i(x_i, x_j), \tag{7.1}$$

where x_i is the donor's private consumption, and x_j is the consumption of some other individual (or group of individuals); j. Imposing the condition $\partial u_i/\partial x_j > 0$ implies an externality relationship in which the consumption of j enters as a positive argument in the utility function of i. In other words, i cares about j. The donor maximises (7.1) subject to the budget constraint:

$$x_i + g_i = w_i, \tag{7.2}$$

where w_i is the wealth endowment of i, g_i is the donor's gift to i, and transfers are assumed costless.

The motivation for giving can be seen by noting that so long as $\partial u_i/\partial x_j > \partial u_i/\partial x_i$, the donor can increase his utility by transferring some of his own income to j. Transfers will take place until the marginal utility of i's income in his own use is equal to the utility associated with a marginal increase in j's consumption. This type of model can be extended to take account of a more specific externality relationship in which j's consumption of a specific commodity (like health care or education), rather than consumption in general, is the relevant variable in i's utility function. The main difference in this case will be in the nature of the commodity transferred.

The externality model provides an intuitively appealing explanation of the existence of direct transfers between donor and recipient, but the full implications of the model can only be seen when it is extended to the case in which the consumption of j generates positive external benefits for a large number of other individuals. In this case, giving by i (or by others) which increases j's consumption takes on the qualities of a public good. If i makes a gift to j which raises his consumption, the gift will also generate positive external benefits for all other potential donors.

Once the publicness of charity is taken into account, the utility function of a representative potential donor, i, takes the form:

$$u_i = u_i(x_i, G), \tag{7.3}$$

where G is the total output of the public good, equal to the contribution of i (g_i) plus the contributions of all others ($\sum_{k \neq i} g_k$).

Assuming the individual takes the contributions of others as given, (7.3) is maximised subject to:

$$x_i + G = w_i + \sum_{k \neq i} g_k \qquad (7.4)$$

The public good model incorporates three important assumptions: (i) that individuals maximise utility, (ii) that the output of charitable activity is a public good, and (iii) that in making a decision about her own gift, i takes the contributions of others as given (the Nash assumption). None of these assumptions appears exceptional, but solving the maximisation problem produces a number of surprising results. Letting n be the size of the group with identical preferences benefiting from the externality, Andreoni (1988) demonstrates that as n approaches infinity:

(a) the proportion of the population contributing to the public good decreases to zero;
(b) only the richest members of the community will contribute;
(c) total donations to the public good increase to a finite value;
(d) average giving decreases to zero.

The intuition behind these results is the fact that if the output of charitable activity is a public good, each individual regards the contributions of others as a perfect substitute for her own gifts. Thus an exogenous increase in the supply of the public good financed by others causes i to reduce her own contribution pound for pound. In the limit average contributions, and the number of contributors, tend to zero. Note that the theory does not predict that total contributions will be zero; at least one individual (the richest) will always give, and for this reason contributions will always be positive. None the less, the total level of contributions in a Nash equilibrium will be Pareto suboptimal. Charitable giving alone fails to achieve optimality because of the pervasive problem of free riding.

Further interpretation of the predictions of the theory depend crucially on the extent of this suboptimality. Hochman and Rodgers (1969) argue that the suboptimality of voluntary provision provides a justification for redistribution through the tax transfer system. Where utility interdependence generates positive externalities which cannot be fully internalised by voluntary activity (be-

TABLE 7.1   Total giving by quintile of net household income, 1984

All households	Quintiles of net income (£/wk)					
	5–67	68–116	117–167	168–231	232+	All
Participation (%)	16.30	25.20	33.70	40.00	47.80	32.60
Average donation (£/wk)	0.97	1.18	1.39	1.08	1.95	1.40
Donation as % income*	2.03	1.29	0.98	0.55	0.63	0.93

*For giving households
Source: Jones and Posnett (1991a).

cause of free riding), compulsory redistribution, affected by government intervention, may be Pareto optimal. The public good theory of philanthropy therefore provides a rationale for welfare spending by government. However, others (notably Sugden, 1982, and Andreoni, 1988) have pointed out that the predictions of the theory appear to be inconsistent with much of the available evidence about the characteristics of charitable giving; to the extent that the validity of the theory itself, and with it this rationale for government intervention, must be in doubt.

The theory predicts that when n is large, both the proportion of the population making a donation to charity and average gifts will be small. In the 1984 Family Expenditure Survey, a total of 32.6 per cent of households reported a positive donation to charity in the two weeks of the survey. Participation increased from 16.3 per cent for households in the lowest quintile of net income to 47.8 per cent in the highest quintile (Table 7.1). Average donations of giving households varied from £50 annually for households in the lowest quintile, to £100 for households in the highest. Data from the Inland Revenue Survey of Personal Incomes (SPI) show that for the 1985/6 tax year, 2.1 per cent of tax units made a (tax-deductible) covenanted donation to charity (Jones and Posnett, 1990, further evidence of participation is given in Table 7.3). Similar evidence of substantial participation and levels of average giving derived from surveys in the United States has been widely interpreted as refuting the predictions of the public good model (Andreoni, 1988; Sugden, 1982).

A further implication of the public good model, first stated formally by Warr (1983), is the proposition that the total provision of a public good is unaffected by redistributions of income within the set of contributors. This neutrality result has important implications for the impact of government spending designed to increase the supply of a public good. If the neutrality theorem holds, any attempt by the government to increase the supply of a public good through spending financed by taxes levied on contributors will fail, because one additional pound of government spending results in an equal reduction in private contributions. Warr (1982) and Roberts (1984) demonstrate that in a pure public good model, government spending crowds out private donations pound for pound, leaving total provision unchanged. Intuitively, this result follows from the fact that in the public good model, it is the total supply of the public good, and not the source of finance, which enters the individual's utility function. For the contributor, forced donations (through taxation) are a perfect substitute for voluntary gifts. When equilibrium is disturbed by the introduction of a tax on i accompanied by a corresponding increase in the provision of the public good, the original vector of consumption is restored by a compensating reduction in g_i. A corollary of this result is the fact that subsidies to private giving will not be effective in increasing the total supply of a public good.

The neutrality theorem which generates the crowding out hypothesis is subject to a number of qualifications. For example, Bergstrom, Blume and Varian (1986) show that if taxes are levied on non-contributors as well as contributors, total provision may be increased by tax-financed spending; crowd out is partial rather than total. A similar result follows if redistribution from a contributor exceeds the size of her gift. None the less, Andreoni (1988) demonstrates that even in the presence of corner solutions (such as those identified by Bergstrom *et al.*), the net effect of government spending, though positive, will be imperceptibly small, and crowd out is still expected to be approximately, if not exactly, pound for pound. 'The only way that the government can have any (significant) impact on the provision of public goods is to completely crowd out private provision. Joint provision is a veil' (Andreoni, 1988, p. 70).

This prediction of the public good model is also at variance with available evidence. Despite known weaknesses of data and methodology (Steinberg, 1985; 1989), available empirical evidence supports the conclusion that the crowding out of private contributions by government spending, though significant, is considerably less than pound for pound. Table 7.2, adapted from Steinberg (1989, p. 150), provides a summary of some of the relevant evidence. The crowd-out parameter, which measures the change in contributions brought about by a $1 change in government spending, varies from −0.66 (Schiff, 1985) to −0.001 (Steinberg, 1983), depending on the measures of government spending and donations. The prediction of total crowd-out of private contributions by government spending is also inconsistent with evidence that many charities receive substantial income in the form of central and local government grants, together with income from investment, sales, and donations (Posnett, 1987; Posnett and Sandler, 1989).

One of the features of the debate surrounding the public good model is the fact that the theory has yet to be rigorously tested. With the possible exception of the evidence relating to crowding out, which is still subject to qualification, none of the predictions of the theory has been tested explicitly except by reference to the general characteristics of charitable giving. Such 'evidence' cannot be taken to be conclusive, but the apparent weaknesses of the public good model have led to a search for alternative explanations, most of which proceed by relaxing one of the central assumptions of the model.

7.2.2. Non-Nash behaviour

A theory of public goods provision in which the assumption of Nash behaviour is replaced by an assumption of non-zero conjectures is discussed by Cornes and Sandler (1984). In principle, a contributor may hold either positive or negative expectations regarding the response of others to an increase in their own gifts. A positive conjectures equilibrium, in which a contributor expects others to increase their contributions in response to an increase in his own gift, will be one in which the extent of free riding is reduced compared with that in a Nash equilibrium. Despite doubts about the consistency of a positive conjectures equilibrium (Sugden, 1985), models of non-Nash bahaviour, particularly in the presence of uncertainty, may prove to be relevant in providing an explanation for some kinds of giving behaviour (for example, the behaviour of individuals who donate time as an input into the fundraising process). The impact of uncertainty, including uncertainty about the response of others, on individual contributions to

TABLE 7.2 Empirical studies of crowd-out

Study	Crowd-out parameter[a]	Measure of government spending	Measure of donations
Abrams and Schmitz (1978)	−0.236[bc]	Federal expenditure on health, education and welfare	Deductions on US federal income tax returns
Reece (1979)	−0.011 to −0.100	AFDC + old age assistance + aid for disabled per recipient	Various, from national survey of philanthropy (US)
Amos (1982)	−0.002 to −0.462	Total transfer income; AFDC; public welfare payments	Deductions on US federal income returns
Steinberg (1983)	−0.001 to −0.003 −0.004 to −0.009[c]	Intergovernment grants for recreation. Intergovernment grants for hospitals (US)	Local United Way allocations to specified service
Jones (1983)	−0.015 to −0.0016[c]	Central and local government spending on social services and housing	Family donations from family expenditure survey (UK)
Schiff (1985)	−0.66[c]	Local government expenditures	Various from national survey of philanthropy (US)
	−0.046[c]	State non-cash welfare spending	
	−0.058[c]	State cash assistance	
Abrams and Schmitz (1984)	−0.30[c]	State and local social welfare payments per $1000 personal income	Deductions on US federal income tax returns
Steinberg (1985)	−0.005[c]	Central and local government spending on social services and housing	Family donations from family expenditure survey (UK)

a Change in donations caused by a $1 increase in government spending.
b Calculated from reported elasticities and available data.
c Reported coefficients different from zero at .05 or better. In some cases, the crowd-out parameter is a non-linear function of reported coefficients and significance tests were not performed for the former.
Source: Adapted from Steinberg (1989), table 8.2.

---

public goods provision is considered by Austen-Smith (1980) and Sandler *et al.* (1987).

7.2.3 Non-utility models

An alternative approach is to relax the assumption of utility-maximising behaviour. Margolis (1982) suggests a model in which individuals have two utility functions: one relating to their own self-interest and one relating to the welfare of the group to which they belong. With a given wealth endowment, the individual allocates separate budgets to 'self' and 'group' activity according to some notion of fairness, and then proceeds to maximise each of these two functions subject to their respective budget constraints. The result is a model of non-selfish behaviour in which the amount of free riding in the provision of public goods is reduced to the extent that contributors take a wider view of social welfare. Sugden (1984) offers a different means of escape from the problem of pervasive free-riding behaviour. Sugden's model is one in which individual behaviour is governed by the dictates of a moral rule: in this case the principle of reciprocity. According to this principle, individual *i* is obliged to make a contribution towards the provision of a public good from which he benefits, providing all other members of the group to which *i* belongs are also making a contribution. The model generates a number of predictions, the most important of which in the present context is the prediction that an increase in endogenous giving will increase, rather than reduce, the gifts of *i*. The theory of reciprocity does not prove that the free rider problem will be overcome in all circumstances, but it does offer a potential explanation for the observation that large numbers of individuals make donations to charity.

Other forms of moral rule might also offer an escape from free riding. An alternative to reciprocity is a Kantian principle by which *i* feels obliged to contribute that amount which corresponds to the amount which she believes others should, ideally, contribute

(Collard, 1978; Harsanyi, 1980). However, this sort of rule is unlikely to be widely accepted if others do not, in practice, make those contributions which i believes they should. Unless the Kantian principle is widely accepted as a basis for behaviour, its impact on the voluntary provision of public goods is unlikely to be substantial.

7.2.4 Private good benefits

A more recent approach to the theory of philanthropy involves a relaxation of the assumption that the output of charitable activity is a pure public good. In these models, individuals are assumed to gain utility directly from contributing to charity, in addition to the public benefits arising from the contributions of others (Steinberg, 1987). An example of this approach is the 'warm glow' theory of altruism outlined by Andreoni (1990). The basis of this approach is the assumption that i gains utility from his own gift to charity (g_i), in addition to the non-rival benefits generated by the total supply of the public good. Letting $G = g_i + \sum_{k \neq i} g_k$ be the total supply of the public good, the individual is assumed to maximise a utility function of the form:

$$u_i = u_i (x_i, g_i, G) \tag{7.5}$$

In this form, g_i enters the utility function twice: once as a part of total giving, once as a purely private good. Retaining the Nash assumption, (7.5) is maximised subject to:

$$x_i + g_i = w_i \tag{7.6}$$

$$g_i + \sum_{k \neq i} g_k = G \tag{7.7}$$

The power of this approach can be seen by noting that since the giving of others (including government grants) is no longer a perfect substitute for i's own gifts, an exogenous increase in G financed by others will not, except in the polar case in which $\partial u_i / \partial g_i = 0$, induce i to reduce his giving by an equal amount. Free riding is no longer pervasive, and the model now predicts that crowd-out of private contributions will be partial, rather than total.

One of the problems with this sort of approach is the fact that the model does not explain why an individual should gain utility directly from contributing to charity. Andreoni (1989), following Becker (1974), suggests that individuals may simply have a taste for giving: 'perhaps they receive status or acclaim, or they may simply experience a "warm glow" from having "done their bit"' (ibid., p. 1448). Posnett and Sandler (1986) offer a more pragmatic approach in which public and private goods are jointly supplied in circumstances in which the purchase of a private good is associated with, and tied to, the finance of a public output. In this model of synthetic joint supply, the purchase of one unit of the private good r from a charity generates βp_r units of the public charitable output G, where p_r is the price of the private good. The purchase of the private good entails a joint donation to charity in fixed proportion β to the individual's expenditure on the good. The utility function of individual i is:

$$u_i = u_i\,(x_i,\, r_i,\, G), \tag{7.8}$$

where $G = g_i + \sum_{k \neq i} g_k,\ g_i = \beta p_r r_i,$ and $\sum_{k \neq i} g_k = \beta p_r \sum_{k \neq i} r_k.$

As a fundraising strategy designed to raise revenue in the face of free-riding behaviour, synthetic joint supply will be successful if a charity enjoys a cost advantage over competitors in the sale of the private good (by means of tax advantages for example), or if the public and private goods are complements in consumption. When the two goods are complementary, an increase in the supply of the public good, financed by others, will lead to an increase in the demand for the private good, and hence to an increase in the income of the charity.

Recent developments in the theory of philanthropy have succeeded in producing a number of rival hypotheses, each of which is consistent with the stylised facts of charitable giving. The rigorous empirical test which might allow rival theories to be distinguished is still lacking. Most of the empirical studies of charitable behaviour have concentrated on estimates of price and income elasticities and, where possible, on the crowd-out effect of government expenditure on private contributions.

7.3   TAXATION AND CHARITABLE GIVING BY INDIVIDUALS

Recent tax reforms in the United States, the United Kingdom and elsewhere have renewed interest in empirical analysis of taxation and charitable giving. The US Tax Reform Act of 1986 saw the elimination of the charitable deduction for non-itemisers, a reduction in the total number of deductions available, a drop in marginal rates, the end of tax deductibility for gifts based on the appreciation of property, and a reduction in the top rate of corporation tax. Similarly, income tax reforms in the United Kingdom have led to a simplification of the tax schedule and a substantial reduction in the highest marginal rate. At the same time, policy-makers have argued that private altruism should replace many activities that have traditionally been funded by the state. To the extent that tax deductibility is a stimulus to charitable giving, these objectives seem to be in conflict.

The US tax reforms have been predicted to cause a dramatic reduction in giving. For example Lindsey (1987) forecasts a reduction in cash donations of between 14.2 and 17.7 per cent, and Clotfelter (quoted in Schiff, 1990) gives similar figures of between 15 and 16 per cent. Schiff (1987) predicts a fall in volunteering of between 6 and 20 per cent and Clotfelter predicts a 5 per cent fall in corporate giving. The size of the predicted fall in revenue suggests a significant cause for concern for the charity sector. However, much of the new empirical research indicates that the models on which these forecasts are based are themselves open to question.

In the United States there is now a long list of empirical analyses of individual giving. Clotfelter (1985) includes a comprehensive survey of the literature, a job that is brought up to date by Steinberg (1990), who identifies twenty-four subsequent empirical studies. Rather than replicating their efforts this chapter concentrates on the issues and arguments raised in the debate. The main focus is on financial donations by individuals; individual volunteering and corporate giving get relatively little attention (see Schiff (1990) for a thorough analysis of volunteering and Clotfelter (1985) for a discussion of corporate giving).

A critical review of the literature reveals that estimation and hypothesis testing are usually constrained by the availability of suitable datasets. This is particularly true of attempts to test for the existence of crowding out, either by other donors or by government expenditure. In general, analysis of tax effects are confined to cross-section surveys and panel datasets, while studies of crowding out and free riding tend to use time-series data. A few US studies attempt to combine the two by using variation in average contributions and public spending between States (see Abrams and Schmitz, 1984; Schiff, 1985; 1990).

A related issue is the link between theoretical models of altruism and empirical demand analysis. The literature betrays something of a gulf between the theory of altruism and empirical models. Most empirical studies are at least implicitly based on variants of the utility model; cross-section studies incorporate price effects as a reflection of rational behaviour and, when the data allow, studies have incorporated crowding out effects. However, there seems to have been little attempt to make an empirical comparison of utility and non-utility theories.

A third theme relates to the tax–price and income elasticities of giving. When Clotfelter (1985) reviewed the state of the empirical literature there was general agreement about the quantitative significance of price and income effects. This view provides a benchmark for more recent work, for instance Schiff (1989, p. 130) notes: 'A consensus has emerged among economists that the price elasticity of giving is slightly greater than 1, whereas the income elasticity is between 0.5 and 0.8.'

However, new econometric methods (Christian and Boatsman, 1990; Reece and Zieschang, 1985; 1989; Jones and Posnett, 1991a,b) and studies using panel datasets (reviewed in Steinberg, 1990) have shaken this consensus. These new results do not necessarily contradict the existence of tax incentives but they do cast doubt on previous estimates of their significance.

7.3.1 Data sources

Studies of individual giving and taxation have used a variety of data sources:

Tax records

The most widely used dataset in US studies is the IRS tax file, an annual cross-section survey derived from individual tax returns.[1] It is often felt that recorded contributions in the tax file will be more accurate than other surveys as the information is required for tax purposes. The UK equivalent is the Survey of Personal Incomes (SPI). For example, the public use tape for the 1985/6 SPI has records for 50 665 tax units on 117 variables. These are extracted directly from tax office records according to a complex stratified sample design.[2] The SPI records the gross annual amount of covenants to charity, which is the dependent variable used in Jones and Posnett (1991b).

Household expenditure surveys

A second source of information on household giving is household expenditure surveys. These have the advantage of a greater range of information on household characteristics than the tax records. Data on charitable contributions from the US Consumer Expenditure Survey for 1972–3 are used by Reece (1979) and Reece and Zieschang (1985). The UK equivalent is the annual Family Expenditure Survey (FES). The FES records three sources of charitable donations: gifts by bank standing order, deductions from pay, and 'casual' giving.[3]

Specialised surveys

Boskin and Feldstein (1977) and Schiff (1985; 1990) use the US National Survey of Philanthropy (NSP). Published in 1974, the NSP covers 2802 households and records their giving in 1973. It covers volunteering as well as cash gifts and has detailed information on the type of gifts, the recipients, and attitudes towards philanthropy, along with a wide range of demographics. The main problem with the NSP is that it is rather out of date. The contemporary relevance of results derived from it depend on the stability of the estimated relationships. In the UK, the Charities Aid Foundation administers an annual Charity household Survey (CHS), which like the NSP offers a rich source of information. So far this dataset has not been used for an econometric analysis of giving.

Other researchers have been able to exploit one-off data sources. For example, Brown (1987) uses a consumer attitude survey from Florida, while Kingma (1989) uses a survey of listeners to National Public Radio in the United States.

Panel data

Steinberg (1990) reports a number of new studies based on panel data. These use the IRS continuous work history file which is available through the Arthur Young tax database.

7.3.2 Empirical models of individual giving

Modern variants of the utility model of altruism, as proposed by Schiff (1985), Steinberg (1986; 1987) and Andreoni (1989), and represented by equation (7.5) and similar specifications, provide the theoretical basis for empirical studies of individual giving. When combined with a budget constraint that models the tax system, they lead to demand functions which depend on price, income, other people's donations and government expenditure, along with relevant demographic characteristics (which of these variables are actually included depends on the available data). The demand equations are often estimated in the log-log form which implies that price and income elasticities are constants.

If donations are tax deductible, as in the US system or the case of covenants in the UK, the net gift made by a taxpayer will be less than the gross sum received by the charity. The opportunity cost of making the donation, in terms of foregone expenditure, is $1-t$ where t is the taxpayer's marginal rate of tax. For higher rate taxpayers this shadow price will depend on the level of gift so that, in principle, the taxpayer faces a piecewise linear budget constraint with segments corresponding to their range of tax brackets.

The utility approach to the determinants of giving suggests that a rational individual will respond to changes in the tax–price in the usual way. So, if giving is a normal good, the own-price elasticity should be negative. In fact the negativity of the tax– price effect could be interpreted as a test for economic rationality in altruistic behaviour.

The price effect also has a normative significance which helps to explain why it has received so much attention in the empirical literature. The key concept here is the notion of treasury efficiency. This implies that deductibility will be efficient, in the sense that the revenue received from individual gifts will be greater than a direct transfer from government, if giving is price elastic.[4]

Steinberg (1990) argues that this traditional view of treasury efficiency needs to be qualified by two recent contributions. First, Slemrod (1989) argues that tax evasion may drive a wedge between the loss of tax revenue, which depends on reported donations, and the money received by charities, which depends on the actual donations. If the level of evasion is sensitive to marginal tax rates, the treasury efficiency rule needs to be adjusted so that 'the elasticity of reported donations exceeds one by an amount proportional to the elasticity of evasion' (Steinberg, 1990, p. 3), thereby weakening the case for deductibility.[5]

The second qualification works in the other direction, strengthening the case for deductions. Adopting the Roberts (1984) framework, discussed above, direct government expenditure would crowd-out individual giving. In this case deductibility may be treasury efficient even if demand is inelastic. In fact with pound for pound crowding out the elasticity simply needs to be negative to guarantee efficiency. Implicit in this argument is the fact that the estimated price elasticity allows for crowding out by other donors.

As well as these efficiency arguments, the use of the charitable deduction has important distributional implications. Higher rate households face a lower tax–price, and hence a greater subsidy for their particular preferences.[6] Some critics advocate alternative policies such as tax credit schemes which are independent of the taxpayer's marginal rate.

The form of the budget constraint when donations are tax deductible raises important methodological issues. Most empirical studies attempt to identify separate estimates of the price and income elasticities of giving. However, with cross-section data this can be confounded by the collinearity of price and income.

On the face of it Table 7.3 suggests a clear gradient in the participation rate and the level of giving. But, on this evidence alone, it would be wrong to attribute this to the independent influence of the tax-price; price depends on the marginal rate and therefore on taxable income. Even using multivariate regression techniques it will be hard to identify separate price and income effects. There are various approaches that might overcome this identification problem:

1. Feenberg (1987) suggests an instrumental variables approach in which the Federal tax-price is instrumented by a Statewide average. Other studies calculate the price using State and local

TABLE 7.3   **Distribution of covenants by tax bracket: 1985/6 Survey of Personal Incomes**

Husband's marginal tax rate	Average covenant (£)	Participation rate (%)	Average covenant (£ per donor)
Basic rate (30%)	4.71	1.8	259.89
40%	35.97	14.0	256.80
45%	52.23	17.9	291.81
50%	68.74	24.8	277.37
55%	84.38	20.5	412.57
60%	152.57	26.5	576.26

Source: Jones and Posnett (1991b).

taxes as well as Federal taxes (see, for example, Feldstein and Taylor, 1976; Abrams and Schmitz, 1985; Christian and Boatsman, 1990). Christian and Boatsman attempt a systematic analysis of the collinearity problem in the context of a log-log demand equation for contributors. They conclude that while their estimated price elasticities are around −2, 'the independent contribution of price in explaining variations in charitable contributions is quite small' (Christian and Boatsman (1990, p. 64).

2. A second approach is to use a structural model of the full budget constraint of the kind developed by Reece and Zieschang (1985; 1989). However, when Reece and Zieschang (1989) find a small and insignificant estimate of the price elasticity, they interpret the result as a symptom of the lack of independent variability confounded by the omission of important demographic variables such as education.

3. The final and most satisfactory approach is to use panel datasets which contain price variation for a particular household over time. This avoids relying on cross-section variation across tax bands to identify the price effect.

It is notable that in the US literature the second and third approaches have both led to price effects that are strikingly different from previous studies (see Table 7.4).[7]

Collinearity of price and income is not the only methodological issue raised by the form of the budget constraint. It is well known

TABLE 7.4　A selection of price and income elasticities from studies using microdata

| | Elasticity | | Dataset | Method | Comment |
	Price	Income			
Cross-income					
Taussig (1967)	−0.04 to −0.1	1.31 to 3.1	US tax file 1962	OLS	Marginal price
Feldstein and Clotfelter (1976)	−1.55	0.80			
Feldstein and Taylor (1976)	−1.09 −1.28	0.76 0.70	US tax file 1962 1970	OLS	Infra-marginal
Boskin and Feldstein (1977)	−2.54	0.69	US NSP		
Reece (1979)	−1.19	0.88	US CES 1972/3	Tobit	
Clotfelter and Steuerle (1981)	−1.27	0.78	US tax file 1975	OLS	
Abrams and Schmitz (1984)	−1.44	0.54	US tax file 1979		Crowd-out
Brown (1987)	−2.53	0.55	Florida survey	Tobit	
Reece and Zieschang (1985)	−0.85	1.43	US CES 1972/3	Utility model	
Schiff (1985)	−2.79	0.76	US NSP	Tobit	
Slemrod (1989)	−1.53 −1.70	0.34 0.26	US Taxpayer Compliance 1982	OLS	Recorded audited
Kingma (1989)	−0.43	0.99	NPR survey	Tobit	
Reece and Zieschang (1989)	ns	0.02 to 0.35	US tax file 1983	Utility model	
Christian and Boatsman (1990)	−2.02	0.10	US tax file 1980	OLS	
Jones and Posnett (1991a)	ns	0.38 to 0.98	UK FES 1984	Type II Tobit	
Jones and Posnett (1991b)	ns	0.50 to 1.65	UK SPI 1985/6	Type II Tobit	
Panel data					
Broman (1989)	−1.03 −0.22 −0.41	0.82 0.24 0.38	US SOI 1979–82	OLS Fixed effects + partial adj.	
Daniel (1989)	−1.31 −0.03 −0.19	0.66 0.48 0.52	US SOI 1979–84	OLS Covariance GLS	

Note: ns – not significantly different from zero (at 5%).

that piecewise linear constraints cause two problems for estimation:

1. Because the marginal price and income depend on the level of donation they are endogenous regressors and, in principle, standard regression techniques are unsuitable. On its own, this problem can be solved by some form of instrumental variable estimator, and the standard solution has been to use the 'first-dollar' or infra-marginal price and income. These depend on the marginal rate the individual would face if he/she made no donation and is therefore independent of his/her level of donation.
2. The second issue is how to deal with the mass points in the distribution of optimal donations that may be caused by clustering of individuals around kink points in the constraint.

The practical importance of these issues is contentious. Clotfelter (1985) argues: 'Despite the theoretical nonlinearity of tax-defined budget sets . . . the average household in practice faces a nearly linear budget set and that the effect of tax deductibility is quite close to that of a simple price decrease' (Clotfelter, 1985, p. 43). But this view is contradicted by Reece and Zieschang (1985) who find that 15.4 per cent of their sample made donations large enough to change their tax bracket, and 14.4 per cent gave enough to change their itemisation status.[8]

The situation seems rather different under the UK system. In Jones and Posnett (1991a) a comparison of marginal rates with and without the deduction of gifts by standing order suggests that in the 1984 FES only nine households (0.1 per cent of the sample) gave enough to alter the price of giving. While in Jones and Posnett (1991b) the evidence from the 1985/6 Survey of Personal Incomes shows that only 134 of the 39 493 taxpaying households (or 0.3 per cent) have infra-marginal prices that differ from their marginal price.

To avoid the complications of dealing with the full range of the budget constraint the standard practice is to linearise around a particular segment. Very few studies have used the marginal price and income as these have the problem of potential endogeneity. Instead most studies use the 'first-dollar' or infra-marginal price and virtual income and linearise around the first segment of the constraint. This instrumental variables approach does not allow for the possibility of mass points around the kinks in the constraint. To allow for these some form of structural model is required. Reece and Zieschang (1985; 1989) use a two-errors model of the full budget constraint.[9]

The tax-schedule approach to the budget constraint corrects for the endogeneity of disposable income but it relies on a static view of individual choice.[10] Other approaches recognise that a problem may also arise from the intertemporal dimension of choice. It has been suggested that some measure of permanent income may be preferable to current income (with or without a tax correction). Reece (1979) uses an average of current and previous year's income before taxes but including the return to home ownership. Feldstein and Clotfelter (1976) and Jones and Posnett (1991a) use the logarithm of total consumption expenditure instrumented by the logarithm of current disposable income (along with relevant demographic variables). The estimated consumption function is used to proxy permanent income. Unfortunately, these studies have not tried to make an explicit comparison of the performance of models that use different definitions of income.

7.3.4 Zero observations

One of the features of the microdata used in US and UK studies is the high proportion of zero observations for charitable contributions. This creates an econometric problem as standard regression analysis will be subject to limited dependent variable bias due to the censoring of the dependent variable at zero.[11]

According to the utility approach a zero observation may occur as a standard corner solution, so that an individual's desired level of donation is zero – even though they may get a positive marginal utility from altruism. However, zero observations are open to other interpretations. These include misreporting and infrequency of expenditure. To take the example of the UK Family Expenditure Survey, donations made by standing order or deduction from pay are likely to be correctly recorded, but with casual donations there may be problems. Some people may simply forget to record the casual gifts they have made, while others may be occasional donors but fail to make a donation during the particular two weeks of the survey. The evidence in Jones and Posnett (1991b) suggests that a similar effect may be at work in the Survey of Personal

Incomes (SPI). Table 7.2 shows a clear gap between the participation rate of higher rate and basic rate taxpayers. This may well reflect the fact that higher rate payers need to record the amount of their covenant to receive their higher rate tax relief, while charities themselves reclaim the basic rate tax. Each of these explanations; corner solutions, misreporting, infrequency, implies a different structural model underlying observed behaviour and hence a different econometric specification.

The treatment of zeros in the empirical literature has evolved through a series of stages which reflect the development of econometric techniques and computing power over the last two decades:

(a) Many early studies simply eliminate the zero observations from the sample. For instance, Feldstein and Taylor (1976) and Feldstein and Clotfelter (1976) estimate log-log demand equations for contributors only. This approach does not solve the problem of zeros. If the zeros correspond to corner solutions and the sample is therefore generated by a standard Tobit model, the appropriate technique would be a truncated regression. However, the choice of a log-log function rules out the possibility of corner solutions. If the zeros are explained by misreporting or infrequency of expenditure a general correction for selectivity bias would be appropriate. In both cases it remains an open question whether the problem is important empirically.

(b) Boskin and Feldstein (1977), and Brown (1987) in one of the models reported in her paper, adopt the apparently pragmatic approach of adding a small positive amount to the recorded contribution before estimating a log-log equation for contributors and non-contributors. This overcomes the computational difficulty of taking the logarithm of zero but it does not solve the econometric problem. Ordinary regression estimation would still face limited dependent variable bias with a proportion of the sample censored at a small positive constant rather than at zero. Again, the use of the log-log form rules out corner solutions.

(c) The conventional wisdom in the recent literature is to use the Tobit model. This approach is adopted by Reece (1979), Reece and Zieschang (1985), Brown (1987) and Schiff (1985;

1990). While the model and estimation technique are theoretically sound, the assumptions made in specifying the model are open to question. In effect the standard Tobit model implies that the process which determines whether or not a person records a donation is the same as the process that determines how much they give. With the utility model this implies that all zeros must be corner solutions.[12]

(d) Critics argue that the Tobit model is too restrictive for many applications using survey data. In particular various generalisations of the model have been proposed (see Blundell and Meghir, 1987). In Jones and Posnett (1991a, b) we use a generalised or Type II Tobit (Amemiya, 1985) and find that its performance is superior to the standard Tobit.

7.3.5 Panel data

The survey datasets discussed so far are all limited to a single cross-section and are therefore hampered by the lack of independent variation in the price and income variables. New evidence is beginning to emerge from panel datasets which suggests that the problem may be of crucial importance. These new developments are reviewed in Steinberg (1990).

A key feature of the panel data is that a particular household's level of giving the tax status can be followed over time. Another important feature is that models can be estimated in a differenced form. This purges any demographic characteristics that remain stable over the survey period, and may make up for the lack of demographic information which has often been accused of causing omitted variable bias in the tax file data.

Steinberg cites two studies in particular, Broman (1989) and Daniel (1989), both of which use the IRS continuous work history file. In both cases, estimation of standard undifferenced models gives price elasticities that are in line with the traditional consensus; Broman gets -1.03 while Daniel gets -1.31. However, when estimators are used that exploit the dynamic nature of the panel very different results emerge. Using a fixed effects estimator, so that the models are estimated in differenced form, Broman finds a price elasticity of -0.22 which is not significantly different from zero. Daniel uses a covariance estimator and a random effects model estimated by GLS. For the covariance estimator the price elasticity is −0.03 and for the GLS estimator it is −0.19.[13] The thrust of these results leads Steinberg to conclude that 'this new evidence from panel data sets strongly challenges the traditional consensus that giving is sensitive to tax rules' (Steinberg, 1990, p. 7).

7.4 PROSPECTS FOR FUTURE RESEARCH

The evidence reported by Steinberg (1990) suggests that important advances will be made in the analysis of panel data. It will be interesting to see how existing results derived from panels stand up to further scrutiny, and how the evidence emerges as new panel data estimators are developed that incorporate the special features of microdata, in particular estimators that allow for limited dependent variables.

Returning to a more theoretical view; it is clear that existing empirical studies take a predominantly partial equilibrium approach. With the exception of Schiff (1990), little analysis has been done of cross price effects. For example, it would be useful to have some indication of the degree of substitution between deductible and non-deductible donations under the UK system. Would non-deductible donations be 'crowded out' by deductible donations if tax concessions were extended, leaving the overall level of giving unchanged?

Corporate giving has been analysed but again in a partial setting. There is scope for investigating the relationship between corporate and private giving. For instance, Schiff (1990) reports speculation that US companies may have responded to the 1986 Tax Reform Bill to make up the expected shortfall in private gifts. To take the argument a stage further, do employees or shareholders take account of the donations made by their companies when deciding on their own level of giving? Finally, there may be an important interaction between lifetime giving and charitable bequests, and hence a potential trade-off between income and estate taxes.[14]

7.5 CONCLUSION

The fact that individuals contribute in large numbers, and in substantial amounts, to organised charities represents something of a paradox. Unfortunately, attempts by economists to resolve this paradox have not, as yet, produced a consensus view. The intuitive appeal of the public good model is challenged by the apparent inconsistency between the predictions of the model and the stylised facts of charitable giving. Other explanations are possible, but each has its weakness. In particular, models which assume that giving generates private as well as public benefits have yet to provide a convincing explanation of what the source of these private benefits might be, and whether public and private benefits are substitutes or complements in consumption. A complete explanation of charitable activity must be able to explain why individuals give to more than one charity, and why certain charities are more successful than others.

The 1986 Tax Reform Act in the USA and similar reforms in the UK and elsewhere have renewed interest in the interaction between tax policy and charitable giving. At the same time, there has been a reassessment of the empirical evidence. To understand these developments it is worth pointing out that the traditional consensus rested on the apparent robustness of price and income elasticities from studies based on similar methodologies and datasets. Perhaps it is not surprising that they obtained similar results. With the use of new techniques and new data sources the consensus has evaporated.

8 Health Care Insurance and Provision

A. J. CULYER

8.1 INTRODUCTION

The focus in this chapter will be on competition and the particular issues addressed will be the merits or otherwise of competitive health care insurance, on the one hand, and competitive health-care provision, on the other. Although some readers may feel it natural to suppose that competition in the one should accompany competition in the other, or a state monopoly of the one accompany a state monopoly in the other, this is not automatically so and it is possible – at least in principle – to combine competition in one market with state monopoly in the other, or private ownership in one and public ownership in the other. The chapter is divided, therefore, into two major sections. Section 2 considers the insurance arguments; section 3 considers the provision arguments.

At the time of writing, these issues are extremely alive in political circles. In the USA, there continues to be concern that the mostly private market there (in both insurance and provision) is both unnecessarily costly and inequitable, with some 50 million (mostly poor and non-white) citizens either uninsured or seriously underinsured and dependent on charity (Farley, 1985; Farley *et al.*, 1990; Pepper Commission, 1990). In Sweden, there is concern that the almost entirely public systems of insurance and provision are both unnecessarily costly and unresponsive to patients' preferences (Saltman and Otter, 1987; Lindgren, 1989; Rehnberg, 1990). In the Netherlands, there is a major public discussion concerning the creation of a more competitive system of public health insurance (van de Ven, 1990). Similar discussions are taking place in France (Launois *et al.*, 1985), Germany (Fisinger *et al.*, 1986; Gitter, *et al.*, 1989; Henke 1990) and most other countries in the developed world. In the UK, the NHS has recently seen the introduction of competition in the public provision system. In the former DDR, the plan is to integrate a completely centralised public insurance and provision system of widely admitted inefficiency and inequity (with an extensive black market in medical care) into the (itself changing) (West) German system. In the other countries of Eastern Europe, reforms of the most fundamental kind are everywhere under active consideration (some in collaboration with the World Health Organisation and the European Community) in response to a univer:al view that the old systems must go, lock stock and barrel, but with no consensus as yet about what is to replace them or how the transition from one to another is to be managed.

There is thus scarcely a country anywhere in which the issues discussed in this chapter are not under active consideration, because of concern about suspected unnecessarily expensive forms of finance, inequity in access and utilisation, inefficiency in provision, and lack of responsiveness to consumer preferences. In some countries, of course, debate relates to more than just one (even all) of these concerns.

8.2 HEALTH INSURANCE

The main issues to be discussed under this head are whether a system of private insurance for health care is more efficient and equitable than a system of social insurance, and what forms of constraint need to be added (such as premium and benefit regulation, compulsion, and cross-subsidy).

The standard welfare economics of health-care insurance is based on the expected utility maximising model (Arrow, 1963; Culyer, 1979; Evans, 1983; 1984). Figure 8.1 shows an individual's utility as a function of income and assumes a diminishing marginal utility (implying a form of risk aversion). Let us suppose that the insurance contract is to cover only the expense of medical treatment when a need arises and that, in any time period, an insurance company knows the probability that the individual in question will

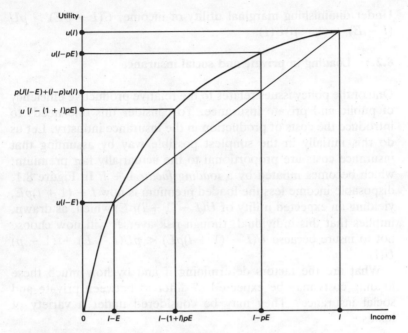

FIGURE 8.1 Welfare economics of health care insurance

need health care and the average expense that this will involve. Assuming for the moment also that the insurer incurs no costs and seeks only to balance annual premium income against annual reimbursements, and that competition between agencies keeps premiums to a minimum, then the premium charged will be the product of the risk of the event occurring (p) and its expected expense (E). For an individual with disposable income I in Figure 8.1, the choice is between insuring by paying an annual premium pE and self-insuring (bearing the risk him or herself) by accepting the uncertain prospect of $(1 - p)I + p(I - E)$, where $I - E$ is disposable income after health-care expenses. Assuming that the utility of income is unaffected by health status, so the $U(I)$ function is the same in sickness and in health, it can easily be seen that actuarially fair health-care insurance is welfare-increasing. Expected utility without insurance is the weighted average of the utilities of disposable income in sickness and in health $pU(I - E)$ $+ (1 - p)U(I)$, and expected utility with insurance is $U(I - pE)$.

Under diminishing marginal utility of income, $U(I - pE) > pU(I - E) + (1 - p)U(I)$.

8.2.1 Loading in private and social insurance

One of the policy issues relates to the relative productive efficiency of public and private insurance. To consider this one needs to introduce the costs of production in the insurance industry. Let us do this initially in the simplest possible way by assuming that insurance costs are proportional to the actuarially fair premium, which becomes inflated by a *loading factor* $1 + l$. In Figure 8.1, disposable income less the loaded premium is now $I - (1 + l)pE$, yielding an expected utility of $U(I - (1 + l)pE)$ which, as drawn, implies that this individual, though risk averse, will now choose not to insure because $U(I - (1 + l)pE) < pU(I - E) + (1 - p)U(I)$.

What are the factors determining if and by how much these loading costs may be expected to differ as between private and social insurance? They may be considered under a variety of heads:

Marketing costs

Competitive insurance firms will include marketing costs that may be absent under social insurance (particularly if the latter is compulsory). This will lead to a higher loading element under private insurance which may or may not be offset by a better matching of benefit packages to individual preferences than is possible under social insurance.

Processing costs

Competitive insurance firms will incur costs of processing applications and determining appropriate premiums. These costs may be lower under social insurance (especially if each has a standard premium under social insurance, or the contribution is linked by formula to income, or social insurance is subsumed under the general tax-raising activity of the state).

Reimbursement costs

Competitive insurers will incur costs in checking claims, pursuing fraud, and reimbursing either providers or patients. Providers too will incur billing costs, whether they bill the insurer directly or the patient. These may be less under social insurance, especially if providers are paid by the social insurance funds or the Treasury on a prospective global budget basis by some form of capitation formula.

Premiums set above minimum cost

This may arise either via monopoly premium setting (which will be absent under truly competitive insurance or with contestable insurance markets) or via X-inefficiency (which may be higher under social insurance than private), but which is also predicted to be absent under contestable markets.

Economies of scale and scope

These may bring about higher unit costs under specialised private health insurance (which loses out on grounds both of scale and scope) than under social insurance, especially if premiums in the latter case are subsumed within the tax system.

Unfortunately, there exists no empirical study of the relative costs of private and social insurance. Some results from OECD (1977) indicate that the purely financial costs are a good deal higher under private insurance and social insurance that also involves extensive billing and reimbursement by patient, episode of care or case. However, these excluded consideration of the welfare losses (if any) that may arise from community premium setting and reduced consumer choice under social insurance.

8.2.2 Optimal deductibles

If l is not simply proportional to the actuarially fair premium but is related, say, to the expected number of claims an insured person may make, then the proportion of the annual premium taken up by loading will be higher for common illness events that cost relatively little, and the optimal benefits package may exclude

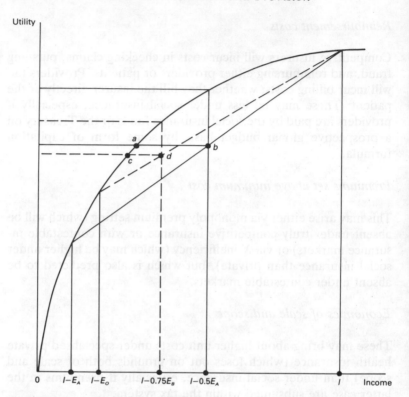

FIGURE 8.2   Insurance and deductibles

insurance against such events. For example, Figure 8.2 shows two
individuals having the same income and the same marginal utility
of income function. E_A is expenditure corresponding to a costly
event with a probability 0.5, E_B is expenditure corresponding to a
less costly event with a probability of 0.75. If the loading element
lies between *cd* and *ab*, welfare is increased with insurance against
E_A but not for insurance against E_B. It may thus be efficient to have
deductibles, such that insurance meets major expenses (and certainly catastrophic ones like cancer treatment) but not minor ones
(like routine dental care or medicines for the relief of flu-like
symptoms) (Arrow 1963).

8.2.3 Adverse selection

Premiums are set according to the insurer's calculated risks for different groups in the community. Because of imperfections in information, it is not possible to 'tailor make' each policy to allow for the specific risks facing any particular individual or family. Consequently, there is some averaging of risks. Figure 8.3 depicts another case in which two individuals are identical save in respect of the probabilities of event E occurring. For A the probability of incurring E is 0.75 and for B it is 0.25. If the event costs £10 000 then, abstracting from loading costs, the actuarially fair premiums are £7500 for A and £2500 for B. However, this degree of detail is, we suppose, unknown to the insurer, who knows only that in a typical year clients like A and B on average cost £5000. The insurer perceives only the average risk (0.5) and sets the premium accordingly. Now suppose that there is also information asymmetry: the insured parties know better their probabilities of needing care than the insurer. Each individual now faces a choice between self-insurance and the sure (financial) prospect $I - 0.5E$ represented by paying the premium. As drawn in Figure 8.3, it can be seen that the low-risk person will prefer self-insurance. This is *adverse selection* (Pauly, 1986; Freund *et al.*, 1989), and is the product of all insurance systems in which the premiums are 'community rated' or regulated by authority at some ceiling. Ignoring the transactions costs of insurance, adverse selection can be seen to be inefficient – there is some actuarially fair (even loaded) premium at which B and the insurer could make a contract. Adverse selection may also create inequities as when, for example, the self-insured are members of a low-income group and fall sick (vertical inequity), or when the perceived low probability is less than the true probability, so that individuals who are truly alike in their relevant characteristics will be treated differently by the system (horizontal inequity).

Adverse selection can be combated by making health-care insurance compulsory. If premiums are set so as to satisfy equity criteria by making them, say, proportional to ability to pay rather than anticipated benefit, and insurers are not able to 'cream-skim' by turning away clients whom they perceive to have a probable expenditure greater than the allowed premium, then compulsory insurance can be equitable in its end effect. It may also be (second-

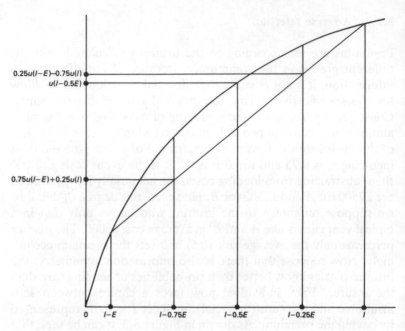

FIGURE 8.3   Insurance and adverse selection

best) efficient if the efficiency gains outweigh the losses from forcing some to insure who perceive the expected benefit to be less than their premium contribution.

8.2.4   Experience rating and cream skimming

A competitive insurance system contains within itself strong incentives for insurers to discriminate in premium setting by utilising whatever information they have on the probability of the insured needing medical care. This is typically historical information relating to past utilisation together with current information on the chronicity of any disease. This has led to the common practice of experience rating which, even if only imperfectly practised, can lead to important horizontal and vertical inequities since the incidence and prevalence of disease are inversely related to family income. Under experience rating, therefore, poor families will typically face higher premiums than better-off families, so their

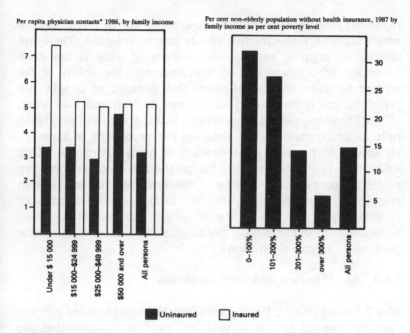

Per capita physician contacts* 1986, by family income

Per cent non-elderly population without health insurance, 1987 by family income as per cent poverty level

■ Uninsured   □ Insured

FIGURE 8.4   **Utilisation, insurance and income in the USA**

*In doctors' surgeries, clinics, hospital emergency departments or outpatient departments.
Source: Pepper Commission (1990) *Final Report*, table 1–2 and figure 1.9.

already low disposable income becomes even lower after health-care insurance premiums have been paid. If they are also less risk averse, or worse informed about sickness events, than the better off (who are usually the better educated) then, in addition to vertical inequity on the payments side, they are less likely to be insured and there will be horizontal inequity in their access to health care at the time of need. To avoid these inequities, compulsory health-care insurance and equitable premium setting are again required, together with measures to prevent cream skimming. US data indicate the significance of these factors, as shown in Figure 8.4, where it can be seen that both underutilisation and underinsurance correlate negatively with income.

It is extremely difficult to prevent cream skimming in premium-regulated insurance markets because there are so many ways in which financially unattractive clients can be rejected. These are difficult to regulate without also destroying what is the main advantage of competitive insurance, namely, the ability of the insured to select from rival offers that package of benefit and premium that is preferred (but see van de Ven and Van Vliet, 1990). These ways of cream skimming include, for example, being rude to unattractive clients, delaying the processing of their applications, or presenting information in a mystifying way. One solution to such problems is to forego the freedom to choose the preferred package by offering a standard benefits package to relevant groups (or everyone) in exchange for compulsory membership of a social insurance system financed either by an earmarked income-related 'health-care tax' (social insurance premium) or general taxation.

8.2.5 Moral hazard and price elasticities

Moral hazard (Pauly, 1968) occurs because being insured encourages the insured person to take less care in ensuring that the undesired state (illness) does not occur (*ex ante* moral hazard), and, when that state does occur, because it encourages the insured person to maximise the use of services up to the point at which the marginal private benefit from doing so falls to zero (*ex post* moral hazard), or is at least lower than the marginal cost of the care. In health-care insurance, the *ex post* variety seems to be the main problem. A caveat is worth noting here: if hospitals and other services set their prices above marginal cost and/or if there are significant marginal external benefits attaching to each individual's health care consumption (Culyer 1971; 1989), then some consumption beyond the point at which price equals marginal value will be optimal.

The effect on the insurance market is predictable. With moral hazard, preferred consumption exceeds the rates at which premiums have been historically set and, provided that providers of care can fully recoup their expenses from the insurer (either directly or via the patient), the provider has every reason to supply this care. This will lead to higher premiums as insurers recalculate the expected costs of events, will drive out some risk-averse individuals from the insurance market, and may cause a rate of utilisation in excess of the optimal rate. Insurers can respond to this in several ways. One, which is increasingly practised in the USA, is for them to adopt a quasi-regulatory role, in which they specify levels of reimbursement prospectively, or set limits on, say, lengths of in-patient stays for each condition, or require internal hospital peer-review procedures to avoid 'unnecessary' care and any that is primarily driven by its earnings potential rather than for the good it does patients. Another, especially used by large US employers who offer health-care insurance as a fringe benefit, is to make special arrangements with Health Maintenance Organisations (involving specified prepayments for a specified package of services) or Preferred Provider Organisations (agencies which contract with a restricted list of providers who offer low-cost services of an agreed standard). Another, commonly adopted by the US public programmes Medicare (for the elderly) and Medicaid (for the eligible poor) is to set fixed rates at which they will reimburse providers for particular treatments (known as Diagnosis Related Groups). Yet another method, more attune with a commitment to market methods of doing things, is to introduce (further) deductibles and, in particular, *coinsurance*, under which the insured party pays a particular proportion of the provider's charges, with the insurer picking up the balance. These out-of-pocket payments in the USA currently amount to about 30 per cent of non-hospital expenses and 10 per cent of hospital expenses.

The effect of coinsurance can be seen in Figure 8.5. With full 'first pound' cover and zero marginal (money) user price, the sick individual may be expected to consume OQ units of health care (say, hospital in-patient days for a particular condition). At this rate of consumption, $MV = 0$. This generates a welfare loss of abQ in the absence of any externality, assuming also that the marginal cost curve corresponds to the social marginal cost curve. Thus abQ is the amount by which the cost of providing Q^*Q units exceeds their value to the consumer ($Q^*abQ - Q^*aQ$). If now the consumer pays a proportion β of the daily cost P, and that is, say, 50 per cent, user price becomes βP, consumption falls from Q to Q' (closer to the 'optimum' Q^*), the 'excess burden' falls by more than half to acd, and total expenditure falls from $OPbQ$ to $OPcQ'$, with the insurer picking up only $\beta PPcd$, implying a lower (future) premium. The 'excess burden' is in fact proportional to the square of the deviation between price and marginal social cost where,

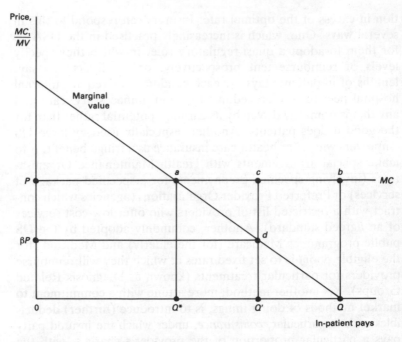

FIGURE 8.5   The effect of coinsurance

with a linear demand curve with a variable elasticity, e, the factor
of proportionality is $0.5eQ/P$ (Newhouse, 1990).

In one of the few thorough empirical attempts to measure welfare effects, Feldstein (1973) estimated that the maximum reduction in the excess burden of 'excess' health insurance in the USA,
associated with raising coinsurance from 33 per cent to 50 per cent,
would have been \$10 billion in 1969 prices after allowing for the
loss of welfare to those who would no longer choose insurance.
However, the implications of this analysis for policy depend crucially on the adequacy of prices as measures of marginal social
cost, on the absence of externalities, on the adequacy of the
demand curve MV as a representation of the consumer's valuation of
health care, and on the adequacy of the estimated price elasticity
of demand. The actual calculation was based on an elasticity estimate that was almost certainly too high by a large factor (hence
producing an upwards bias in the estimated welfare loss). The
most recent evidence on demand elasticities suggests that for all
types of care they lie in the range -0.2 to -0.1 (Manning *et al.*,

1987). These researchers also found, however, that the average elasticities were larger for the poor, for children, and especially for the children of the poor (Lohr *et al.*, 1986). The elasticities were derived in a massive RAND experiment which set a limit on annual out-of-pocket expenditure of $1000, after which the insurer paid everything. This would evidently reduce the elasticity compared with a situation in which there was no expenditure limit. The experiment (like Feldstein's study) also did not allow for the effects that changing utilisation may have on doctors' decisions. The extent to which coinsurance reduces utilisation depends on the doctors' responses to this potential threat to their incomes (Evans, 1974; 1976) and on their opportunity for *supplier induced demand*. Patients in the experiment did not make up a very large proportion of any doctor's practice. But, if they had, as would be the case for a system-wide change in coinsurance rates, there would have been the possibility of the generation of sufficient additional demand to maintain doctors' incomes and, of course, reduce the observed price elasticity. We are thus dealing with a situation in which it may be dangerous to infer the size of demand elasticities on the basis of an essentially *partial equilibrium* analytical framework, when there is *a priori* reason to expect some general equilibrium effects which are not captured in the model.

These possible demand-inducing responses have been subject to relatively little detailed empirical work and that which has been done reports mixed results – for example, in Ontario where, as in the USA, the typical doctor is paid on a piece rate rather than by salary, it has been found that higher doctors' fees (per item of service) correlated positively with the use of the procedures of tonsillectomy and hysterectomy (as fees rose so more procedures were used), negatively in diagnostic curettage and cholecystectomy, and statistically insignificantly in many other cases (Labelle *et al.*, 1990). The supplier inducement hypothesis predicts that the relationship between fee changes and use of procedures will be negative. An earlier study (also Canadian) found a much stronger response by doctors (Beck, 1974).

8.2.6 Conclusions

Since so much depends upon empirical evidence that is simply not available, there is lots of room for different observers to take quite different views about the best way of organising health-care insurance, especially when to empirical uncertainties one adds quite different views about equity in health and health-care payments, and about the relative priority to attach to equity compared to efficiency. The principal issues have, however, been laid out in this section in sufficient detail for the reader to begin to form a judgement. It is to be hoped also that the importance of the issues, and their practical significance as matters of current policy debate, will encourage researchers to address the unresolved issues, especially those that are amenable to empirical assessment.

8.3 PROVISION

8.3.1 Provider markets in health care

The general favour in which economists hold competition arises from the theory of perfect competition or, more generally, the theory of contestability. Competition for the ownership of firms, in the product or service market, and ease of entry and exit, imply that firms will maximise net worth, which in turn implies that output, in the absence of production externalities, will be produced at least cost. It also implies that, provided demand is appropriately expressed, and there are markets for everything, the right outputs will be produced at the right rates and volumes. There are manifest hazards in transferring these presumptions to the health-care sector (Culyer and Posnett, 1990).

(a) There is no market force promoting net worth (or profit) maximisation in a provider industry that is overwhelmingly non-profit and it is clearly possible for non-profit organisations (even if they are still maximising something) to pursue objectives that are counter to the objectives of government policy and also counter to efficiency – whether by providing whatever is provided at higher cost than is necessary or providing an inappropriate set of outputs.

(b) There may not be sufficient well-informed demanders or sufficient alternative providers (incumbents or new entrants) for inefficient providers to feel sufficient pressure to improve cost-effectiveness, or for new providers to anticipate sufficient reward to warrant entering the market.

(c) The conditions required for contestability of markets, especially under 'natural' monopoly, are often absent and political considerations often make them difficult to create.
(d) To judge whether the output mix is appropriate and cost-effectively produced requires information that is often lacking and, where some exists, highly imperfect.
(e) In systems where there are overall budget limits, as in the United Kingdom, Sweden or Canada, overall output optimality will be highly contingent on the permitted levels of public and private expenditure.

In this section the main empirical results will again come from the USA, though particular attention will later be paid to the UK experiment in provider competition introduced as the result of Department of Health (1989). The strategy will be to examine the evidence on the effects of competition in the USA and then to speculate about the means by which its adverse effects can be avoided elsewhere, while simultaneously harnessing its good effects. In addition, the important distinction between the *public expression of demand* and the *public or private provider response* to that demand will be examined.

8.3.2 Hospital competition

Suppose that the insurance arrangements adopted are such that the provider is reimbursed retrospectively for whatever costs of care are implied by the controlling physician's choices in each patient's case. For simplicity let us also assume that there is no direct incentive for the physician to generate demand in order to maintain his or her income. Under these circumstances one expects hospitals that are profit-maximisers to seek to attract clients not through price competition, since whatever price is set will be reimbursed anyway, but through non-price competition. A necessary condition for this is, of course, that price be set above marginal cost, as may be predicted to be the case whenever there is any degree of monopoly, but which may also be more generally the case unless insurers require patients or their referring physicians to seek out the lowest cost option, which for the moment we assume not to be the case.

As the hospitals compete for patients either directly or through physician referrals, some of the more obvious modes of attracting them will include offers of higher quality care, more convenient location, more lavish hotel-style non-clinical facilities, shorter waiting times, and longer in-patient stays (at least as long as the patient – being insured – wants at zero price and as long as possible from the hospital's point of view, as long as the daily billed charge exceeds the hospital's perceived opportunity cost of marginal days). The higher quality care is most likely to be advertised (both to patients and their doctors) in terms of additional inputs and procedures, both diagnosing and treating, which will be perceived as welfare increasing by clients even though the relation between such procedures and ultimate outcomes in terms of 'getting better' or 'getting worse slower' may be tenuous or non-existent. All these forms of non-price competition are cost-raising but, so long as the costs can be passed on to the insurer, there is no financial incentive to limit them. Moreover, there is no mechanism for pushing any of these dimensions of activity towards an optimal rate. Further, the same incentives confront non-profit hospitals too.

A common model employed has been based on the postulate that non-profit hospitals jointly maximise quantity and quality of service (e.g. Newhouse, 1970). While models of this genre imply that hospitals will minimise the unit costs at each level of activity, the levels of activity will again typically exceed the optimum be-cause the demander has every reason to demand any service having a positive perceived marginal value, while the payer (the insurance company) merely pays for whatever costs are implied by the interaction of patients' demands (mediated by physicians) at zero user-price and the providers' supply decisions (moral hazard).

In the United States, up to about 1982, when hospital reim-bursement on a retrospective cost-plus basis was the norm, experi-ence seems broadly to confirm these predictions. Robinson and Luft (1985; 1987) found that hospitals in more competitive mar-kets, as judged by hospital density, had higher costs per day and per case than those in less competitive markets after adjusting for case-mix, scale, local wage rate differences and ownership type (contrary to the usual predictions about where X-inefficiency is to be expected). Moreover, unit cost increased monotonically with the number of neighbouring hospitals. Other studies have found greater duplication of clinical services in more competitive mar-kets (Luft *et al.*, 1986), which can be directly counter to better

quality care as judged by ultimate health outcomes, since it seems
to be the case that below certain volumes of particular types of
patient, there are outcome losses attributable to insufficient 'learn-
ing by doing' or frequent experience in the handling of particular
surgical procedures (Flood *et al.*, 1984).

In this connection it is worth pointing out that there are very
large variations in the rate of medical intervention between different health-care systems *and also* within systems, even when due
allowance has been made for differing population characteristics
such as age, sex and morbidity differences. For example, McPherson (1988) reported age-standardised rate of hysterectomy (per
100 000 population at risk) of 700 in the USA, 600 in Canada, 450
in Australia, 250 in the UK and 110 in Norway. Within the UK,
McPherson *et al.* (1982) found a variation between 7.5 and 27.5
per 10 000 population at risk in tonsillectomy rates between
Health Districts, 7.5 to 15 in hysterectomy, 4.5 to 9.5 in prostac-
tectomy, 1 to 4.6 in haemorrhoidectomy. Similar variations have
been found in other studies. These may reflect what has become
known as a 'surgical signature' in which the uncertainties, judgements and preferences of particular doctors vary (Wennberg and
Gittlesohn, 1982) but in general the reasons for these variations
are poorly understood, though the international variations are
often related to bed and doctor to population ratios (a kind of
Say's Law of health care). Small area variations within systems
almost certainly derive in large part from the substantial discretion
exercised by doctors in most health-care systems (Sanders *et al.*,
1989). The variations clearly have expenditure implications for the
ultimate payers. McPherson (1988) estimated that if eight common
surgical procedures (hysterectomy, cholecystectomy, pros-
tatectomy, tonsillectomy, inguinal hernia repair, lens operations,
appendicectomy and haemorrhoidectomy) had been used at the
rates in Canada or the USA, UK expenditure would have risen
from £176 million to £455 million or £447 million respectively
(1986 prices).

It is important to appreciate that the practice of medicine is in
large part more of an inexact art than a precise science: 'the
medical decisionmaking process is a complicated interaction of
scientific evidence, patient desire, doctor preferences, and all
sorts of exogenous influence, some of which may be quite irrelevant' (McPherson, 1989). For example, a pathologist can test

via autopsies whether a diagnosis made prior to death was correct, wrong or missed (namely, the disease revealed at autopsy had not been anticipated clinically). Cameron and McGoogan (1981) found that, of 1322 diagnoses covering twenty-six diseases, 46.5 per cent were correct, 39.8 were wrong and 13.7 had been missed. Of the wrong diagnoses, in 83 per cent of cases the actual condition was the main cause of death; of the missed diagnoses, in 19.7 per cent of cases the actual condition was the main cause of death. Moreover, there is clear evidence that some procedures either do little good for some patients and may even generate net harm, yet they continue in use. Cholecystectomy (an operation for gall stones) is such a case (Gracie and Ransohoff, 1982; Bouchier, 1983; Roos and Danzinger, 1986), as are tonsillectomy (Roos, 1979; Paradise *et al.*, 1984), haemorrhoidectomy (*The Lancet* editorial, 1975), hysterectomy (Sandberg *et al.*, 1985) and many others. Although there are great difficulties in establishing what surgery really is unnecessary (Pauly, 1979), difficulties that are compounded by the so-called 'placebo effect' by which the mere fact of receiving medical attention seems to yield a benefit, this brief survey suggests at the very least the underlying technology for determining health production and cost functions is rather inadequate.

These variations and their cost consequences are a complicating factor in assessing the efficiency (or otherwise) of policies to promote competition. No assessment of competition has yet taken account of them. It seems, however, that some of the apparent inefficiencies of provider competition are attributable to the payments mechanism on the demand side rather than to the fact of competition itself. After about 1982, US policies towards 'cost control' emphasised changes in the form of hospital reimbursement (with price controls) and explicit price competition through selective contracting between payers and providers (Arnould and De Brock, 1986). The common feature that all these measures had is that they set the hospital's reimbursement *prospectively*. For example, in the case of the state programmes for Medicaid, historic cost information was used together with planned case volumes; in the case of the Federal Medicare programme, fixed prices per case in 467 diagnosis and related groups (DRGs) were established. Two programmes of selective contracting for Medicaid patients have been used in California and Arizona. If these measures are to reduce cost per case, they need, of course, to be set at levels lower than current costs. Since the more competitive markets are those where unit costs have been highest, it is in these markets that one predicts the greatest effect. Melnick and Zwanziger (1988) and Zwanziger and Melnick (1988) found that cost per case fell after the introduction of selective contracting in California in the competitive markets and rose (but at a slower rate than before) in the less competitive markets (see also Robinson and Luft, 1988). With all the prospective reimbursement schemes, there seems to have been a reduction in the annual rate of hospital cost inflation for the hospitals most affected by it (Feder *et al.*, 1987) though not all studies have found an effect (e.g. Melnick and Zwanziger, 1988).

An important question is, of course, whether these cost reductions represent real gains in efficiency. For example, one way of reducing costs under a DRG system is to exercise greater selectivity by admitting relatively low-cost patients in each category – a form of cream skimming. Another way of reducing cost per case (but not necessarily total costs) is to discharge patients earlier and, perhaps, with less regard to the adequacy of the convalescent facilities at home or of other community support services (which are particularly important for the elderly and for those living alone). Evidence on the former (known as 'DRG creep') does not seem to indicate significant cream skimming. By contrast, there is strong evidence on falling lengths of stay (in a country with already the shortest lengths of hospital stay in the developed world) – a reduction of over 6 per cent after the introduction of DRHs according to Rosko and Broyles (1987), while other studies such as DesHarnais *et al.* (1987) and Feder *et al.* (1987) report larger proportionate reductions in length of stay.

There is some evidence that patients on discharge are on average more sick than previously (Carroll and Erwin, 1987) but little to suggest that their changing overall care package resulted in worse health outcomes. A marked increase in the use of 'subacute' care facilities on discharge has been noted, with a decline in discharges to the patient's own home (Morrisey *et al.*, 1988). The terminally ill seem also to have been discharged from acute care facilities, as evidenced by a significant decline in the number of deaths in hospital, as distinct from hospice or nursing home (Sager *et al.*, 1989).

Prospective reimbursement seems also to have brought about a reduction in the number of hospital admissions (DesHarnais *et al.*, 1987; Melnick and Zwanziger, 1988). This may have arisen because of the increasing use of second opinions (in the USA unlike the UK, the admitting doctor is usually the doctor the patient first sees; under the UK system by which the GP refers to a named hospital doctor, a second opinion is built into the admission procedure in nearly all cases). Several studies have shown that the use of second opinions has reduced the rate of surgical intervention (e.g. Grayboys *et al.*, 1987) without adverse effects on eventual health outcome. There is also evidence of a shift from in-patient to outpatient care, from traditional in-patient surgery to day-case surgery, and a tendency for the severity of case-mix to rise, which suggests that there has been no great cream skimming, but which has tended to cause the average cost per case to fall less than it otherwise would have due to reductions in length of stay, and in some cases to cause it to rise somewhat.

8.3.3 Prospects for competition in the United Kingdom

The UK reforms are based on the key distinction between *purchasers* and *providers*. Here we shall focus on the hospital system. There are two types of purchaser: health authorities funded on an adjusted capitation basis for the population in their catchment area, and GPs of two further kinds, those with special funds for the purchase of diagnostic and elective surgical procedures from hospitals, and non-fundholders reliant mostly on capitation payments for the patients registered with them who refer to hospital in the traditional way. There are two types of NHS provider: Trusts, which are funded directly by the Department of Health and which are managerially independent of health authorities, and Directly Managed Units in which the provider side is integrated with the purchasing side under a health authority. In addition, purchasers may contract for services from a third provider source: the private sector.

The principal defects of competition in the USA had their origins in three features of the provider market:

1. Absence of an effective budget constraint on purchasers (whether insurers or consumers), which arose from low or zero

price at the point of use and encouraged cost-raising non-price competition amongst providers

2. Retrospective hospital cost reimbursement by third party payers which simultaneously permitted demand at low prices to be met and covered all costs incurred as specified by providers, thus further encouraging high activity and raising cost per case

3. Poor information about quality, whether interpreted in input/ process terms (inputs per unit of activity) or outcome terms (effective impact on health) and imperfect incorporation of these considerations in contracts between payers and providers.

In the UK, although (money) price will be effectively zero for the consumer (which will permit the internalisation of any externalities in health care), both purchasing GPs and purchasing authorities will be expenditure capped, and so the first adverse feature of the US market will be absent. Moreover, under the UK arrangements, budgets for providers will be set largely *prospectively* by the authorities with whom they contract and the prices of items charged on a service by service, or case, basis will again be known in advance by purchasers, so the effects of retrospective payments systems will also be absent. The effectiveness of competition in the UK hospital market is therefore likely to depend on the following factors:

(a) The ability of health authorities and GPs to articulate the needs of their local communities for health care, by identifying prevailing patterns of morbidity and mortality that are amenable to effective medical care, and to assess the relative cost-effectiveness of providers' offers, in order to maximise the impact of available resources on needs (efficiency) constrained by local interpretations of equity.

(b) The ability of contractors to measure and monitor the quality of care in order to avoid cream skimming and, in general, to raise what are commonly perceived to be quality standards that are lower than they need be.

(c) The ability of purchasers to assess the 'reasonableness' of purchasers' offer prices, particularly when there is local monopoly.

(d) The ability of regional authorities and the Department of

Health to ensure that purchasing authorities do not enjoy monopsonistic gains taken in the form of either exploitative behaviour of providers or, as may be more likely, of X-inefficiency in the identification of needs and the revelation of a demand pattern that reflected the relevant social concerns.

Of these, the first and the last are crucial for, no matter how competitive or cost-effective the provider side, if it responds to poorly specified needs, or inequitably demanded services, the system will remain inefficient and inequitable, even if it becomes more responsive to consumer preferences in respect of hotel and other services complementary to direct medical treatment. Just as in the USA, the principal defects of the provider side have their roots in imperfections on the demand side, so is it in the UK. In principle, the structure is one that is *enabling* in the sense that it does not *build in* a systematic demand-side failure, nor indeed, *ensure* or provide any formal mechanism for guaranteeing that the expressed demands derive from consumer's preferences, inter-preted by collective or personal agents (authorities and doctors) in the light of the best epidemiological information about effective-ness, nor that they also take proper account of equity considera-tions. A system design that provides for the public, collective setting of resource constraints, within which individual clinical judgement is exercised by doctors as agents for individual patients, may be a necessary condition for efficiency and equity in health care, but it is not sufficient. Moreover, the public discussion of equity in the NHS is only just beginning and there is substantial haziness both about the meaning of the concept and how it ought best to be operationalised (Mooney, 1983; Lockwood, 1988; Culyer and Posnett, 1990; Wagstaff, 1991).

It is quite possible that over time the balance between public and private *provision* of health care may alter substantially – for example, if it were to turn out to be the case that private providers were better able to respond to the demands of authorities and GPs than public providers. Although this would represent a major departure from the traditional view of the NHS in Britain as a public service, it does not necessarily imply that the objectives of the NHS would be less well served thereby – this depends again quite crucially on the ability and willingness of *purchasers* to behave in an appropriate fashion. However, the available information on the relative cost-effectiveness of private providers (whether non-profit or for-profit) and public providers suggests that the cost (and quality) advantage often lies with the latter (Stoddart and Labelle, 1985) so that any shift in the public–private mix on the provider side is likely to become manifest only in the very long run. Within public provision, however, there are likely to be more substantial shifts as purchasers select from amongst a wider set of providers than before, trading off, for example, distance and ease of visiting against waiting times, quality and relative cheapness. One also predicts greater responsiveness to consumer preferences for complementary services.

8.4 CONCLUDING COMMENTS

The recurring theme of this chapter has been the centrality of the demand side in evaluating the prospects for competition in the health-care field. The environment created by insurance, whether private or social, and the ways in which need and the demand for care are related and revealed by individuals and collective agencies, are crucial because they provide the signals and the rewards/ penalties for the supply response. There is reason to believe that a social insurance method of finance can be both more equitable and efficient than private insurance, but whether, within such a framework, the paying agencies (in the form, in the UK, of health authorities and GPs) will follow their own objectives without regard for wider (or higher) notions of social welfare, remains to be seen. These issues might have light shed upon them by public choice theory, though there has been to date no systematic analysis of this sort in the health-care field. The next few years will provide ample international evidence as different systems evolve, and an ample agenda for further research in health economics. In this, it will be important to examine the detailed institutional frameworks within which the various players act their parts and research will have to embrace health-care capital markets (Mayston, 1990a), health-care labour markets (Mayston, 1990b), as well as the interdisciplinary areas concerned with health-care needs and the effectiveness of health care in its impact on health.

9 The Economics of Education: Changing Fortunes

HOWARD GLENNERSTER

9.1 THE RISE AND DECLINE OF THE ECONOMICS OF EDUCATION

From the mid-1950s to the early 1970s the economics of education blossomed. Blaug's (1976) authoritative bibliography on the subject listed ninety-five items published in the period up to and including 1955. The 1966 edition contained 800 items in all, the 1976 edition 2000. As someone working in the field at the time, I well remember the excitement and the pace of development in the subject. The best introductory text is still Blaug (1970). Yet in the succeeding decade the subject stagnated, just as the public education budget did in the UK and USA. The stagnation in spending can be explained in various ways. The post-war birth-rate boom subsided. So, too, did investment in higher education after the Sputnik[1] scare faded. The student rebellions of 1968 played their part. There was a disenchantment with the economic pay-off from education that the economists had predicted. With reduced education budgets went reduced research budgets. Yet the decline in the economics of education went much deeper than that. It was intellectual not just financial. The subject was deeply flawed and it paid the price.

176

9.1.1 The human capital tradition

American economists Becker (1964) and Schultz (1963) exploited the basic idea that education was a neglected element in explaining economic growth. Moreover, the decision an individual made to continue his or her education was analogous to the decision an entrepreneur made to invest in capital equipment. The individual incurred costs. There were the costs of the tuition or schooling, represented by the fees paid, and there were the opportunity costs of not entering the labour force, taking time out to study. There were also financial rewards in the higher earnings that such individuals would gain.

The US census had income data and educational experience of individuals, which enabled economists to produce evidence that more highly educated individuals did indeed earn more over their lifetimes. On average each additional year of schooling raised that person's lifetime earnings profile. Recent American evidence is shown in Figure 9.1. Those additional earnings streams could be discounted back to a present value. How much would I pay to have

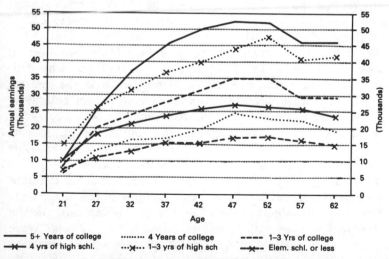

FIGURE 9.1 Earnings by age and education in 1987, US males

Source: Burtless (1990) derived from US Bureau of the Census, Current Population Reports, Series P-60.

that additional stream of earnings now? That capital sum can then be compared to the cost of the additional education. Was it financially worth it as an investment? Lo and behold, on average, the figures showed the investment produced a positive return and a substantial one too. Individuals were therefore acting rationally by staying on in the education system and they would continue to do so up to the point where their private rate of return tended to equate to other ways of investing their financial resources.

What was true of individuals was also true of nations. In so far as individuals' higher earnings reflected their higher productivity, as was the case in a reasonably competitive labour market, their extended education added to the productive capacity of the economy, and this came to be called the social rate of return to education. Not only could this general statement be made. It was possible to go on to calculate what the social rate of return was to investing in different types and levels of education. What was the economic return from a developing country investing in primary versus secondary or tertiary education? What was the return on science as opposed to humanities courses at university? What was the return on postgraduate versus undergraduate courses? World Bank reports and economic advisers to the UK government began to produce such indicators. Cost-benefit analysis came to education (for an international review see Psacharopoulos, 1981).

In another important contribution Becker (1964) was able to build on Marshall's (1890) insight and show not only why individual firms in a free market would not invest in the general training of their employees since other firms would compete those employees away, but also showed that employees would carry the cost privately in reduced wages during apprenticeship. Specific training tied to the firm would be undertaken in a free market as its benefits could not leak but that was distinctly limited.

Once invented these models could be replicated for different countries and for different kinds of education and training. They were always the subject of some fairly heroic assumptions. Did the differential earnings reflect differential marginal products? Were cross-sectional analyses of age earnings profiles a good indication of the additional earnings graduates would actually gain? How did teenagers actually make educational decisions? Blaug's (1976) masterly review of the human capital literature and its empirical support to that date has never been bettered. Despite his early enthusiasm this review was subtitled 'A Slightly Jaundiced Survey'.

9.1.2 Screening

In the early 1970s the sceptics moved from criticism to alternative theoretical models to explain the available evidence. In the United Kingdom, Peter Wiles (1974) published a paper expounding what he called the 'External-Test-Not-Content-Hypothesis'. A series of papers was published on both sides of the Atlantic, not casting doubt on the individual's rationale for staying in education, but on how to interpret the broader economic significance of what was happening (Arrow, 1973; Spence, 1973; Stiglitz, 1975).

The burden of this theory was to show that employers would be acting rationally if they used higher education as a way of selecting out the able and persistent young people who could stay the academic race. The qualities so revealed and signalled to employers were difficult and expensive for employers to find out for themselves. Hence they relied on the formal education system to do it for them free. Such graduates need not have learned anything at university but so long as university did a good grading job and gave good signals, it was worth employers using that information to recruit graduates to more highly paid jobs and if the selection process had sorted out good people they would be paid more in their later careers. The same can be said of a general training scheme like the UK government's Youth Training Scheme. It may provide little in the way of additional skills but may be used as a screening mechanism. Gleeson (1989) notes that 'for some, YTS has become the only way into employment [although] there is little evidence that the content of YTS courses is the main contributary factor'.

This was a worrisome theory. The main underlying message of the human capital school to governments had been – invest in education and you will increase the productivity of the nation and raise the growth rate. The screening theorists were suggesting that the private rates of return to education were no guide to the social rates. We might have too much education, not too little. Arrow (1973) pointed out that if college were a mere screening device, abolition of higher education or at least charging economic fees could bring about real efficiency gains for the economy as a whole. This was a highly convenient idea at a point when politicians wanted to cut the education budget for wider economic and political reasons. Stiglitz (1975) put education alongside dress, gender and race as screening devices. Perhaps one reason British employers need higher education less is that they have another very good screening device to choose those in whom they are interested – class and the Public School (that is to say the private) system of education. If accent and social class will do as a way of sorting out promising managerial material why worry about a degree?

There then followed a period in which empirical tests of the two theories were tried. An American study (Taubman and Wales, 1973) conveniently split the difference. Roughly half the net earnings differentials they observed they associated with screening factors. Riley (1979) claimed that his data supported the hypothesis in some occupations and not others. In Britain, Layard and Psacharopoulos (1974) found little empirical support for the thesis. Indeed, they argued that because the dispute is about the reasons why earnings of graduates and others are higher, market evidence is of little help. Burtless (1990) in a later review is still of the view that, 'no economist has proposed a statistical test that can reliably distinguish between the human capital and screening theories'.

9.1.3 Manpower requirements

At the other end of the intellectual spectrum, and especially in Europe, economists tried to tell governments how many people to train and educate. It was not a silly thing to want to do. Unlike the United States, European governments paid for university education and hence needed to know how much to provide and in what subjects. The planned economies of the East, which then seemed so good at these things, had an economic plan, perhaps five years ahead, and so could read off how many engineers or doctors they wanted. The educational institutions could then be financed to produce those numbers. In a modified form something similar operated in the semi-planned economies like Sweden. Various attempts were made to do that in the United Kingdom and even more in the developing world. Most had disastrous consequences. Places in science were expanded in British universities only to find that there was no demand. It was decided that Britain had too many doctors, and medical schools were cut causing a doctor shortage in the 1960s. It was decided that places in teacher training colleges could be cut because the birth-rate was falling. It proceeded to rise sharply, causing a teacher shortage in the 1960s. The best recent review of the later literature on manpower forecasting is to be found in Psacharopoulos (1987).

9.1.4 Efficiency and schools

The economics of education was more than rate of return analysis, of course. The problem was that other components in the subject field were not significant enough. There was strangely little work on the largest element in the education budget – schools. Since human capital theory depended on analysing increments to education beyond compulsory school leaving ages there was little you could say about schooling, a major weakness when it came to the practical usefulness of the economics of education.

There was some good pioneering work on the production functions of schools or what mix of inputs produced the best outcomes (Burkhead, 1967). Was it better teachers, or more teachers, or books or equipment? The problem here was not the theory but the data and the results. The information on how schools used what resources was weak. In the UK no statistics were kept on what each school actually spent. Compared to that, the social data on pupils was relatively rich and swamped the economic variables. For a review of the early literature see Glennerster (1972a). The latest, mainly American, work is reviewed by Psacharopoulos (1987).

Instead of pursuing this interesting range of work, economists left the field to sociologists and psychologists. Coleman (1966) and Jenks (1972) in the USA concluded that differences in school resources explained less than 5 per cent of the variation between pupils' performance. It was left to Rutter *et al.* (1979) and Mortimore (1988) in the UK to pursue the task of measuring differential school effectiveness more deeply. We return to their work later.

9.1.5 Spending and finance

Another important element in that early work was, what may be called, the social accounting of education. It may seem odd now but there was, at that time, no description of what was being spent on all levels of education, publicly and privately, and how those spending levels had changed over time. Nor was there any consistent account of how the total education budget was financed. In the UK, Wiles (1956) had the first go, but Vaizey (1958) produced a historical account of education spending and the share of economic activity devoted to it over time. In truth education had done remarkably well up to that point. In 1972 I was able to write (1972a, p. 4):

> [E]ducation has grown more rapidly than consumers' expenditure in every period [of government since the Second World War] . . . Over the last decade [from 1960 to 1970] in real terms we spent less on tobacco, less on newspapers and magazines, 10 per cent more on food, 35 per cent more on radios, TVs and electrical goods and 44 per cent more on alcoholic drink. That is the measure of the affluent consumer society. Yet we spent 51 per cent more on education in the same period again in real terms. Only our expenditure on cars and telephones rose faster.

This rate of expansion continued until the first oil crisis and in the UK came to a shuddering halt in 1976. Figure 9.2 shows how education spending in the UK in real terms stood still for a decade. Because the numbers in each age group varied over time, the impact was sharpest on the age group that was growing at the time, those between 18 and 24. For them resources fell by as much as 25 per cent per head. The share of the GDP devoted to education fell from 6.4 per cent in 1974/5 to 4.9 per cent in 1988/9 (Glennerster and Low, 1990).

9.1.6 Distributional issues

Another small strand in this tradition was the attempt to measure the distributional impact of education spending. Who gained most from the state's heavy involvement in this sector of the economy? The classic work of its kind was Hansen and Weisbrod's (1969) study of the large and generous state-supported system of higher education in California. His broad conclusion was that the higher the income of the families the more they benefited from the public subsidies to higher education. Social factors led children from higher income groups to participate disproportionately in higher

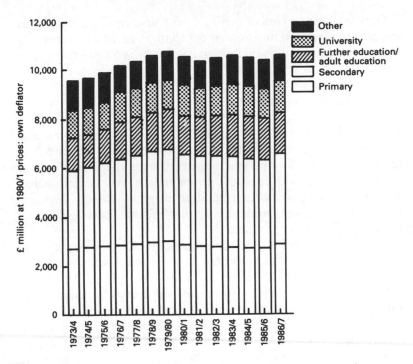

FIGURE 9.2 Current public expenditure on education by function, United Kingdom

education, and hence disproportionately to derive benefit from the high spending on the University of California. This conclusion was challenged by Pechman (1970) who argued that though higher income families derived more benefit from higher education they also paid higher taxes. Glennerster (1972b) concluded much the same as Weisbrod in an analysis of the expansion of higher education in the UK in the period of the Labour government 1964–70. A more detailed analysis with similar results was undertaken by Le Grand (1982). Children from professional families received five times as much public money from the education budget as unskilled working-class children. This was almost entirely the result of differential take up in post-school education. Recent work at the LSE by Hills (1991) suggests that the middle class does well from higher education even when its higher tax burden is taken into account.

Quite a different kind of writing on the finance of education was the prescriptive literature arguing for changes in the way education *should* be financed. It is that which has flourished more recently in a different political climate.

9.1.7   Vouchers and all that

It is probably true that Tom Paine (1791) was the first to advocate something like a voucher for education. At least, he favoured reducing taxes on poor people to the minimum and argued that all poor families should receive four pounds a year which would enable them to pay for their children to go to school; the local ministers of religion should certify that this had been done. His book was burned for his pains.

Milton Friedman's classic exposition of limiting the state's role to the finance of education and not its provision was first set out in 1955 and revised in *Capitalism and Freedom* (1962). The central theme of the book is that a large state apparatus is incompatible with political freedom and democracy and this is especially true of education where state employees have the power to shape young minds. On the other hand, Friedman accepted that not all families could afford to buy education for their children out of their basic incomes or not at a level that was economically optimal. Hence, he was prepared to see the state give a tied grant to parents to enable them to buy a standard level of education. If they wanted more than that they could add to the value of the voucher and spend it at any educational establishment. The expectation was that private schools would move in to meet this parental demand just like firms do in any other market.

The idea was taken up in Britain by Peacock and Wiseman (1964) and West (1965) writing for the Institute of Economic Affairs. Though Friedman had advanced the case in terms of political freedom and a minimal state, there was another efficiency argument inherent in his model. That was formally spelt out in a papers by Stubblebine (1965) and Pauly (1974). The argument predated the public choice literature we shall discuss later. It was possible to think of parents with a wide range of preferences for spending on education for their children. Some would have high preferences and want to see the state spend perhaps £2000 per year on the schooling of their child. Others may see no reason to spend anything much. For good reason voters are not prepared to see that happen and the state enforces a minimum expenditure. What it decides to spend will be the outcome of a political compromise. The median voter's preference for education spending may prevail. For the average and below-average preference parent they will be satisfied or more than satisfied with the spending their child receives at a state school. High preference parents will be frustrated. They will see a mean electorate not giving their child the education they desire for it. The very rich can opt out of state education and pay twice, once in taxes, the other from their own pocket to get the schooling they want. Average families will not be able to do that, but they might if they had a voucher and could simply top it up to buy slightly better education for their child. Those denied that possibility and those forced to pay twice suffer a welfare loss. Such a scheme would, of course, increase inequality of opportunity between children, but as West (1965) suggested, nobody seriously believes in that anyway.

Numerous different models for a voucher scheme were developed on both sides of the Atlantic. In evidence to the Layfield Committee (UK, 1976) on local government finance, Maynard (1975) was able to summarise all these variants and suggest that, at the very least, the United Kingdom government should change the law to allow local authorities (Kent was to be the county), to experiment with a voucher scheme. The Layfield Committee said this was beyond their terms of reference.

To be frank, before the late 1970s the whole voucher debate was strictly for the seminar room.

9.1.8 Loans

Much the same could be said about student loans. The discussion sprang from a recognition of capital market failures in the finance of higher education. Banks were not prepared to lend to young people enough to pay the full cost of their higher education. Outside a slave society they had no collateral for their loan. Rich parents could provide security but that was only a minority solution. The human capital evidence showed that, on average, such students would do well financially and the distributional studies showed that those who benefited were disproportionally middle-class children. This was one area, therefore, on which some on the left and right of the normal policy debate came to agree on an income-related repayment scheme for those who had gone through higher education, Prest (1966) and Glennerster *et al.* (1968). Nobody took much notice.

9.1.9 A balance sheet

In the mid-1970s the economists of education limped off the field at half time with a none-too-promising score line. They had set out to explain human investment decisions and been confronted with an alternative hypothesis they could not refute. They had predicted that investment in higher education would bring the rewards of a faster growth rate which it did not apparently do. They had failed with manpower planning. They had ignored schooling and failed to have anything helpful to say about how to improve schools. Their proposals on vouchers and loans fell on deaf ears. Yet education prospered as never before. That was not to last. Public spending cuts were at hand and some of the things economists had been saying began to fall on more fertile ground.

9.2 THE NEW ECONOMICS OF EDUCATION AND ITS POLICY IMPACT

Several things have happened to the economics of education in the period since 1976 and the cuts that accompanied the economic crisis of the time. In the first place, much of the same kind of work continued. The best reviews of the latest work in the old tradition is to be found in Psacharopoulos (1987) and Cohn and Geske (1990). We concentrate here on new trends in the subject and new policy issues.

9.2.1 The demand for post-school education

Blaug (1976) had noted that 'the demand for education remains a curiously neglected subject in the vast empirical literature exemplifying the human capital approach'. This was a gap that British work began to fill. First, it managed to explain in a convincing way what had puzzled many educationalists – the rapid falling off in school staying on rates and the demand to enter higher education.

After rising sharply in the 1950s and 1960s staying on patterns stabilised for nearly a decade and a half. The projections of places needed in higher education were continually revised downwards. Various explanations were offered, modern teaching methods in school, comprehensive education, the image of universities. Pissarides (1982) was able to show that the reasons were largely economic. The costs of staying on had risen: there had been a rise in the earnings of teenagers; and the value of student support had fallen in real terms. Pissarides showed that earnings of graduates slipped relative to manual earnings and overall earnings growth had slowed down. So the private rate of return to staying on at school fell, and the demand for higher education fell with it.

More recently, earnings differentials have grown again and so too have real earnings. The demand for higher education has risen as the model predicted. This has opened the way for more work by economists seeking to explain both the comparatively low level of demand for post-school education in the UK and its wide social class variation (Williams and Gordon, 1981; Robertson and Symons, 1988; Micklewright *et al.*, 1989). Young people from families who have not themselves been through college view the experience differently. Those from manual workers' homes require higher potential earnings differentials to encourage them to enter higher education. Parents who have been to college may pass on a view about the consumption benefits of higher education. Certainly staying on rates in England and Wales are highly affected both by fathers' previous occupation and by parents' household income. Rice (1987) finds the income variable holds more for girls than for boys. This suggests that to give an educational maintenance allowance to encourage staying on at school would work for girls but may not have much impression on boys' staying on rates. In short, there is a promising and continuing area of work here with policy relevance (see Bennett *et al.*, 1992).

Earnings differentials appear to be critical in explaining overall staying on rates. If staying on rates are low in the UK perhaps the reason lies with employers. If they value and reward graduates or trained personnel the evidence suggests the derived demand for training will result. If they do not, young people learn this very quickly. There may be little governments can do to affect this. But in so far as government policy seeks to save public expenditure by making children's schooling more expensive for familes, by reducing child allowances, or lowering the level of student support, it is likely to have significant effects on the already low rates of take up by poorer families and by girls.

9.2.2 Vocational training

Work in Britain in the 1980s shifted away from an almost exclusive concern with higher education during the 1960s and turned to post-school training. Most notably this was true of the work of Professor Prais (see Prais, 1987; Prais and Wagner, 1988; Prais and Steedman, 1987) at the National Institute for Economic and Social Research. He illustrates with detailed case studies the way other countries in Europe organise their training of 16–18 year olds and beyond. This is where the UK appears so different. For historical reasons we have chosen to give low priority to the general training needs of this group which individual employers will not meet. Policy has begun slowly to take account of this view.

9.2.3 Public choice theory and quasi markets

The political and welfare economic arguments for a voucher scheme had, as we saw, fallen on stony ground in the 1960s. The study of education was to be powerfully influenced by another more general set of theories about the public sector as a whole – public choice theory (Mueller, 1989). This field took off in the United States in much the same way as the economics of education had in the 1960s. It included within its ambit economic theories of voting behaviour, the economics of democracy, and the economics of public bureaucracies.

Its first contribution was largely to remove the halo effect that attached to education spending *per se*. The contention was that education spending was pushed up by public sector workers and bureaucrats who were able to monopolise access to the democratic process and manipulate it to increase rewards for themselves without producing comensurate gains in output (Borcherding, 1977). Teachers were paid more by education, experience and district size, and for none of these was there evidence that this was related to productivity or quality. Public sector services were devoid of an efficiency test.

Much the same broad conclusion was drawn from Hirschman's

(1970) much more subtle book. He discussed the problems public service consumers faced if they did could not exercise the sanction of exit or taking their custom elsewhere. Without that kind of sanction public services merely had to rely on 'voice' or what Friedman (1962) had called 'cumbrous political channels'. Hirschman, unlike Friedman, did not actually suggest that relying on the market would always be better. Indeed, using the education voucher example, he suggests it may not be. A mix of market and non-market methods, with the occasional application of the exit sanction to inefficient organisations, is actually what he favoured. However, in the climate of the Thatcher years the case that public sector institutions, including schools, must be inefficient *a priori* was readily accepted. Thus the burden of the argument for vouchers shifted to a means of encouraging efficiency within the state school sector by introducing competition.

The other strand in the original case meant giving vouchers to all parents, including those with children at private schools, in order to encourage the growth of the private sector and relieve the purses of middle-class families burdened by school fees. The new Conservative Secretary of State for Education, Sir Keith Joseph, soon found that this was not the most popular policy with Her Majesty's Treasury. It would have increased public expenditure on education at a stroke by 6 per cent or more, as those who spent their own money on education would have had their bills, or part of them, paid by the Exchequer. Only a limited subsidy was given to 35 000 pupils at assisted place schools.

9.2.4 Quasi-markets for schools?

In the 1988 Education Act the Conservative government did introduce a series of changes which went some way to introducing market-type mechanisms into British education. Two separate sets of quasi-market reforms were included in the Act, one related to schools, the other to higher education.

All secondary schools and all but small primary schools will be funded according to a formula the central department has to approve. Any pupil signing on at a local state school will trigger a payment by the local authority to the school, which is free to administer the resulting budget as it pleases. A proportion of the total sum available for schooling in the Local Education Authority will be kept by the local authority to provide common services, special units for disruptive pupils, educational psychologists, inspection and central administration, before the the rest is allocated by formula. Local authorities must spend less than 15 per cent of their 'Potential Schools Budget' on these common services. The new devolved system goes by the name, Local Management of Schools (LMS). (For an explanation and analysis of the first phase see Lee, 1990.) In the case of schools which opt out of local control (only sixty out of 29 000 at the time of writing), the same formula is applied to determine how much they receive in grant from central government. However, this grant is then topped up to compensate such schools for not receiving the Local Education Authority's central services.

Parents have the right to choose to which school to send their child and cash follows the child according to the formula. The net effect of these measures resembles the kind of voucher scheme once advocated by Christopher Jenks in the United States (Mecklenburger and Hostrop, 1972) which confined vouchers to the state school system.

Nevertheless, the new scheme falls short of a full market solution for at least four reasons.

1. No money can escape to the private sector.
2. There is no free entry for new providers. Capital expenditure for new places and new schools must be approved by the local authority and the central department in Westminster. Central government's watchdog, the Audit Commission, has been pressing local education authorities to economise by closing more schools. Spare capacity to meet changes in demand will be limited. There is really no mechanism to replicate free entry on the one hand, or bankruptcy on the other, to keep the market truly competitive.
3. Choice by parents is limited because in the very same Act the government required all state schools to follow a common curriculum. One of the persuasive arguments advanced by proponents of the voucher scheme was that parents disagreed about what constituted a good education. That was the case for parental choice (Coons and Sugarman, 1978).
4. Teachers' salaries, the largest slice of the school budget, are still

set on a national salary scale limiting the freedom of school managing bodies to arrange their budgets.

For all these reasons many, in the Conservative Party and beyond, would like to see the next government take these reforms to their logical conclusion and formula fund all schools, private and public, direct from central government (see for example the *Independent* newspaper's Charter for Change, 5 June 1991). Schools would then be left to go bankrupt and other capitalist risk-takers would enter the market offering new educational services. What is the theoretical case for and against the existing reforms and their possible extension?

9.2.5 Local management of schools

The theoretical case for LMS is that it reduces X-inefficiency (Leibenstein, 1966; 1973). Senior managers are ill-informed about day to day issues. Decisions about book purchase or equipment or staffing, taken in a distant County Hall by those who do not have to suffer the consequences of their actions, are likely to be poor because information is lost passing up the chain of command, and the incentives in a central bureaucracy are to simplify allocation rules and not to reflect local situations. LMS provides a mechanism for determining the optimum range of services that should be provided at a central local authority level. The argument is that schools should purchase central services only when they need them and these should be charged at cost. Critics object that these services are needed most by schools in disadvantaged areas, English as a second language, for example. That objection can be met by the response that formula funding should take account of such factors and leave the school free to decide whether to buy the services or to do the work itself.

The theory of decentralised budgeting implies that local managers should have the capacity to set their own salary levels untied by national salary scales. That reasoning has been applied to the comparable opted out hospitals which can set their own salary scales. Critics raise two kinds of objections.

It is suggested that local bargaining would give an unfair advantage to schools in areas with a high tax base. That would not, however, be the case if schools in deprived areas received a higher weighting in the funding formula, and central government either funded schools direct or gave Local Education Authorities with such schools an additional grant. The second objection is that local bargaining removes from the state a powerful monopsony position in its negotiations with teachers unions. Where the balance of advantage lies in that situation is difficult to judge. Local bargaining may tend to increase the public sector pay bill. This has to be weighed against the efficiency gains of decentralised budgeting; and monopsony power is not efficient in any case. It may have held down teachers' salaries unnaturally.

So far, then, the case for local management of schools seems to hold up well to theoretical examination. There is also recent empirical support from a large survey of academic results in the USA, where decentralised schooling systems showed better results (Chubb and Moe, 1990).

What of the case for extending the principle of the market further? Local decentralised school budgeting is a necessary but not a sufficient condition for a true quasi-market.

9.2.6   Competition and schooling

Two aspects require particular attention: efficiency, and selectivity.

Efficiency

Advocates of full competition between schools have always argued that the case for state involvement in education only extended to its responsibility to empower parents to buy education, and to ensure that, as future citizens, all children acquired basic skills. Beyond that schools were no different from other service providers (Friedman, 1962; Peacock and Wiseman, 1964; West, 1965; Maynard, 1975). Under the UK schools market now emerging, the government will ensure that an acceptable standard of common education is provided by means of the National Curriculum, assessment tests and a system of inspection overseen by Her Majesty's Inspectors of Schools. With such enhanced information on output, it is claimed, parents and pupils will be able to make an informed judgement about the services offered by competing schools. The most efficient will gain pupils and resources, the others will decline. This is the traditional form of efficiency competition between producers we hope to find in free markets – 'E' competition for short. It is, however, not the only form of competition.

Selectivity

Health economists are fully aware that the health-care market is characterised by another form of competition, selection bias, adverse selection or 'S' competition for short (Akerlof, 1970; Pauly 1986, Summers, 1989; Barr, 1992). The same is true of insurance markets more generally (Pauly, 1974). An analogous problem arises with schooling, though it is not generally discussed in the same theoretical literature.

It is vital for health-care providers to exclude high cost, high risk patients from their group of users. It is thus not surprising to find that an enormous amount of attention is paid in marketing and in competition with other health-care providers, to ensure that a minimum number of these high cost patients are attracted. Schools are in a similar position. Work by Professor Rutter and colleagues (1979) produced elaborate and effective measures of what constituted 'good' secondary schools. What went on in schools, however, explained only about 5 per cent of the variance in pupil achievements. An even more detailed longitudinal study of the differential effectiveness of primary schools in London was able to explain 9 per cent of the variance in pupils' reading achievements and 11 per cent of mathematical attainment by reference to schools' effects (Mortimore *et al.*, 1988). These are higher figures than achieved in comparable American studies but are still relatively small compared to the 64 per cent of variance explained by initial attainment and social background. Any school entrepreneur acting rationally would seek to exclude pupils who would drag down the overall performance score of the school, its major selling point to parents. There would then emerge schools, each catering for distinct bands of ability. The precise structure would depend on the optimum mix of selectivity and size in any given location. Whether that would be a good or a bad result gets us into a wider debate about education policy. Some would welcome that result, others would not. What economic theory suggests is that a pure internal market between schools would not produce a neutral outcome in this respect.

9.2.7   Poor information, joint products and externalities

So far we have seen that an internal market will, other things being equal, produce a selective system of education, selective according to the attributes that determine school performance most strongly, that is inherited ability and class. Does this matter?

There is still dispute about the research evidence but, on balance, it would seem that the introduction of non-selective schooling in Britain in the 1960s and 1970s did raise the educational outcomes of the schooling system especially for the average and below average child (Glennerster and Low, 1990). Schools with mixed ability intakes also achieve better results than those with restricted ability mixes (Rutter *et al.*, 1979). Because parents are not in a position to know the value added by different schools, standardising for the differential intake schools may have, they will get systematically misleading information about the efficiency of the schools between which they must make choices. It would certainly not be in the interests of the selective schools to reveal this kind of information.

Advocates of the market can reasonably respond at this point that there are ways round all these problems. The formulae for funding schools can be so weighted that schools which take less able children receive more money. This sounds like an answer and has intrinsic equity merit, but in this context it assumes that moderate additional resources will produce enhanced exam results that will bid up the results the school achieves to levels it would have reached if it had not taken the slow learner or working-class child. Unfortunately, all the evidence suggests that this is not so. Even when large additional sums have been spent on schools with significant numbers of deprived children, the results improve only by small amounts or, in much early research, not at all (Coleman, 1966; Rutter *et al.*, 1979; Hanushek, 1986). Even if we take the more optimistic results, their responsiveness to money spent is so low that we cannot rely on a weighted formula to solve the problem of selection.

Advocates of non-selective education argue that such a system produces externalities of several kinds. A common local school fosters local community ties. Such schooling helps to reduce social class divisions. This may be disputed. A socially inclusive local education system is incompatible with a socially exclusive one. It would seem that the choice between the two has to be a collective choice. An internal market which was completely unconstrained would inevitably preclude that choice by producing a selective system. In so far as Local Education Authorities did succeed in obtaining a mixed entry to their schools, parents would be able to judge the relative merits of schools' performance starting from a level, as opposed to a staggered, start. It would be necessary, in any system that enabled choice to take place, for the Local Education Authority to produce studies of the relative performance of schools in value added terms taking account of the social and other characteristics of invididual schools, as the Inner London Education Authority (ILEA) did before it was abolished. Parents would then be free to choose between schools that differed in ways that did not produce negative externalities. They could choose between those that offered more or less formal discipline, religious denominational instruction, single-sex schoolng, sports or music or any mixture of the above.

9.2.8 Sunk costs

Arguably the best way to learn whether a school fits a particular child is to try it out. That is the way we choose between supermarkets or hairdressers but it is not so easily done with schools just because part of the raw material is the child. Moreover, part of the quality of the education process comes from the child being settled and happy in the school. Frequent changes will disrupt that process and could do long-term damage. Parents are therefore quite rational to show loyalty to the school of their initial choice rather than exercising frequent exits and shopping around strategies. Traditions and an ethos in a school community are assets not easily or quickly gained. For a school to decline and go bankrupt over a long period will cause considerable educational and social costs to the pupils caught up in its demise. New entrants will find it takes a long time to build a new school community. The sunk costs, in short, are high. This is not to deny that useful market signals can be produced by new parents opting for other schools and demand slackening. It does suggest that simple market pressures will not be enough. Professional advice and support, which can identify a school at risk and help it to take corrective action early before decline sets in, are important adjuncts to a more market led system.

9.2.9   The case for a managed market

The case so far has been that schooling has some peculiar characteristics that do not adapt readily to a full market solution. Schooling can be reconciled with an element of market discipline but only with a number of safeguards. These require the Local Education Authority to play a significant role. It would be:

(a) To choose a pattern of education provision, selective or non-selective, in line with local parents' collective choice.
b)   To plan a structure of schools in the area, taking account of expected demographic change and the preferences revealed by parents' choice of school.
(c) To support schools with a good inspection and advisory service which can diagnose those in trouble and give special and early support to prevent a long terminal illness.
(d) To provide other services on demand at a market price.

If this were done, there would be no case for schools to opt out of a local authority with supportive and marketing functions alone. Indeed, schools that did opt out of such a system would only be acting rationally as free riders, trying to avoid the costs which must be incurred to keep such a system in equilibrium, or to evade the choice of the local community that has determined on non-selective education.

9.2.10   Higher education and post school training

How far do similar factors operate in post-school education? My contention is that the considerations that apply here are rather different. On balance, the case for applying market-type mechanisms is stronger. Yet government policy has been hesitant and confused.

Those aged 16 to 18 are in a transition period of near adulthood. The state does not insist they shall be educated but is unhappy if they are not at least being trained. Government has moved to force those not in work to attend some kind of training by withdrawing rights to social security benefit unless young people enter an approved training programme. It might be better to go the whole way and raise the compulsory school or training age to 18. Compulsory education or training linked to job experience could be financed through a basic training voucher. Government policy looks as if it is stumbling in that direction.

From the age of 18 we are dealing with adults, not parents acting as proxy demanders, with the state having some residual role to protect the child and ensure that he or she has enough education to become a fully independent individual.

The balance between private benefits and public good has shifted by adulthood. The aim of public policy is to ensure that individuals invest optimally in their own human capital and have the resources to do so. The citizenship goals that attach to community schooling become irrelevant as young people want to move away from home.

Selective institutions become the norm, and competition between institutions to provide the best or most appropriate courses has always been a feature of higher and further education.

The social goal remains that of ensuring that young and older adults alike are not prevented from investing in their own futures and hence in the economy's productive capacity. Such is the case for treating post-school education as any market commodity.

9.2.11 Markets or quasi-markets?

Yet here too there are difficulties. The capital market has never been able to handle human capital efficiently, outside a slave society. Though banks will lend money to students without security they will only do so to a limited extent, insufficient to support an individual through an expensive training, tuition costs included. Only students who could rely on rich parents to secure the risk can finance themselves this way. Hence governments have come to provide free or heavily subsidised higher education. Typically, in Europe, these subsidies have been given to institutions of higher education to reduce their tuition costs. In Britain, individuals have been subsidised to cover their living costs too.

Three issues have dominated debate on the finance of higher education ever since the the Robbins Committee (1963) reported.

1. Should state financial support for higher education be given to students or institutions?
2. Should that support take the form of an outright subsidy or a returnable loan?
3. Should financial support for teaching be separated from research?

The full quasi-market approach suggests that the state should support *students*, not subsidise *institutions*. Colleges and universities should compete for students and their bursaries. This would minimise the X-inefficiencies of higher education institutions, free them from centralised regulatory control and potential political control, and give students real choice enabling good teaching institutions to prosper (this case is powerfully argued by Barnes and Barr, 1988). Students should repay the cost of their support in so far as they derive private gain from the investment. Individuals would weigh the costs of higher education against its expected returns. Government should support fundamental research at those institutions that are doing it well not spread an indirect subsidy thinly, mixed up with the funding of student numbers.

In some respects, recent policy has moved in that direction. Throughout higher education grants to cover teaching are separated from research. If an institution accepts a student up to a quota it will trigger a teaching grant. If it takes more than this quota it will receive a fee paid by the LEA, by a research council or by the individual. This represents an incentive to expand but at a low income per student. The true market solution would be for the government to offer a national scheme of bursaries on a subject by subject basis that would be sufficient to pay for tuition and living costs. It would then be for the student to choose which courses best suited and had the best reputations.

Government did opt to move gradually towards a loans system that would replace the present system of student grants. New top-up loans are available to supplement lower real grants. The government argued, with good reason, that one of the obstacles to expanding higher education in a period of severe limits on public expenditure, was the very high unit cost of higher education in the UK; and our relatively generous system of student support was one element in that high cost (UK, 1988). Its solution was to introduce a mortgage-type repayment scheme which saved minimal amounts of money even in the long run and cost money in the short run, while probably acting as a deterent to some students as well (Barr, 1989). My own long-preferred solution has been a graduate tax which avoids presenting students with a future burden unrelated to their capacity to pay. The case set out in Glennerster *et al.* (1968) is set in its modern context by Barr (1989).

9.2.12 In brief

The economics of education ought now to be moving near the centre of debate. Education is near the top of the political agenda again, and many of the perceived solutions to present ills are seen to lie in applications of simple market remedies. The difficulty is that economic theory suggests that these remedies may be worse than the cure, at least as far as schools are concerned. That may not be the message some politicians will want to hear.

10 Political Economy, Applied Welfare Economics and Housing in the UK

DUNCAN MACLENNAN and KENNETH GIBB

10.1 INTRODUCTION

Theoretical welfare economics has been concerned, for more than a century, with efficient resource allocation and the basis of criteria for ranking and selecting distributional outcomes. The growing formalisation of the literature has contributed much needed consistency and clarity. However, theoretical clarity is often achieved by making simplifying assumptions which isolate the specific set of relationships under study from broader social, political and even economic processes. Political economy, in the traditional sense of the term, has become much less widely practised with the advent of formal welfare economics.

Much of the debate between 'New Right' and 'Left' and indeed 'Old Left' and 'New Left' in Britain over the last two decades has been closer to 'political economy' than 'welfare economics' in scope and language. In effect, over the last two decades, the nicely calculated more or less of applied welfare economics (embracing cost-benefit analysis, policy incidence, etc.) has had little effect on public policy in contrast to the broad faiths of 'the property owning democracy', 'competition', 'deregulation', 'privatisation' and, more recently, citizenship. It is the adoption and implementation of such ideas that have dramatically altered the welfare state and the housing system in Britain.

These observations may then raise the question, why bother with applied welfare economics? Outside the realms of academic journals is it only the economists role as 'Preacher' (to use Stigler's phrase) which matter? Indeed, in the mass media of newspapers and television, economists, at their point of greatest impact on individual citizens, succumb to the pressure to produce assertive sound bites, usually with value judgements implicit and empirical conclusions unqualified.

In such a context applied welfare economics becomes, in our view, a critical link between textbook theory and publicised polemic. Technically competent, empirically rigorous studies with explicit statements of the inherent value judgements are a *sine qua non* of rational policy development, they are the essential balance of 'realism' to ideologically based 'visions'. However, such analysis is a necessary but not sufficient condition for rational policy development – clarity of social objective and a propensity to place evidence ahead of prejudice are also required.

The housing sector in Britain has been significantly impacted by pre-1970s ideologies, was a core component of the development of the welfare state, and has been central to the shifts of the 1980s. This indicates much about how the changing political economy of the decade affected the sector, and indeed whether the housing and related policies pursued were consistent with broad policy objectives, and/or were inconsistent with other competing political economic agendas.

The chapter develops this analysis in a number of stages. The next section outlines the importance and meaning of housing and the likely public policy problems which arise from housing and housing systems. The third section briefly reviews the range of instruments available to intervene in housing markets. The fourth and largest section of the paper briefly reviews the empirical evidence on the economic aspects of British housing policy. The concluding section considers major issues for future consideration.

10.2 HOUSING – AN ECONOMIC PERSPECTIVE

10.2.1 Housing matters

Housing, as a durable asset, is consumed, financed and produced. Households, in Britain, commonly pay between a sixth and a third of their incomes on housing. In consequence, housing rents and prices have a direct and major impact on disposable incomes. And with two-thirds of Britons now home-owners, private dwellings now constitute around a half of personal sector wealth. At the same time, in 1989, mortgage debt amounted to more than half the value of GDP, and with asset values exceeding mortgage debts by £750 billion the sector was, and is, the locus of a large 'monetary overhang'.

The construction industry, with residential development as its major activity, generally employs close to 1 million people. Investment in the construction and renovation of houses absorbs a fifth of gross fixed capital formation, thereby contributing over 4 per cent of GDP.

Housing systems also matter at more disaggregated scales of analysis. The quality, price and availability of housing shapes the character of cities and regions, with major contrasts across the country, and impacts on mobility between places. And, of course, price and availability shape the well-being of different socio-economic groups, for instance the elderly and, now most visibly, the homeless. The housing system therefore influences not only the scale and growth of national and local economies but also the acceptability, in social terms, of economic outcomes.

The bias of British housing research and policy, until well into the 1980s, has been to focus upon 'housing problems' as social difficulties requiring expenditure actions. At the same time, it was widely assumed, apart from in relation to housing investment programmes varied as part of Keynesian demand management policies, that the housing sector was led by other economic change. There is some merit in this emphasis if it is noted that economic growth and not housing policies has been the major source of housing progress in Britain.

However, it is an oversimplified view. Recent experience, as discussed in section 10.4, makes clear that the massive economic influence of the housing sector can influence patterns of growth and inflation. And such imbalance may partly stem from housing and related policies.

This starting point, from an economics perspective, is in no way intended to diminish the social importance of addressing housing problems. For much of the post-war period the dominant perceived problem, from 1945 to 1975, was the shortage of housing to meet the 'needs' of low and, even, middle-income households. Even before the advent of Thatcherism (see, for instance, the Labour government's Green Paper of 1977: Housing Strategy Committee, 1977), it was recognised that broad shortages had been resolved and that housing quality and urban regeneration, 'special needs', tenure choice and subsidy targeting were the emerging issues. Thatcherism, in many respects, highlighted these issues and developed radical (and we do not equate radical with efficient) policy measures to address such issues. At the end of the 1980s it is apparent that the housing 'problem' agenda is evolving into a new phase, in part consequent upon the income distribution and housing policy thrusts of the last decade. Homelessness, as defined by a variety of parties, has doubled since 1985 and according to Shelter now affects 400 000 plus households in Britain (though this estimate is double that of the government). Repossession of homes and long-term mortgage arrears rocketed between 1988 and 1991, and it is widely estimated that 80 000 homes were repossessed in 1991, and twice that number of owners accumulated at least six months of arrears. These difficulties, and a higher real cost of housing than a decade ago, have to be set against progress in housing quality, urban regeneration and tenure choice achieved in the last decade. As in so many other aspects of Britain in the 1980s, real growth in housing conditions has to be set against the apparently growing inequality of outcomes – and this is clearly the setting for a renewed debate on the political economy of British housing policy.

The starting point for an applied welfare analysis is a clearer understanding of what housing is and how it is produced and allocated.

10.2.2 Housing as a commodity

Most areas of applied economics have specialised assumptions about goods and markets which help to minimise the reductionism of the core, underlying theoretical model. Housing is no exception, indeed the rather complex nature of housing as a commodity is what makes housing market analysis challenging. But it also means that 'preachers' striding down from the high plains to economic theory with a backpack of simplications quite often miss the subtleties of the local terrain and in consequence ramble around the subject area to no great purpose. The important characteristics of housing are set out below.

10.2.3 Commodity complexity

Housing is a complex rather than simple commodity. A house is composed of a range of capital and land components assembled to meet a range of household wants. A house provides shelter (roofs, walls, floors), comfort (windows, heating), space and structures to pursue a range of household activities (entertaining, wine-making, listening to CDs, etc.) and privacy (from family, friends and neighbours). The choice of a particular physical unit also implies a joint choice of location and neighbourhood. Location, choice, unlike much of the emphasis of much urban economics, is not merely concerned with the travel to work costs of household members in the labour force. Access to shopping, leissure, social and public service sites all influence the choice of dwelling. The immediate characteristics of the local neighbourhood also shape what households are prepared to pay for housing units.

Commodity complexity creates a number of technical difficulties for economic analysts. The price and income elasticities of demand for commodities are important parameters in assessing policy impacts. Commodity complexity combined with locational factors makes it almost impossible to make a convincing estimate of the price elasticity of demand for housing, let alone its component parts.

Complexity, with houses varying in character, also raises difficulty for the efficient design of social housing policies. If, for distributional/merit good reasons, the state wishes to ensure some minimum level of housing consumption, it may be essential to spell out which attributes are to be consumed. But separate market vouchers, allowances for 'rooms', 'quality', 'location' are not feasible. On the other hand, direct, tied provision by social landlords may mean that social planners fail to recognise changes in preferred commodity bundles over time.

10.2.4   Locational aspects

Some of the attributes of housing may have positive and negative effects on other neighbours and citizens. Most obviously, building houses on scarce countryside may inflict welfare losses on the overall population of an urban area. Domestic heating systems with low private costs may have high social costs (namely, the contemporary fashion to have style enhancing 'living flame fires' for which two-thirds of the energy escapes up the chimney, yet impressed neighbours rate it higher than global warming). Failure of an individual to maintain the interior and exterior of his or her home may create negative externalities for neighbours (under certain information arrangements this may generate the classic prisoner's dilemma problem of urban renewal). If the image of a whole neighbourhood becomes progressively deteriorated then there may be negative externality effects for other urban residents. The image of an overall city may then suffer, as with Glasgow in the 1960s and Liverpool in the 1980s, and further contribute to an erosion of the local economic base.

Housing externalities are visibly capable of creating a negative dynamic for households, cities and neighbourhoods, but the task of identifying such causal chains and linkages has hardly begun, though such issues have been of growing relevance in contemporary housing problems. But clearly housing originated externalities have individual and collective income, productivity and growth effects which may shape the long-term distribution of income. Most obviously, in the 1980s a number of labour market studies in Britain and the USA have indicated that 'address discrimination' is used as a screening device by employers to reduce their hiring costs.

The housing system, because of its locational aspects, is also important in shaping how societies cope with income inequalities. Where rich and poor are forced, by history and geography, to live in close proximity, the rich cannot easily escape the poverty-induced externalities of the poor. This argument has been widely recognised in relation to epidemics of disease in crowded Victorian cities. But it may be equally pertinent today, and not just in American cities; geographic separation through the housing system is the main mechanism by which affluent Britons avoid the distress of seeing the roofless in cardboard boxes, the prospect of random, unwelcome encounters with drug pushers, drug victims, HIV sufferers and street criminals. And it is the mechanism by which they often seek to live amongst households like themselves, so that their children are taught in classes with few disadvantaged children, and so on.

This point is made not self-righteously, but rather to point up that the housing system, through locational sorting of incomes, not only reflects the income distribution but is also a mechanism for choosing to sustain distributions which generate poverty externalities.

There is also, arising from commodity complexity, a warning in this for applied welfare economics. The complexities of housing, externalities and economic development effects mean that the costs and benefits of housing policies are seldom contained in the housing sector, but spillover into other sectors, areas and the future.

10.2.5 Durability

Housing is also a durable good. Physical structure may last for centuries and values may not significantly decline in real terms even across generations. This means that housing should be examined both in terms of its consumption aspects and its investment potential. The UK tax system has failed to make this distinction in the way it treats occupied housing. It grants tax relief on the first $30 000 of a mortgage loan (although there is no logical reason for any such ceiling) but it fails to tax the return made to investors in the form either of capital gains or rental income returns. Even more pointedly, housing policy in Britain facilitates low-income consumption of rental housing, but middle-income purchase of assets and this has a major long-term impact in reinforcing differences in wealth.

The interaction between consumption and investment characteristics requires that policy analysis should distinguish between short-run housing expenditure decisions and long-run economic costs. The housing literature typically uses a long-run equilibrium concept, a modified form of the user cost of capital (Meen, 1987; Smith, Rosen and Fallis, 1988; Muth and Goodman, 1989). Following Meen, the real user cost of housing capital, stripped to the essentials, equals:

$$([(1 - \theta)i - p] + \delta - g)V \tag{10.1}$$

where θ is the household's marginal tax rate, i is the nominal interest rate, p is the general rate of inflation (so $[(1 - \theta)i - p]$ is the post tax real interest rate), δ is the rate of depreciation, g is the real capital gains rate and V is the asset price of housing. The user cost of housing capital refers to the opportunity cost of tying up capital in the form of housing plus the *rate* of depreciation *minus* the real capital gain accruing to housing. It is quite possible, in periods of negative real interest rates, for the user cost to be itself negative, and this would be associated with a high investment demand for housing. Policy analysis, however, tends to focus solely upon annual expenditure.

Complexity, Location and Durability are the three major aspects of 'housing' which make it distinctive from the applied economics perspective. These features also interact to shape the operational characteristics of housing markets. The first important aspect of the market is that housing supply (leaving aside turnover of the existing stock) is inelastic in the short term and long period elasticity estimates are also low. Construction lags need not imply 'market failures', rather they reflect recognition lags (exacerbated by commodity complexity), lags in securing local land (locational specificity of demand) and the complex task of building in numerous components (commodity complexity). Obviously, land planning by the state may have a major impact on the availability and price of housing.

A second major feature of most housing markets is that commodity complexity, particularly in view of the large-scale asset investment being made by households, requires consumer search. Commodity complexity (particularly where the true nature of some attributes cannot be established until after a transaction) creates an information asymmetry between sellers and buyers and this results in a housing 'information' industry of valuers, estate agents, etc. There may then be a complex matching process operating in the market in which there are significant costs in reaching equilibrium – and they should not be ignored in welfare economic analysis. For instance, a major consequence of rent controls is to generate an allocation process largely shaped by information flows and costly search (see Maclennan, 1982); indeed the 'process' costs may be the critical welfare economic cost relating to rent controls, though they have been ignored by most economists.

The spatial component of housing demand, and demand

growth, interacts with the spatial fixity of existing stock and lags in new construction to make it likely that housing markets, defined at a local scale, will be out of equilibrium in the short term. And the short term may last a long time – Maclennan (1988) argues that submarkets in Glasgow in 1976 had price differentials (after he-donic adjustment) which were only gradually eroded by new construction over a decade. Another implication of slow stock equilibration is that housing shortages (defined in social terms) may not be removed quickly and that interim/emergency policy measures may be required in the housing sector (consider, for instance, the emergency housing response to earthquakes or a changing political will to deal with homelessness).

The paragraphs above give a flavour of the important aspects of housing. They also hint at the reasons why governments have sought to intervene in housing markets and this issue is examined further below.

10.3   INTERVENTION IN THE HOUSING MARKET

At the most general level, intervention in a market might be justified under three areas of concern: efficiency, equity (fairness) and macroeconomic/economic development. This chapter emphasises the first two classes of concern but also notes aspects of the third.

10.3.1   Efficiency

Free markets generate technically efficient resource allocations where there is perfect competition in supply, where there is perfect information, no market failures exist and/or there is evidence that significant state failure would occur if there was direct housing provision by the public sector (this latter argument being particularly relevant to the UK housing context). The overall social efficiency of free markets is also recognised in such circumstances if the ethical judgements that individuals are the best judge of their own welfare and that the distribution of income is fair can all be accepted.

It is important to distinguish between problems arising from operationally inefficient housing markets and those arising from income inequality manifested in a correspondingly unequal distribution on housing consumption. This distinction is important in analysing British housing policy and many practitioners fail to make it, often contributing to a hostility towards market solutions. It is widely accepted by economists that income transfers are generally superior to tied aid as a form of redistribution. But there are important structures and instruments in British housing policy, rent controls and social housing for instance, which were created when this argument was either not recognised or deemed not to be practicable. That is, for many housing analysts and practitioners tied housing subsidies (often not means tested) were regarded as a key redistribution mechanism. Changing these perspectives and structures is a key aspect of housing subsidy reform in Britain. A further complication is that spending and other measures directed at the housing sector may not have solely housing goals, but may have health, employment, urban regeneration etc. objectives. 'First best' policy for housing is compromised by such concerns. However, the merit of an economic perspective on these issues is that it places the burden of proof with those trying to justify intervention and it does not accept history or political acquiescence as good grounds for the misuse of scarce resources. But does the housing market conform to the technical/structural requirements of a market system likely to generate Paretian outcomes?

10.3.2 Perfect competition

In any local housing market there are usually large numbers of buyers, sellers and market agents – that is, the system is likely to be competitive. However, there are a number of important caveats. In the market sector slow-supply-side responses may create periods of seller power not just in new supply but in the secondhand market. The market in such contexts may be more accurately labelled as 'imperfectly monopolistically competitive – but competitive none the less. Ball (1983) argued that there was evidence of concentration in the housing construction industry and Maclennan (1982) has argued that spatial or local monopolies can easily exist within an apparently competitive national housing market. In the rented housing market the assumption of equal power between tenant and landlord may not be realistic (Barr, 1987). Once the tenant becomes attached to his 'home' the landlord can exploit the power differential by raising rents. This is one instance where some form of regulation would provide a more efficient outcome.

10.3.4 Externalities

The housing system, as noted above, is characterised by the pervasive effects of negative and positive externalities, where a cost-benefit imposed by one agent on another cannot be compensated for or recompensed. For example, if there are two neighbours and person A upgrades his/her property, this will increase the value of both properties. It A does not have a sufficient marginal valuation of carrying out the up-grading work to outweigh its cost (only counting his utility) the work will not be done. But if the benefit to B is greater than the cost, the project may well be efficient but not take place because A does not incorporate B's utility into the decision.

External effects are important to a whole range of housing quality questions such as urban renewal, neighbourhood re-habilitation and the basic housing development process. If an area retains a reputation that it no longer deserves, it will continue to bear the cost of the reputation, and otherwise profitable opportunities will be passed up. The general health externality arising from Victorian slum housing was a major reason for government intervention (Gibb and Munro, 1991). Again, however, public provision is not necessarily required: coordination may be the efficient role of the state where it attempts to resolve the non-cooperative game problems faced in examples such as that found by A and B. Rent control legislation led to long-term investment in private rented housing requiring a substantial risk premium requirement. It may not be risky in the 1990s to provide rental units, but potential suppliers do not see the market that way and continue to charge 'unnecessary' risk premia. A subsidy from the state to provide market rents could be justified by this form of externality. The policy problem in relation to housing externalities in Britain is one of abiding ignorance. Although they have been recognised as significant for a century, and prompted large programmes, they are seldom measured and weighted explicitly in spending decisions.

10.3.5 Perfect information

Efficient markets depend on full knowledge of prices and qualities of goods offered in the market. Health is a good case where this requirement breaks down and expert assistance (and government intervention) is required. Specific institutions such as estate agents and surveyors have developed to supply housing information and reduce transactions costs. Barr (1987) argues that most of these kinds of informational problems can be solved by the market. He argues that the state should confine itself to regulating the minimum standards of professional bodies and home insurance schemes. However, complex selling chains and repeat surveys on traded homes suggest that there is some way to go in ensuring competitive efficiency in the transaction trades.

10.3.6 Missing markets

There are two areas of relevance to housing where private markets fail to produce a good service, even though the cost of providing it is less than what individuals are willing to pay. In the capital market some households are debarred from secured loans because of institutional convention, despite the absence of economic justification. A spatial example of this was building society 'redlining' where certain areas were precluded from mortgages. This can equally happen due to statistical screening practices at the point of mortgage application. Barr (1987) argues that is a justification for the public provision or guarantee of loan finance.

Similar to the externality problem of coordination, there is the related issue of *complementary markets*. Such a market exists where a market only operates for a combination of products but not for each one independent of the other. Imagine a world where people drank coffee with sugar and did not use either product for anything else. In reality there are many cases where large-scale public – coordination is required. Take the example of land redevelopment such as the London Docklands Development Corporation – if markets were complete then the prices themselves would perform this coordinating role. Exactly the same market failure exists for run-down peripheral estates and the inner cities (and dealing with such problems now absorbs half the national housing budget).

Taken together, these observations about the relative efficiency of the housing market indicate evidence of market failure and of a need for regulations, minimum standards and perhaps some form of subsidy provision. They would not, it would appear, provide a rationale for public provision. In any case, none of the points so far raised has dealt with the question of whether a public sector housing system with an administrative allocation system and no clear guidance on rent-setting in relation to market rents can provide an efficient comprehensive housing service. This raises the political (and not simply technical) question about the efficiency and governance of social housing (considered further below).

10.3.7 Equity

The government may feel it should intervene in the housing market in order to alter households' access to housing, or simply to redistribute resources so that all households can attain some standard of housing provision. If it was felt that households were not aware of the externality effects of their poor housing or that they did not have sufficient information to consume an efficient amount of housing, then there may be a case for some form of intervention on grounds of equity if it could be shown that these problems disproportionately affect particular socio-economic groups (Barr, 1987).

If the problem relates to simply not having enough income, the question is really whether redistributional policy should be based on cash transfers or through in-kind subsidies. In other words, every modern society has some form of poverty provisions and these include shelter requirements. What is the better form of housing support: person-related and in cash, or through dwelling-tied provision or property? It was indicated above, under fairly general assumptions, that cash transfers do not interfere with relative prices (Le Grand and Robinson, 1982). But against this view underpinned by consumer sovereignty is the 'merit good' case. In housing terms, it is argued that there are direct consumption externalities resulting from the poor increasing their housing consumption (more than would be the case under cash transfers) and that taypayers benefit from the direction of their income in such a meritorious fashion (and indeed have clear tax-donor preferences). If individual preferences are overridden by the preferences of the donors (for whatever reason), then in-kind transfers may be more socially efficient.

In summary, the efficiency arguments do not of themselves offer a case for public provision although they do point to the need for regulations, minimum standards and the like. We have argued, however, that the housing system can be plausibly argued th represent a second best system and that therefore departures from marginal cost pricing is quite justified on efficiency grounds, given the twin existence of distorting subsidies to owner occupiers and non-market rents in the social rented sector. The equity arguments for intervention depend on one's view of the appropriate degree of redistribution but there clearly is a case for some degree of intervention.

The chapter now moves on from the abstract world of the case for market intervention. British housing *has* endured more than seventy years of large-scale intervention where billions of pounds have been invested in public ownership of housing, as much has been lost through the ravages of rent controls, and the economy has suffered from the diversion of investible funds into (frequently secondhand) owner occupation rather than productive forms of investment. In the following section we consider the political economy of housing policy by looking at specific areas of difficulty in the housing market.

10.4 MAJOR CONCERNS IN UK HOUSING POLICIES

10.4.1 Tenures

Housing policy and subsidy arrangements in Britain have been organised historically on a housing tenure basis. Although reform in Britain must aim at a more tenure neutral system of subsidies and finance there is merit in examining existing policies tenure by tenure. The pattern of housing tenure in Britain in 1989 is indicated in Table 10.1.

10.4.2 Owner occupation

A key aspect of government policy since 1979 has been the extension and support of owner occupation, premised on the

TABLE 10.1   Housing tenure, September 1989, Great Britain
(percentage)

	No. of dwellings (000s)	Owner occupied	Local authority	Private rented	Housing association
England	19 289	67.8	21.8	7.6	2.8
Wales	1 157	70.6	20.3	7.2	1.9
Scotland	2 108	46.6	44.8	5.8	2.7
Great Britain	22 554	66.0	23.9	7.4	2.7

Source: Housing and Construction Statistics, September 1989.

(questionable) assumption that owning is superior to renting, especially from councils. It was also a feature of the decade 1979–89 that rising real house prices were regarded as a sign of economic success. Owner occupation has grown in the UK from 55.3 per cent in 1979 to 66 per cent in 1989. This has been achieved largely as a result of one specific housing policy, the Right to Buy of council tenants at substantial price discounts (averaging more than 46 per cent of capital values, see: Maclennan, Gibb and More, 1991). It is this large discount rather than sale *per se* which raises economic concerns. The upsurge in owning has also been the result of income growth, significant tax-based subsidies and the short-to medium-run effects of financial deregulation in the mortgage market. Given what appears to be a highly inelastic supply side, all these factors have also had a role to play in the boom and now collapse of the housing market. The start of the 1990s has been characterised by record levels of home repossessions and a continuing growth in mortgage arrears.

The Right to Buy (RTB) policy had two ends: to further the government's core 'property-owning democracy beliefs' and to recycle capital receipts to meet public sector borrowing policy targets. Not only did the massive discounts (based on length of tenancy) have limited economic rationale, but the government's 'creative' use of local authority receipts treated durable assets just as if they were a form of current spending. Little thought has been given to the resale consequences of the now privately owned council houses. There is now substantive empirical evidence (Forrest and Murie, 1990) that RTB sales have been of higher than average quality council dwellings to higher than average income tenants. The net result of the policy for the local authority, for most of the period when unable to spend all their RTB receipts freely, has been undoubtedly to further the gap in economic status between those owning and those still renting. Indeed, the lack of social mix in the local authority sector is borne out by comparison of owners and tenants in the Rowntree study (Maclennan, Gibb and More, 1990) which indicates that council tenants are more likely to be elderly, dependent on benefits, single parents, disabled, unemployed, living alone and to reside in neighbourhoods they do not like. The RTB sales will have often taken place in the best neighbourhoods but their long term relet potential, of course, is removed from the allocations system.

The positive income elasticity of demand for housing meant that fast growth regions in southern Britain saw substantial increases in housing demand in the 1980s. Apart from income effects, demand was greatly boosted by the effects of mortgage market deregulation. The 1980s saw the most fundamental of changes in the mortgage market. Previously, queueing was required to allocate mortgages since there was minimal price competition between building societies and weak competition from the banking sector. The flow of funds for loans depended on the inflow of retail market savers' deposits. The end of the 'corset' on bank lending in 1981 allowed banks into the market, the interest rate cartel collapsed, and societies were liberalised by the 1986 Building Societies Act. This change enabled access to wholesale funding, personal banking services and the largest societies the opportunity to convert into banks. The industry is highly concentrated but offers a wide and expanding range of mortgage and investment products, revolutionising the market in a quite unprecedented way.

Deregulation impacted on demand in two distinct ways. Most obviously, considerably more funds were available for mortgage lending, essentially making the supply of funds perfectly elastic at the going spread of mortgage rates. Loans as a multiple of income grew steadily in the mid-1980s and 100 per cent mortgage loans became increasingly common, especially for first-time buyers. The second influence on the housing market was the phenomenon of equity withdrawal. Housing equity can be released through trading up or down, on inheritance, and since the 1980s, by taking out additional loans, secured on your property but not for housing purposes. In 1988, the market value of the UK housing stock minus the stock of outstanding loans was of the order of £700 billion. The sum of £22 billion was released in 1988 with significant macroeconomic effects on consumer spending, imports and reduced levels of savings. The long-term housing demand consequences of overexposure and mortgage debt problems are presently all too apparent.

Owner occupation, with respect to other housing tenures and other forms of asset, enjoys favourable tax treatment which stokes up demand for housing, distorts allocative decisions, is vertically and horizontally inequitable and has potentially severe macroeconomic repercussions. Real capital gains and the income from owning property in untaxed. From a consumption point of view, mortgage interest payments attract tax relief up to the first £30 000 of the mortgage, and this costs the exchequer something in the region of £8 billion annum. The Community Charge removed an excise-based property tax, and in December 1991, the government decided to widen further the tax expenditures enjoyed by temporarily removing stamp duty (a 1 per cent tax on all houses above £30 000) on all properties up to £250 000.

There is now substantial evidence about the formal incidence and distribution of these tax expenditures (ibid.). Since mortgage loans reflect ability to pay (as a multiple of earnings) but real house price inflation over time erodes the link between mortgages and prices (and this has a distinct regional profile), it is intuitive that mortgage interest tax relief (MITR) is directly proportional to incomes, but this is not so for capital gains or income tax exemptions. In 1989, the average level of MITR for the six regional areas in the JRF Study was £513 with the top 30 per cent of income groups receiving more than three times that received by the bottom 30 per cent. MITR went disproportionately to younger households and tended to rise the further out households located from city centres. The authors estimated that exemption from capital gains was worth an average of £3403 in 1988, based on some strong assumptions, and that this had a strong north–south profile, but was more positively related to house prices than to current incomes. It was households in the peak earning ages who enjoyed the most capacity to earn large capital gains and there was a clear jump in capital gains made once households located more than 15 kilometres from the city centre.

However, formal subsidy incidence ignores the effect of housing supply elasticities on the economic or effective incidence of tax-based subsidies. Considerable, but unsystematic, evidence suggests that because of technical, seasonal and planning reasons, housing supply is relatively unresponsive, especially in the tightly zoned South East. If this is the case, much of these tax giveaways will be capitalised into higher house prices. So, not only do these tax expenditures have significant demand, public expenditure and (arguably) inequitable consequences, they may push house prices up, in the opposite direction from the espoused objective of using MITR to ease first-time buyer housing costs.

Since 1989, house prices have fallen in the UK as a whole and particularly in southern England (by up to a quarter). Sustained high mortgage rates, followed on by record mortgage repossessions and long-term arrears have created a visible housing crisis (as opposed to the less visible underfunding and deterioration of urban social housing for more than fifteen years). The debt consequences of overborrowing and the fallacious belief that ever-rising real house prices was a worthy policy objective have now been most cruelly exposed. The owner occupied market for housing has collapsed so extensively in parts of the UK that some commentators have suggested that there may be two years' supply of unsold housing on the market.[1] By offering a new tax subsidy in the stamp duty holiday and a commitment to pay Income Support direct to lenders, the government seeks to tackle the symptoms rather than the cause of the housing market crisis. The causes are inelastic supply, irrational and unfair subsidy and a lack of sensible renting and financing alternatives. Until politicians recognise the sources of the present problems, they cannot hope to design fair and efficient solutions.

10.4.3 Private renting

The standard example of the damaging effects of price controls is the competitive model of rent controls wherein the free market long-run equilibrium price is set above the level of rent controls. Robinson (1979) uses a stock adjustment model of the rental market (encapsulating the inelasticity of supply) and this demonstrates that there is no finite lower limit on the size of the active rental stock. This is because there is a necessary flow of new housing required to maintain a depreciating stock. Frankena (1975) showed that if landlords operate with the rent control as a constraint on revenue rather than profit, by cutting back on maintenance and other variable costs, then the same absolute level of profit can be made in the short run at the expenses of deteriorating quality of the stock.

In the period after 1979, housing policy has attempted to reinvigorate private renting in deregulating new tenancies and pumppriming new investment in rented property through the subsidised business expansion scheme (BES). So far, the results have not been encouraging. The BES may have added 8000 units to the private rented sector in its first two years (Crook *et al.*, 1991) but that is only a small proportion of the net decline in private renting in Britain in that period. In any case, BES properties have only to be let for five years to attract maximum tax relief – there is considerable uncertainty as to whether the stock will remain on the market after this period.

Maclennan *et al.* (1990) found that across their six case study areas private renting housed different groups and that the mix varied from region to region, such that in the North, around half of the sample were older, often poor and lived in small, inner-city houses which were typically of relatively poor quality. In Bristol and London, the largest group was made up of small, average and above average income households residing in adequate market tenancies. Deregulation of tenancies only applies to around 50 per cent of the market (the rest has effectively been *de facto* deregulated for years). Rates of return in the most attractive private renting scenario examined, Bristol, made around 7 per cent (including assessed capital gain). This was still not competitive with the rest of the economy in 1988–9.

While deregulation of rents is a necessary condition of new investment, there are further steps that have to be taken. First, there has to be a recognition that private renting plays a specialised and multifaceted role in the housing system. Policy to improve easy access housing to lubricate the labour market will not be appropriate for the elderly living in unfurnished rented housing. Second, acknowledgement has to be made of the widespread distrust of private landlordism. Reputation and credibility remain a stumbling block to increasing demand in the rental market. The government can counteract this by setting up a monitoring system based on landlord licensing. Third, housing in Britain is taxed under the assumption of infinite life. This means that landlords can receive no depreciation allowances, putting them at a severe disadvantage to other forms of business. Fourth, the Housing Benefit system will play a critical part if the private rented sector is to meet an increased demand for its form of provision. At the moment, Housing Benefit is too inflexible when it comes to meeting market rents and as a result of poverty trap problems (marginal tax rates can still be as high as 99.9 per cent), the benefit system institutionalises immobility. More flexible systems, such as the dual taper Housing Benefit system which reduces the marginal tax rate at little extra cost to the Treasury (see Hills, 1991), are an absolute prerequisite if private renting is going to return from the margins of the housing system to be simply a minority but vital housing tenure.

It is only at this point, with these policy reforms in place, that designing appropriate capital subsidy mechanisms for private renting can be considered. Any grant system would have to be introduced in a way that was consistent with policy mechanisms and objectives for the rest of the housing system. The key question remains whether it is possible to build cross-party consensus on a constructive role for private renting. Until that emerges, and until private renting is seen as a valid part of housing, the suggested reforms cannot take place.

10.4.4 Social housing

Over the decade 1979 to 1989, the government succeeded in cutting public expenditure in real, absolute and not just proportional terms. The bulk of these reductions, as tax expenditures grew in home ownership, were borne in the council sector. In 1989, councils spent only one-eighth of what they had done in 1979 on new housing provision. As council-tied subsidies were reduced real average rents rose by 54 per cent. However, with means-tested Housing Benefits replacing traditional tied subsidies this meant that middle rather than low-income tenants were faced with real increases in net of subsidy rents. By the end of the decade more than two out of three council tenants received Housing Benefit assistance. Until after 1989, capital funding for housing associations, the alternative 'third arm', was hardly increased. Over the decade as a whole spending by government on housing fell from 8 to 3 per cent of public expenditure totals.

Much of the onslaught on council housing was justified by the government in terms of their broad political economy. But there was, and is, a concern on the part of practitioners and tenants that all was not well with council housing. It is arguable that the Conservative administrations of the 1980s did not cause the problems of council housing, though they may have frustrated their solution.

Applied economic analysis of council housing in Britain has been largely notable for its absence and much that is written about the sector is polemical. But there is sufficient research evidence now available to suggest that pre-1980s, even late 1980s, council housing was a badly designed system from an economic standpoint. The key features of the system were development processes, pricing and financial accounting and management effectiveness.

10.4.5 Development

In the 1950 and 1960s, often with annual output exceeding 200 000 units, council building to meet 'needs' and effect slum clearance came to house one-third of Britons. These developments adopted a narrow conception of 'needs' usually defined in simple Shelter terms, and ignoring locational, neighbourhood and other aspects of housing demand. Deep subsidies induced tenants to accept highly constrained choice options. Fast development on a large scale meant the widespread replication of technical and social errors. It is difficult to accept that a market led process would have produced consistent errors, or indeed a system in which three tenants had been given an effective voice. The development ethos often meant that organisational and financial structures were not well designed to manage assets effectively.

From 1919 onwards the financial arrangements for council housing made major elements in common. First, subsidies were fixed on a per house basis in nominal terms at the date of construction (until 1978). Subsidies and rents from all dwellings and estates were pooled into a single account (the Housing Revenue Account). The HRA, until 1980, was required not to be in surplus even though capital assets were entered at historic cost values. Further, until 1990, local tax revenues could be used to balance the account and, from 1980 to 1990, surpluses withdrawn from it (though this is still possible in the Scottish legislative framework).

The average rent level for a particular council depended not only on service costs but also history and political choices in relation to local tax revenues. And, of course, the spatial pattern of council housing development within cities, and indeed across regions, meant that it became a major local political concern and device. At the start of the 1980s, all British cities with more than 500 000 residents had at least half of housing provided by the council. In Glasgow, where two-thirds of the 1981 population lived in some form of public housing, half the local political wards had more than 75 per cent council housing, and 75 per cent had more than half. In such a context the concerns of applied economics were swept aside by broader political economy questions.

Intra and interregional differences in rents clearly did not reflect key economic considerations and this hampered regional labour mobility. But there were also major allocative distortions within individual councils. Councils were, and are, relatively free to select their own dwelling pricing criteria (usually bundling property and service charges into a single figure). The JRF analysis for 1989 revealed that hedonic pricing equations which usually explain 50–75 per cent of variations in market prices *never* explained more than a quarter of the variation in rents within councils. It is hardly surprising that half the population of tenants are now in houses mismatched to household size and that up to a third of tenants are frustrated at being unable to secure variations in service quality for which they would pay. The subsidy received by a tenant in a given type of dwelling depends on the pricing scheme, the structure of the HRA and Housing Benefit. As a result of the systems in place council subsidies are essentially disorderly. They vary from region to region; the JRF analysis indicates that, defined as the gap between market and gross rents (before Housing Benefit), they varied from 2 to 100 per cent between London and Glasgow and after benefit payments by 33 and 70 per cent. These are large and unsystematic differences.

Poorer tenants do receive larger absolute subsidies than more affluent tenants. Whilst the average subsidy to council tenants was close to the average value of MITR for owners (but not in all regions), owners with incomes in excess of £5200 per annum generally received higher subsidies than renters with such incomes. When it is recalled that there may be poverty-trap effects for renters and a larger component of tied subsidy for renters, it is clear that the British housing subsidy system distorts tenure choices in favour of owning for all but the largest income households.

The effectiveness of housing management service provision by councils has been researched in the 1980s (see Maclennan *et al.*, 1989). The evidence is largely that finance and subsidy systems have not promoted a widespread efficient use of resources. Some councils chose to be businesslike, participative and decentralised. Many others did not. Central government policy and advice for housing management has been progressive in nature in the 1980s. Performance monitoring and tenant participation reports are now required annually of authorities. 'Ring-fencing' of Housing Revenue Accounts has prompted more businesslike relationships between council departments. The setting of service standards proposed in the citizens' charter and the proposed advent of compulsory competitive tendering for management services are likely to induce further improvements.

There has been a growing realisation since the mid-1980s that Britain is likely to need a large social rented housing sector into the next century. The changing nature of the income distribution suggests that low-income households will not be adequately housed, nor their rundown estates upgraded, without major public subsidies. The 1988 Housing Act, however, opened up possibilities for achieving this without re-establishing council monopolies.

With the agreement of tenants, alternative landlords may now take over individual houses (Tenants Choice) or estates, or even councils transfer all their stock to alternative landlords (Large Scale Voluntary Transfers). More than a dozen English councils have now undertaken LSVT. The 'ring-fencing' subsidy required is constructed to achieve this objective (through a complex series of yet more distortions) and further transfers are likely. To date, the only major alternative landlords have been housing associations – the tax and subsidy regime still precludes private landlords from entering this emerging market. In this respect the government's attempts to create a more competititve structure for social housing appear rather half-hearted.

Looking to the future, much more attention needs to be given to how alternative landlords price houses and manage them in order to avoid further major difficulties in two decades' time. We are not convinced that Britain has yet found a fair and long-term feasible model for social housing or, alternatively, rental housing which meets social objectives – basic economic questions are still being avoided.

10.5 THE REFORM AGENDA IN THE 1990s

The reform proposals set out in the second report of the Duke of Edinburgh's Inquiry (1991) broadly meet with our approval, though a stronger case could have been made for grant-aided housing investment where favourable externalities can be produced.

The major challenges are to produce a competitive, efficient and fair system of housing subsidies in Britain. Tenure should be de-emphasised as a policy objective and replaced by more explicit concerns about adequacy, accessibility and affordability.

Systematic pricing criteria are required across all the rental sectors and the owned sector. The main form of support should be a redesigned form of income-related housing allowance (with 'traps' minimised) which should be available in all tenures. Where capital grants are required, say in urban regeneration, they should be competitively tendered across all social and private landlords who would be subject to licensing and inspection.

Such a policy thrust would require the phasing out of mortgage interest tax relief. Government and Opposition not only both lack courage but insight in this respect. Wilcox (1991) has indicated that the macroeconomic consequences would be favourable, and first-time buyers would suffer little as new allowances and lower house prices came into play. The welfare economic arguments are clearer. What is also becoming clearer in the early 1990s is that the political economy of reform is changing. The present system is creating a sufficient number of signs of distress, on the council estates, in cardboard city and bed and breakfast homes, and in a collapsed housing market that change is almost inevitable. The government cannot allow its gains in home ownership to continue to crumble alarmingly. And in this respect it makes little sense to continue to give two-thirds of housing tax reliefs to the richest one-third of owners who would, arguably, retain past voting and tenure patterns following the reforms suggested.

Housing subsidy policy in Britain now has to evolve and not return to older approaches. Future governments would do well to ally economic principles of subsidy design to a growing use of markets and a restructured, competitive rental housing sector embracing social and private participants.

End-Notes

CHAPTER 3

1. The German data precede the reunification with East Germany.
2. The woman will generally require her employer's permission to defer retirement.
3. The retirement pension, for instance, was £1.30 for a single person in 1948; over the next fifteen years it was uprated five times, reaching £2.875 in March 1963.
4. The result of the indexation formula for the basic pension was to create a 'ratchet', whereby the effect if price inflation exceeded the rate of earnings increase in any one year was to give an unintended increase to the real pension. The operation of the ratchet is best shown by example. Suppose that pensions are £100 in period 0; that in period 1 earnings rise by 100 per cent, with no increase in prices; and that in period 2 prices rise by 100 per cent with no increase in earnings. Over the whole period real earnings remain unchanged; but pensions have been increased to £200 in period 1, and to £400 in period 2. The real pension, unintentionally, has doubled whilst real earnings remained constant. The effect operated on a number of occasions in the later 1970s.
5. Benefits were not necessarily uprated each year; nor was each uprating necessarily exactly in line with earnings increases. Benefits were raised more rapidly than earnings just before some elections (e.g. 1959 – 'You've never had it so good') or, as in 1974, just after an election in fulfilment of a manifesto pledge. But the effect in the long run was to maintain the relativity of benefits to pre-tax average earnings almost exactly.

CHAPTER 5

1. Some notable recent papers in this literature are Meyer (1989), Mofitt (1989), and Atkinson (1990). A now rather old important survey paper is that by Danziger *et al.* (1981). See also references to more recent surveys in Barr (1992).

2. For a discussion of the job search model see Lippman and McCall (1976), Hey (1979), Pissarides (1985).
3. Katz and Meyer argue that the impact of this dummy variable could represent the actions of employers with preplanned policies of recalling previously laid-off workers at the end of their benefit period.
4. This section draws on a more extended analysis in Dustmann and Micklewright (1992).
5. In the fuller analysis on which we have drawn here we consider both risk aversion and discounting. Note that uncertainty is not technically essential to our results in a risk-neutral framework; the same results could be obtained with a *certain* job for the wife in the second period but at a lower wage.

CHAPTER 7

1. Taussig (1967) uses the 1962 tax file data, Feldstein and Taylor (1976) use 1962 and 1970, Clotfelter and Steurle (1981) use 1975, Feenberg (1987) uses 1982, Reece and Zieschang (1989) use 1983.
2. All these tax datasets raise the issue of sample stratification. The selection of tax records is weighted so that those on high incomes and special groups like the self-employed are overrepresented. Any estimation techniques should take account of this sample design if the estimates are to be representative of the underlying population of taxpayers. Many US studies seem to have ignored this issue or have concentrated on specific income groups. For example, in Reece and Zieschang (1989) results are presented for the full sample and also for the first three quartiles of the income distribution. Jones and Posnett (1991b) use weighted estimators so that each observation's contribution to the log-likelihood function is weighted by the inverse of its sampling fraction.
3. Aggregate figures from the FES are also used for time-series analysis of total giving in Jones (1983) and Steinberg (1985).
4. Using data from the US Taxpayer Compliance Measurement Program for 1982 on audited tax returns and comparing them to the unaudited tax file, Slemrod concludes that 'overstatement is apparently less price responsive than actual giving' (Slemrod, 1989, p. 522).
5. The Treasury approach is a rather naive view in which efficiency is simply defined in terms of the revenue received by the charities. More elaborate optimal tax models, where the policy-maker's objective is to maximise social welfare are presented in Atkinson (1976) and Feldstein (1980).
6. This suggests an interesting empirical issue. If data are available on the recipients of individual gifts, it would be possible to analyse the impact of the distribution of income on the type of charities that benefit.
7. Christian and Boatsman (1990) note that collinearity does not affect the predictive power of the regression model provided the linear relationship remains stable. However, by its nature, tax reform

alters the relationship between taxable income and marginal rates.

8. Under the US system a further complication is added by the tax-payer's decision whether or not to itemise deductions. The information on contributions by non-itemisers in the US tax files is limited and non-itemisers have often been excluded from the analysis. This is sampling according to the dependent variable and may cause selection bias. One solution to this problem is to include only those who would have itemised irrespective of their charitable contribution (see Clotfelter and Steuerle, 1981). Clotfelter (1989) argues that there is no evidence for a separate 'itemisation effect'. Whereas Dye (1978) finds that a dummy variable for itemisation status seems to play the same role as the price variable. A similar result occurs in Jones and Posnett (1991a) where a dummy variable for taxpaying households seems to have the same explanatory power as the price variable. In Jones and Posnett (1991b), controlling for the distinction between basic rate and higher rate taxpayer's eliminates any price effect on participation or the level of giving by covenant.

9. As well as using an own-price, Schiff (1990) uses the net wage $W(1 - t)$ as a cross price for voluntary donations in the demand function for cash donations (and vice versa for voluntary donations).

10. In his equation for hours volunteered Schiff (1990) tries to avoid a similar simultaneity problem by using a measure of 'full' or 'potential income'. Here the individual infra-marginal net wage $w(1 - t)$ is calculated first and then potential labour income is calculated by multiplying the net wage by 2000 which is intended to represent the number of hours if the individual worked full time all year round. This avoids simultaneity with hours volunteered (and actual hours worked) but it seems to imply that full income (labour and non-labour) will be highly collinear with the net wage variable (and the price variable $1 - t$).

11. In the US National Survey of Philanthropy 12 per cent make no cash donation and 68 per cent make no donation of time. In the 1984 FES 67.4 per cent of households make no donation and in the 1985/6 SPI only 7.5 per cent of the unweighted sample of tax units record a covenant (this corresponds to a weighted participation rate of around 3 per cent).

12. This model is taken one step further by Reece and Zieschang (1985; 1989) when they specify the full budget constraint. In the likelihood function for their model, zero observations are explained by the joint probability of observing a zero donation and the individual's desired donation being on each of the possible kink points or linear segments of the constraint.

13. Similar results are reported by Clotfelter (1980) who finds a cross-section price elasticity of -1.401 but only -0.388 in a first difference model. He concludes that 'it is inappropriate to use elasticities from cross section equations to simulate short-run changes in charitable giving' (Clotfelter, 1980, p. 335). Broman also estimates a model

with fixed effects and partial adjustment of contributions. Her findings contradict those of Clotfelter who argues that there are 'substantial lags' in adjustment to tax changes.

14. Watson (1984) discusses some theoretical implications of the timing of gifts over the life cycle.

CHAPTER 9

1. The first Soviet satellite, Sputnik I, was launched in 1957.

CHAPTER 10

1. Adrian Coles, speaking at a housing statistics conference, November 1991, London, Royal Society of Arts.

Bibliography

Aaron, H. J. (1982) *Economic Effects of Social Security* (Washington DC: Brookings Institution).

Abrams, B. A. and Schmitz, M. D. (1978) 'The "crowding-out" effect of governmental transfers on private charitable contributions', *Public Choice*, 33, 29–37.

Abrams, B. A. and Schmitz, M. D. (1984) 'The crowding-out effect of governmental transfers on private charitable contributions: cross-section evidence', *National Tax Journal*, 37, 563–8.

Ainley, P. and Corney, M. (1990) *Training for the Future* (London: Cassell).

Akerlof, G. (1970) 'The market for lemons: qualitative uncertainty and the market mechanism', *Quarterly Journal of Economics*, 84, 488–500.

Akerlof, G. A. (1978) 'The economics of tagging', *American Economic Review*, 68, 8–19.

Allen, S., Watson, A., Purcell, K. and Wood, S. (eds) (1986) *The Experience of Unemployment* (London: Macmillan).

Amemiya, T. (1985) *Advanced Econometrics* (Oxford: Basil Blackwell).

Amos, O. M. (1982) 'Empirical analysis of motives underlying individual contributions to charity', *Atlantic Economic Journal*, 10, 45–52.

Andreoni, J. (1988) 'Privately provided goods in a large economy: the limits of altruism', *Journal of Public Economics*, 35, 57–73.

Andreoni, J. (1989) 'Giving with impure altruism: applications to charity and Ricardian equivalence', *Journal of Political Economy*, 97, 1447–58.

Andreoni, J. (1990) 'Impure altruism and donations to public goods: a theory of warm-glow giving', *Economic Journal*, 100, 464–77.

Arnould, R. J. and De Brock, L. M. (1986) 'Competition and market failure in the hospital industry: a review of the evidence', *Medical Care Review*, 43, 253–92.

Arrow, K. A. (1973) 'Higher education as a filter', *Journal of Public Economics*, 2, 193–216.

Arrow, K. A. (1981) 'Optimal and voluntary income distribution', in S. Rosefielde (ed.) *Economic Welfare and the Economics of Soviet Socialism: Essays in Honor of Abram Bergson* (Cambridge: Cambridge University Press).

Arrow, K. J. (1963) 'Uncertainty and the welfare economics of medical care', *American Economic Review*, 53, 941–73.

Ashton, P. (1984) 'Poverty and its beholders', *New Society*, 18 October.
Atkinson, A. B. (1969) *Poverty in Britain and the Reform of Social Security* (Cambridge: Cambridge University Press).
Atkinson, A. B. (1970) 'On the measurement of inequality', *Journal of Economic Theory*, 2, 244–63.
Atkinson, A. B. (1976) 'The income tax treatment of charitable contributions', in R. E. Grierson (ed.) *Public and Urban Economics: Essays in Honor of William S. Vickrey* (New York: D.C. Heath.
Atkinson, A. B. (1983a) *The Economics of Inequality* (Oxford: Oxford University Press).
Atkinson, A. B. (1983b) *Social Justice and Public Policy* (Hemel Hempstead: Harvester Wheatsheaf).
Atkinson, A. B. (1985) 'How should we measure poverty? Some conceptual issues', ESRC Programme on Taxation, Incentives and the Distribution of Income, Discussion Paper 82.
Atkinson, A. B. (1987) 'Economics of the welfare state: introductory comments', *European Economic Review*, 31, 177–81.
Atkinson, A. B. (1987) 'Income maintenance and social insurance', in A. J. Auerbach and M. J. Feldstein (eds) *Handbook of Public Economics: 2* (Amsterdam: North-Holland).
Atkinson, A. B. (1989) *Poverty and Social Security* (Hemel Hempstead: Harvester Wheatsheaf).
Atkinson, A. B. (1990) 'Institutional features of unemployment insurance and the working of the labour market', STICERD, London School of Economics, Welfare State Programme Discussion Paper 50.
Atkinson, A. B., Gomulka, J., Micklewright, J. and Rau, N. R. (1984) 'Unemployment benefit, duration and incentives in Britain: how robust is the evidence?'. *Journal of Public Economics*, 23, 3–26.
Atkinson, A. B. and Micklewright, J. (1990) 'Unemployment compensation and labour market transitions: a critical review', STICERD, London School of Economics, TIDI Programme Paper 143.
Atkinson, A. B., Maynard, A. K. and Trinder, C. (1983) *Parents and Children* (London: Heinemann).
Atkinson, A. B. and Stiglitz, J. E. (1980) *Lectures in Public Economics*, (London: McGraw-Hill).
Auerbach, A., Hagemann, R., Nicoletti, G. and Kotlikoff, L. J. (1989) *The Economics of Ageing Populations: The Case of Four OECD Economies* (Paris: OECD).
Auerbach, A. J. and Kotlikoff, L. J. (1990) 'Demographics, fiscal policy and US saving in the 1980s and beyond', in L. H. Summers (ed.) *Tax Policy and the Economy: 4* (Cambridge Mass.: MIT Press).
Austen-Smith, J. D. (1980) 'Individual contribution to public goods', *Economics Letters*, 5, 359–61.
Ball, M. (1983) *Housing Policy and Economic Power* (London: Methuen).
Barnes, J. and Barr, N. (1988) *Strategies for Higher Education: The Alternative White Paper* (Aberdeen: Aberdeen University Press).
Barr, N. (1981) 'Empirical definitions of the poverty line', *Policy and Politics*, 9, 1–21.

Barr, N. (1987) *The Economics of the Welfare State* (London: Weidenfeld & Nicolson).

Barr, N. (1989) *Student Loans: The Next Step*, David Hume Paper No. 15 (Aberdeen University Press).

Barr, N. (1990) 'Economic theory and the welfare state: a survey and reinterpretation', STICERD, London School of Economics, Welfare State Programme Paper 54.

Barr, N. (1992) 'Economic theory and the welfare state: a survey and interpretation', *Journal of Economic Literature*, 30, 741–803.

Barr, N. and Coulter, F. (1990) 'Social security: solution or problem?', in J. Hills (ed.) *The State of Welfare* (Oxford: Oxford University Press).

Beck, R. G. (1974) 'The effects of copayment on the poor', *Journal of Human Resources*, 9, 129–42.

Becker, G. S. (1964) *Human Capital* (New York: National Bureau of Economic Research).

Becker, G. S. (1965) 'The allocation of time', *Economic Journal*, 75, 493–517.

Becker, G. S. (1974) 'A theory of social interactions', *Journal of Political Economy*, 82, 1063–93.

Beckerman, W. and Clark, S. (1982) *Poverty and Social Security in Britain since 1961* (Oxford: Oxford University Press).

Bennett, R., Glennerster, H. and Revèson, D. (1992) 'Investing in Skill: to stay on or not to stay on', *Oxford Review of Economic Policy*, 8(2).

Bergstrom, T., Blume, L. and Varian, H. (1986) 'On the private provision of public goods', *Journal of Public Economics*, 29, 25–49.

Bernheim, B. D. (1987) 'Social security benefits: an empirical study of expectations and realisations', National Bureau of Economic Research, Working Paper 2257.

Berthoud, R. and Kempson, E. (1990) *Credit and Debt in Britain* (London: Policy Studies Institute).

Birch, R. C. (1974) *The Shaping of the Welfare State* (London: Longman).

Blaug, M. (1970) *An Introduction to the Economics of Education* (Harmondsworth: Penguin).

Blaug, M. (1976) 'The empirical status of human capital theory: a slightly jaundiced survey', *Journal of Economic Literature*, September, 827–56.

Blaug, M. (1978) *Economics of Education: A Selected Annotated Bibliography* (Oxford: Pergamon Press).

Blundell, R. and Meghir, C. (1987) 'Bivariate alternatives to the Tobit model', *Journal of Econometrics*, 34, 179–200.

Bodie, Z. (1989) 'Inflation insurance', National Bureau of Economic Research, Working Paper 3009.

Bodie, Z. (1990) 'Pensions as retirement income insurance', *Journal of Economic Literature*, 28, 28–49.

Borcherding, T. E. (1977) *Budgets and Bureaucrats: The Sources of Government Growth* (Durham, NC: Duke University Press).

Boskin, M. J. and Feldstein, M. (1977) 'Effects of the charitable deduction of contributions by low and middle income households: new evidence from the National Survey of Philanthropy', *Review of Economics and Statistics*, 59, 351–4.

Bouchier, I. A. D. (1983) 'Brides of quietness: silent gallstones', *British Medical Journal*, 286, 415–6.

Bradshaw, J., Mitchell, D. and Morgan, J. (1987) 'Evaluating adequacy: the potential of budget standards', *Journal of Social Policy*, 16, 165–82.

Bradshaw, J. and Wakeman, I. (1972) 'The poverty trap up-dated', *Political Quarterly*, 43, 459–69.

Broman, A. (1989) 'Statutory tax rate reform and charitable giving: evidence from a recent period of reform', *Journal of the American Tax Association*, 10, 7–21.

Brown, E. (1987) 'Tax incentives and charitable giving: evidence from new survey data', *Public Finance Quarterly*, 15, 386–96.

Brown, J. C. (1990) *Victims or Villains? Social Security Benefits in Unemployment* (York: Joseph Rowntree Memorial Trust).

Brown, M. and Madge, N. (1982) *Despite the Welfare State: A Report on the SSRC/DHSS Programme of Research into Transmitted Deprivation* (London: Heinemann Educational Books).

Buchanan, J. M. (1968) 'What kind of redistribution do we want?', *Economica*, 35, 185–90.

Burkhead, G. *et al.* (1967) *Input and Output in Large City High Schools* (Syracuse NY: Syracuse University Press).

Burtless, G. (1990) 'Current proposals for school reform: an economist's appraisal', Martindale Centre, Lehigh University.

Cameron, H. M. and McGoogan, E. (1981) 'A prospective study of 1152 hospital autopsies: analysis of inaccuracies in clinical diagnoses and their significance', *Journal of Pathology*, 133, 285–300.

Carroll, N. V. and Erwin, W. G. (1987) 'Patient shifting as a response to Medicare prospective payment', *Medical Care*, 25, 1161–7.

Central Statistical Office (1990) *Social Trends 20* (London: HMSO).

Child Poverty Action Group (1982) *The Poverty of Taxation* (London: CPAG).

Child Poverty Action Group (1988) *National Welfare Benefits Handbook* (London: CPAG).

Child Poverty Action Group (1989) *Rights Guide to Non-Means-Tested Benefits* (London: CPAG).

Christian, C. and Boatsman, J. (1990) 'Cross-sectional price elasticity estimates of the charitable contributions deduction', in S. M. Jones (ed.) *Advances in Taxation* (Greenwich, Conn.: JAI Press).

Chubb, J. E. and Moe, T. M. (1990) *Politics, Markets and America's Schools* (Washington DC: Brookings Institution).

Clotfelter, C.T. (1980) 'Tax incentives and charitable giving; evidence from a panel of taxpayers', *Journal of Public Economics*, 13, 319–40.

Clotfelter, C. T. (1985) *Federal Tax Policy and Charitable Giving* (Chicago: University of Chicago Press).

Clotfelter, C. T. (1989) 'Tax-induced distortions in the voluntary sector', *Case Western Reserve Law Review*, 39, 663–94.

Clotfelter, C. T. and Steuerle, C. E. (1981) 'Charitable contributions', in

H. J. Aaron and P. J. A. (eds) *How Taxes Affect Economic Behavior* (Washington, DC: Brookings Institution).

Cohn, E. and Geske, T. G. (1990) *The Economics of Education* (Oxford: Pergamon Press).

Coleman, J. S. (1966) *Equality of Educational Opportunity* (Washington DC: US Government Printing Office).

Collard, D. (1978) *Altruism and Economy* (Oxford: Martin Robertson).

Commission, P. (1990) *A Call for Action* (Washington DC: US Government Printing Office).

Coons, J. and Sugarman, S. (1978) *Education by Choice: The Case for Family Control* (Berkeley: University of California Press).

Cornes, R. and Sandler, T. (1984) 'The theory of public goods: non-Nash behaviour', *Journal of Public Economics*, 23, 367–79.

Cowell, F. A. (1981) 'Income maintenance schemes under wage-rate uncertainty', *American Economic Review*, 71, 692–703.

Cowell, F. A. (1985) 'Welfare benefits and the economics of take-up', ESRC Programme on Taxation, Incentive and the Distribution of Income, Discussion Paper 89.

Creedy, J. and Disney, R. (1985) *Social Insurance in Transition* (Oxford: Clarendon Press).

Crook, A., Kemp, P., Anderson, I. and Bowman, S. (1991) *The Business Expansion Scheme and Rented Housing* (York: Joseph Rowntree Foundation).

Culyer, A. J. (1971) 'The nature of the commodity "health care" and its efficient allocation', *Oxford Economic Papers*, 23, 189–211.

Culyer, A. J. (1979) *Expenditures on Real Services: Health* (Milton Keynes: Open University Press).

Culyer, A. J. (1980) *The Political Economy of Social Policy* (Oxford: Martin Robertson).

Culyer, A. J. (1989) 'The normative economics of health care finance and provision', *Oxford Review of Economic Policy*, 5, 34–58.

Culyer, A. J. (1991) 'Conflicts between equity concepts and efficiency in health: a diagrammatic approach', *Osaka Economic Papers*.

Culyer, A. J., Maynard, A. K. and Posnett, J. P. (eds) (1990) *Competition in Health Care: Reforming the NHS* (London: Macmillan).

Culyer, A. J. and Posnett, J. W. (1990) 'Hospital behaviour and competition', in A. J. Culyer, A. K. Maynard and J. P. Posnett (eds) *Competition in Health Care: Reforming the NHS* (London: Macmillan).

Daniel, J. (1989) 'Price and income elasticities of charitable giving: new evidence from a panel of taxpayers', *mimeo*.

Danziger, S., Haveman, R. H. and Plotnick, R. (1981) 'How income transfer programs affect work, savings, and the income distribution: a critical review', *Journal of Economic Literature*, 19, 975–1028.

Dasgupta, P. S. and Maskin, E. (1986) 'The existence of equilibrium in discontinuous economic games I and II', *Review of Economic Studies*, 53, 1–41.

Davy-Smith, G., Bartly, M. and Blane, D. (1990) 'The Black Report on socioeconomic inequalities in health: 10 years on', *British Medical Journal*, 301.

Deacon, A. and Bradshaw, J. (1983) *Reserved for the Poor* (Oxford: Martin Robertson).

Department of Health and Social Security (1985a) *Reform of Social Security*, Vols 1–3, Cmnd 9517–9 (London: HMSO).

Department of Health and Social Security (1985b) *Reform of Social Security: Programme for Action*, Cmnd 9691 (London: HMSO).

DesHarnais, S., Kobrinski, E. and Chesney, S. (1987) 'The early effects of the prospective payment system on inpatient utilization and the quality of care', *Inquiry*, 24, 7–16.

Diamond, P. A. (1977) 'A framework for social security analysis', *Journal of Public Economics*, 8, 275–98.

Diamond, P. A. and Mirrlees, J. A. (1978) 'A model of social insurance with variable retirement', *Journal of Public Economics*, 10, 295–336.

Dilnot, A. W., Kay, J. A. and Morris, C. N. (1984) *The Reform of Social Security* (Oxford: Oxford University Press).

Dilnot, A. W. and Kell, M. (1987) 'Male unemployment and women's work', *Fiscal Studies*, 8, 1–16.

Donnison, D. (1982) *The Politics of Poverty* (Oxford: Martin Robertson).

Duke of Edinburgh (Chairman) (1991) *Inquiry into British Housing* (London: National Federation of Housing Association.)

Dustmann, C. and Micklewright, J. (1992) 'Means-tested unemployment benefit and family labour supply: a dynamic analysis', European University Institute, Working Paper ECO 92/69.

Dye, R. F. (1978) 'Personal charitable contributions: tax effects and other motives', *Proceedings of the 70th Annual Conference on Taxation*, National Tax Association, 311–21.

Ellwood, D. T. and Summers, L. H. (1986) 'Poverty in America: is welfare the answer or the problem?', in S. H. Danziger and D. H. Weinberg (eds) *Fighting Poverty* (Cambridge, Mass.: Harvard University Press).

Ermisch, J. (1984) *Housing Finance: Who Gains?* (London: Policy Studies Institute).

Ermisch, J. (ed.) (1990) *Housing and the National Economy* (Aldershot: Avebury).

Evans, E. J. (ed.) (1978) *Social Policy 1930–1914: Individualism, Collectivism and the Origins of the Welfare State* (London: Routledge & Kegan Paul).

Evans, R. G. (1974) 'Supplier-induced demand – some empirical evidence and implications', in M. Perlman (ed.) *The Economics of Health and Medical Care* (London: Macmillan).

Evans, R. G. (1976) 'Modeling the objectives of the physician', in R. D. Fraser (ed.) *Health Economics Symposium* (Kingston: Queen's University Industrial Relations Centre).

Evans, R. G. (1983) 'The welfare economics of public health insurance: theory and Canadian practice', in L. Soederstrom (ed.) *Social Insurance* (Amsterdam: North-Holland).

Evans, R. G. (1984) *Strained Mercy: The Economics of Canadian Medical Care* (Toronto: Butterworths).

Falkingham, J. (1989) 'Dependency and ageing in Britain: a re-examination of the evidence', *Journal of Social Policy*, 18, 211–33.

Fallis, G. (1985) *Housing Economics* (Toronto: Butterworths).

Farley, P. J. (1985) 'Who are the underinsured?', *Milbank Memorial Fund Quarterly*, 63, 476–503.

Farley, P. J., Cornelius, L. J. and Goldstone, D. E. (1990) 'Health insurance of minorities in the United States', *Journal of Health Care for the Poor and Underserved*, 1, 9–24.

Feder, J., Hadley, J. and Zuckerman, S. (1987) 'How did Medicare's prospective payments system affect hospitals?', *New England Journal of Medicine*, 317, 867–73.

Feenberg, D. (1987) 'Are tax models really identified: the case of charitable giving', *National Tax Journal*, 42, 629–33.

Feldstein, M. S. (1973) 'The welfare loss of excess health insurance', *Journal of Political Economy*, 81, 251–80.

Feldstein, M. S. (1974) 'Social security, induced retirement and aggregate capital formation', *Journal of Political Economy*, 82, 905–26.

Feldstein, M. (1980) 'A contribution to the theory of tax expenditures: the case of charitable giving', in H. J. Aaron and M. J. Boskin (eds) *The Economics of Taxation* (Washington: Brookings Institution).

Feldstein, M. and Clotfelter, C. T. (1976) 'Tax incentives and charitable giving in the United States: a microeconomic analysis', *Journal of Public Economics*, 5, 1–26.

Feldstein, M. and Taylor, A. (1976) 'The income tax and charitable contributions', *Econometrica*, 44, 1201–21.

Fisinger, J., Kraft, K. and Pauly, M. V. (1986) 'Some observations on greater competition in the West German health-insurance system from a US perspective', *Managerial and Decision Economics*, 7, 151–61.

Flood, A. B., Scott, W. R. and Ewy, W. (1984) 'Does practice make perfect?: the relation between hospital volume and outcomes for selected diagnostic categories', *Medical Care*, 22, 98.

Forrest, R. and Murie, A. (1990) *Selling the Welfare State: The Privatisation of Public Housing* (London: Routledge).

Frankena, A. (1975) 'Alternative models of rent controls', *Urban Studies*, 12, 303–8.

Freund, D., Rossiter, L. F. and Fox, P. D. (1989) 'Evaluation of the Medicaid competition demonstrations', *Health Care Financing Review*, 11, 81–97.

Friedman, M. (1962) *Capitalism and Freedom* (Chicago: University of Chicago Press).

Garcia, J. (1985) *The Econometric Analysis of Cross-Section and Panel Data Models as Applied to Labour Supply Models*.

Garcia, J. (1989) 'Incentive and welfare effects of reforming the British benefit system: a simulation study for the wives of the unemployed', in S. Nickel, W. Narendranathan, J. Stern and J. Garcia (eds) *The Nature of Unemployment in Britain* (Oxford: Oxford University Press).

George, V. and Wilding, P. (1976) *Ideology and Social Welfare* (London: Routledge & Kegan Paul).

236   *Bibliography*

Gibb, K. and Monro, M. (1991) *Housing Finance in the UK* (Basingstoke: Macmillan).

Gitter, W. H., Hauser, H. *et al.* (1989) *Structural Reform of the Statutory Health Insurance System* (Bayreuth: University of Bayreuth).

Gleeson, D. (1989) *The Paradox of Training: Making Progress out of Crisis* (Milton Keynes: Open University Press).

Glennerster, H. *et al.* (1968) 'A graduate tax', *Higher Education Review*, 1, 26–37.

Glennerster, H. (1972a) *Willing the Means* (London: Campaign for Educational Advance).

Glennerster, H. (1972b) 'Education and Inequality', in H. Glennerster (ed.) *Labour and Inequality* (London: Fabian Society).

Glennerster, H. and Low, W. (1990) 'Education' in J. Hills (ed.), *The State of Welfare* (Oxford: Clarendon Press).

Gordon, M. (1988) *Social Security Policies in Industrial Countries: A Comparative Analysis* (Cambridge: Cambridge University Press).

Gracie, W. A. and Ransohoff, D. F. (1982) 'The natural history of silent gallstones: the innocent gallstone is not a myth', *New England Journal of Medicine*, 307, 798–800.

Grayboys, T. B. and Headley, A. (1987) 'Results of a second-opinion program for coronary artery bypass surgery', *Journal of the American Medical Association*, 258, 1611–14.

Gueron, J. M. (1986) *Work Initiatives for Welfare Recipients* (New York: Manpower Demonstration Research Corporation).

Halpern, J. and Hausman, J. (1984) 'Choice under uncertainty: a model of applications for the social security disability insurance program', MIT, *mimeo*.

Halpern, J. and Hausman, J. (1986) 'Choice under uncertainty: labour supply and the decision to apply for disability insurance', in R. Blundell and I. Walker (eds) *Unemployment, Search and Labour Supply* (Cambridge: Cambridge University Press).

Hansen, W. L. and Weisbrod, B. A. (1969) 'The distribution of costs and direct benefits of public higher education: the case of California', *Journal of Human Resources*, 4, 176–91.

Hansen, W. L. and Weisbrod, B. A. (1978) 'The distribution of subsidies to students in California public higher education: reply', *Journal of Human Resources*, 13, 137–9.

Hanushek, E. A. (1986) 'The economics of schooling: production and efficiency in public schools', *Journal of Economic Literature*, 23, 1141–77.

Harsanyi, J. C. (1980) 'Rule utilitarianism, rights, obligations and the theory of rational behaviour', *Theory and Decision*, 12,115–133.

Hausman, J. (1981) 'Exact consumer surplus and deadweight loss', *American Economic Review*, 71, 662–76.

Hay, J. R. (1976) *The Origin of the Liberal Welfare Reforms, 1906–1914* (London: Macmillan).

Hayek, F. A. (1978) *Law, Legislation and Liberty* (London: Routledge & Kegan Paul).

Henke, K.-D. (1990) 'What can Americans learn from Europeans? – a response', *Health Care Financing Review*, Annual Supplement, 93–6.

Hey, J. (1979) *Uncertainty in Microeconomics* (Oxford: Martin Robertson).

Hey, J. and Mavromaras, K. (1981) 'The effect of unemployment insurance on the riskiness of occupational choice', *Journal of Public Economics*, 31, 105–29.

Hill, M. (1990) *Social Security Policy in Britain* (Aldershot: Edward Elgar).

Hills, J. (1990) *Changing Tax: How the Tax System Works and How to Change it* (London: CPAG).

Hills, J. (1991) *The Thirty Nine Steps to Housing Finance Reform* (York: Joseph Rowntree Foundation).

Hirschman, A. O. (1970) *Exit, Voice and Loyalty* (Cambridge, Mass.: Harvard University Press).

Hochman, J. M. and Rodgers, J. D. (1969) 'Pareto optimal redistribution', *American Economic Review*, 59, 542–57.

Holzmann, R. (1988) 'Ageing and social-security costs', *European Journal of Population*, 3, 411–37.

Housing Strategy Committee (1977) *Housing for All* (London: National Economic Development Office/HMSO).

Hurd, M. D. (1990) 'Research on the elderly: economic status, retirement and consumption and saving', *Journal of Economic Literature*, 28, 565–637.

Inquiry into British Housing (1991) *Second Report* (York: Joseph Rowntree Foundation).

International Labour Office (1984) *Into the Twenty-First Century: The Development of Social Security*, (Geneva: ILO).

Jackson, D. (1972) *Poverty* (London: Macmillan).

Jenkins, S. and Millar, J. (1989) 'Income risk and income maintenance: implications for incentives to work', in A. Dilnot and I. Walker (eds) *The Economics of Social Security* (Oxford: Oxford University Press).

Jenks, C. (1972) *Inequality* (New York: Basic Books).

Jones, A. M. and Posnett, J. W. (1990) 'Giving by covenant in the UK', in Charities Aid Foundation (ed.) *Charity Trends* (London: CAF).

Jones, A. M. and Posnett, J. W. (1991a) 'Charitable donations by UK households: evidence from the Family Expenditure Survey', *Applied Economics*, 23, 343–51.

Jones, A. M. and Posnett, J. W. (1991b) 'The impact of tax deductibility on charitable giving by covenant in the UK', *Economic Journal*, 100, 1117–28.

Jones, P. R. (1983) 'Aid to charities', *International Journal of Social Affairs*, 10, 3–11.

Katz, L. F. and Meyer, B. D. (1990) 'The impact of potential duration of unemployment benefits on the duration of unemployment', *Journal of Public Economics*, 41, 45–72.

Kell, M. and Wright, J. (1990) 'Benefits and the labour supply of women married to unemployed men', *Economic Journal*, 100, 119–29.

238   *Bibliography*

Kesselman, J. R. and Garfinkel, I. (1978) 'Professor Friedman, meet Lady Rhys-Williams: NIT vs CIT', *Journal of Public Economics*, 10, 179–216.

Kingma, B. R. (1989) 'An accurate measurement of the crowd-out effect, income effect and price effect for charitable contributions', *Journal of Political Economy*, 97, 1195–207.

Knight, F. H. (1921) *Risk, Uncertainty and Profit* (Boston, Mass.: Houghton Mifflin).

Labelle, R. J., Hurley, J. and Rice, T. (1990) 'Financial incentives and medical practice: evidence from Ontario on the effect of changes in physician fees of medical care utilization', Hamilton, McMaster University, CHEPA Paper 90–4.

Lancaster, K. (1966) 'A new approach to consumer theory', *Journal of Political Economy*, 74, 132–57.

Lancet Editorial (1975) 'To tie; to stab; to stretch; perchance to freeze', *The Lancet*, ii, 645–6.

Launois, R., Majnoni d'Intagnano, B., Stephan, J. and Rodwin, V. (1985) 'Les réseaux de soins coordonnés (RSC): propositions pour une réforme profonde au système de santé', *Revue Française des Affaires Sociales*, 39, 37–62.

Layard, R. and Psacharopoulos, G. (1974) 'The screening hypothesis and the returns to education', *Journal of Political Economy*, 82, 985–8.

Lazear, E. P. (1986) 'Incentive effects of pensions', in D. A. Wise (ed.) *Pensions, Labor and Individual Behavior* (Chicago: University of Chicago Press).

Le Grand, J. (1982) *The Strategy of Equality* (London: Allen & Unwin).

Le Grand, J. and Robinson, R. (1982) *The Economics of Social Problems* (London: Macmillan).

Lee, T. (1990) 'Carving out the cash for schools', University of Bath, Social Policy Paper 17.

Leibenstein, H. (1976) 'Allocative efficiency versus X-efficiency', *American Economic Review*, 56, 392–415.

Leibenstein, H. (1983) 'Competition and X-inefficiency: a reply', *Journal of Political Economy*, 81, 765–77.

Leimer, D. R. and Lesnoy, S. (1982) 'Social security and private saving: new time-series evidence', *Journal of Political Economy*, 90, 606–42.

Lindbeck, A. (1985) 'Redistribution policy and the expansion of the public sector', *Journal of Public Economics*, 28, 309–28.

Lindgren, B. (1989) *Consumer Choice and Provider Competition in Swedish Health Care – Is It Possible?* (Lund: Swedish Institute for Health Economics).

Lindsey, L. (1987) 'Individual giving under the Tax Reform Act of 1986', *The Constitution and the Independent Sector Spring Research Forum* (Washington, DC: CISRF).

Lippman, S. A. and McCall, J. J. (1976) 'The economics of job search: a survey. Part 1: Optimal job search policies', *Economic Inquiry*, 14, 155–89.

Lockwood, M. (1988) 'Quality of life and resource allocation', in M. Bell and S. Mendus (eds) *Philosophy and Medical Welfare* (Cambridge: Cambridge University Press).

Lohr, K. N., Brook, R. H., *et al.* (1986) 'Use of medical care in the Rand health insurance experiment: diagnosis and service-specific analyses in a randomized controlled trial', *Medical Care*, 24, Supplement.

Luft, H., Robinson, J. and Garrick, D. (1986) 'The role of specialized services in competition among hospitals', *Inquiry*, 23, 83–94.

Mack, J. and Lansley, S. (1985) *Poor Britain* (London: Allen & Unwin).

Mack, J. and Lansley, S. (1991) *Breadline Britain, 1990s* (London: HarperCollins).

Maclennan, D. (1982) *Housing Economics*, (London: Longmans).

Maclennan, D. (1988) 'Real Estate Economics' (Wharton Share of Real Estate), mimeo.

Maclennan, D. and Clapham, D. (1989) *The Nature and Effectiveness of Housing Management in England* (London: HMSO).

Maclennan, D., Gibb, K. and More, A. (1991) *Fairer Subsidies, Faster Growth: Housing, Government and the Economy* (York: Joseph Rowntree Foundation).

Maclennan, D., Gibb, K. and More, A. (1990) *Paying for Britain's Housing* (York: Joseph Rowntree Foundation).

McPherson, K. (1988) *Variations in Hospitalization Rates: Why and How to Study Them* (London: Kings Fund Institute).

McPherson, K. (1989) 'International differences in medical care practices', *Health Care Financing Review*, Annual Supplement, 9–20.

McPherson, K., Wennberg, J., Hovind, O. and Clifford, P. (1982) 'Small area variation in the use of common surgical procedures: an international comparison of New England, England and Norway', *New England Journal of Medicine*, 307, 1310–14.

Manning, W. G. and Newhouse, J. P., *et al.* (1987) 'Health insurance and the demand for medical care: evidence from a randomized experiment', *American Economic Review*, 77, 251–77.

Margolis, H. (1982) *Selfishness, Altruism and Rationality* (Cambridge: Cambridge University Press).

Marsh, D. C. (1980) *The Welfare State: Concept and Development* (London: Longman).

Marshall, A. (1890) *The Principles of Economics* (London: Macmillan).

Maynard, A. K. (1975) *Experiment with Choice in Education* (London: Institute of Economic Affairs).

Mayston, D. (1990a) 'Managing capital resources in the NHS', in A. J. Culyer, A. K. Maynard and J. P. Posnett (eds) *Competition in Health Care: Reforming the NHS* (London: Macmillan).

Mayston, D. (1990b) 'NHS resourcing: a financial and economic analysis', in A. J. Culyer, A. K. Maynard and J. P. Posnett (eds) *Competition in Health Care: Reforming the NHS* (London: Macmillan).

Mecklenburger, J. A. and Hostrop, R. W. (eds) (1972) *Education Vouchers from Theory to Alum Rock* (Illinois: Homewood).

Meen, G. (1987) 'The impact on the UK housing market of alternative mortgage regimes, seminar presented at the centre for Housing Research, University of Georgia.

Melnick, G. A. and Zwanziger, J. (1988) 'Hospital behavior under competition and cost-containment policies', *Journal of the American Medical Association*, 260, 2669–75.

Meyer, B. (1989) 'A quasi-experimental approach to the effects of unemployment insurance', National Bureau of Economic Research, Working Paper 3159.

Micklewright, J. (1990) 'Why do only a quarter of the unemployed in Britain receive unemployed insurance?', STICERD, London School of Economics, TIDI Programme Paper 147.

Micklewright, J. (1989) 'Has Britain an early school leaving problem?', *Fiscal Studies*, 10, 1–16.

Ministry of Reconstruction (1944) *Social Insurance, Cmd 6550* (London: HMSO).

Mitchell, B. R. and Deane, P. (1962) *Abstract of British Historical Statistics* (Cambridge: Cambridge University Press).

Mitchell, O. S. (1988) 'Worker knowledge of pension', provisions, 6, 21–39.

Moffitt, R. (1989) 'Demographic behaviour and the welfare state: econometric issues in the identification of the effects of tax and transfer programs', *Journal of Population Economics*, 1, 237–50.

Moffit, R. (1992) 'Incentive effects of the US welfare system: a review', *Journal of Economic Literature*, 30, 1–61.

Mooney, G. H. (1983) 'Equity in health care: confronting the confusion', *Effective Health Care*, 1, 179–85.

Morrisey, M., Sloan, F. and Valvona, J. (1988) 'Medicare prospective payment and post hospital transfers to subacute care', *Medical Care*, 26, 685–98.

Mortimore, P. *et al.* (1988) *The Junior School Project; Part C: Understanding School Effectiveness* (London: Inner London Educational Authority Research and Statistics Section).

Muellbauer, J. (1990) 'The great British housing disaster and economic policy', IPPR, London, Research Report 4.

Mueller, D. C. (1989) *Public Choice II* (Cambridge: Cambridge University Press).

Muth, R. and Goodman, A. (1989) *The Economics of Housing Markets* (Berne: Harwood Academic).

Nagy, G. (1991) 'Unemployment benefits in Hungary – first experiences', *Mozgo Vilag*, 96–103.

Newhouse, J. P. (1970) 'Toward a theory of non-profit institutions: an economic model of a hospital', *American Economic Review*, 60, 64–74.

Newhouse, J. P. (1990) 'Pricing and imperfections in the medical care marketplace', Paper presented at the World Congress of Health Economics, Zurich.

Nichols, A. L. and Zeckhauser, R. (1982) 'Targeting transfers through restrictions on recipients', *American Economic Review, Papers and Proceedings*, 72, 373–7.

Nichols, D., Smolensky, E. and Tideman, T. N. (1971) 'Discrimination by waiting time in merit goods', *American Economic Review*, 16, 312–23.

Nickell, S. J. (1979) 'The effect of unemployment and related benefits on the duration of unemployment', *Economic Journal*, 89, 34–49.

Nozick, R. (1974) *Anarchy, State and Utopia* (Oxford: Basil Blackwell).

O'Higgins, M. (1985a) 'Welfare, redistribution and inequality – disillusion, illusion and reality', in P. T. Bean, J. Ferris and D. K. Whynes (eds) *In Defence of Welfare* (London: Tavistock).

O'Higgins, M. (1985b) 'Inequality, redistribution and recession: the British experience, 1976–1982', *Journal of Social Policy*, 14, 279–307.

O'Sullivan, A. (1984) 'Misconceptions in the current housing subsidy debate', *Policy and Politics*, 12, 119–44.

O'Sullivan, A. (1985) *Supply Response in Housing?*, University of Glasgow, *mimeo*.

OECD (1977) *Public Expenditure on Health* (Paris: OECD).

OECD (1988) *Ageing Populations: The Social Policy Implications* (Paris: OECD).

OECD (1990) *OECD Economic Surveys: New Zealand, 1988–89* (Paris: OECD).

Okun, A. M. (1975) *Equality and Efficiency: The Big Tradeoff* (Washington DC: Brookings Institution).

Olsen, E. (1969) 'A competitive theory of the housing market', *American Economic Review*, 59, 612–22.

Oppenheim, C. (1990) *Poverty: The Facts* (London: Child Poverty Action Group).

Paine T. (1791) *The Rights of Man* (Harmondsworth: Penguin).

Paradise, J. I., Bluestone, C. D. and Bachman, R. Z. (1984) 'Efficacy of tonsillectomy for recurrent throat infection in severely affected children', *New England Journal of Medicine*, 310, 674–83.

Parker, H. (1982) *The Moral Hazard of Social Benefits* (London: Institute of Economic Affairs).

Parker, H. (1989) *Instead of the Dole* (London: Routledge).

Pauly, M. V. (1968) 'The economics of moral hazard: comment', *American Economic Review*, 58, 531–7.

Pauly, M. V. (1974) 'Overinsurance and public provision of insurance: the roles of moral hazard and adverse selection', *Quarterly Journal of Economics*, 88, 44–62.

Pauly, M. V. (1979) 'What is unnecessary surgery?', *Milbank Memorial Fund Quarterly*, 57, 1.

Pauly, M. V. (1986) 'Taxation, health insurance, and market failure in the medical economy', *Journal of Economic Literature*, 24, 629–75.

Peacock, A. T. and Wiseman, J. (1964) *Education for Democrats* (London: Institute of Economic Affairs).

Peacock, A. T. and Wiseman, J. (1967) *The Growth of Public Expenditure in the United Kingdom* (London: Allen & Unwin).

Pechman, J. (1970) 'The distributional effects of public higher education resources in California', *Journal of Human Resources*, 5, 361–70.

Pechman, J. and Timane, M. (1975) *Work Incentives and Guarantees: The*

New York Income Tax Experiment (Washington DC: Brookings Institution).

Pepper Commission (1990) *A Call for Action*, US Bipartisan Commission on Comprehensive Health Care (Washington DC: US Government Printing Office).

Piachaud, D. (1971) 'Poverty and taxation', *Political Quarterly*, 42, 31–44.

Piachaud, D. (1979) *The Cost of a Child* (London: Child Poverty Action Group).

Piachaud, D. (1981) 'Peter Townsend and the Holy Grail', *New Society*, 10 September, 419–21.

Piachaud, D. (1987) 'Problems in the definition and measurement of poverty', *Journal of Social Policy*, 16, 147–64.

Pissarides, C. A. (1982) 'From school to university: the demand for post-compulsory education in Britain', *Economic Journal*, 92, 654–67.

Pissarides, C. A. (1986) 'Job search and the functioning of labour markets', in D. Carline, C. A. Pissarides, W. S. Siebert and P. J. Sloane (eds) *Labour Economics* (London: Longman).

Posnett, J. W. (1987) 'Trends in the income of registered charities, 1980–85', in Charities Aid Foundation *Charity Trends 1986/7* (London: CAF).

Posnett, J. W. and Sandler, T. (1987) 'Joint supply and the finance of charitable activity', *Public Finance Quarterly*, 14, 209–22.

Posnett, J. W. and Sandler, T. (1989) 'Demand for charity donations in private non-profit markets: the case of the UK', *Journal of Public Economics*, 40, 187–200.

Prais, S. J. (1987) 'Educating for productivity: comparisons of Japanese and English schooling and vocational preparation', *National Institute Economic Review*, 119, 40–56.

Prais, S. J. and Steedman, H. (1987) 'Vocational training in France and Britain: the building trades', *National Institute Economic Review*, 116, 45–55.

Prais, S. J. and Wagner, K. (1988) 'Productivity and management: the training of foremen in Britain and Germany', *National Institute Economic Review*, 123, 34–47.

Prest, A. R. (1966) *Financing University Education* (London: Institute of Economic Affairs).

Psacharopoulos, G. (1987) *Economics of Education: Research and Studies* (Oxford: Pergamon Press).

Quigley, J. (1979) 'What have we learned about urban housing markets?', in P. Mieszkowski and M. Strazheim (eds) *Current Issues in Urban Economics* (Baltimore: Johns Hopkins University Press).

Reece, W. S. (1979) 'Charity contributions: new evidence on household behaviour', *American Economic Review*, 69, 142–51.

Reece, W. S. and Zieschang, K. (1985) 'Consistent estimation of the impact of tax deductibility on the level of charitable contributions', *Econometrica*, 53, 271–93.

Reece, W. S. and Zieschang, K. (1989) 'Evidence on taxation and charitable giving from the 1983 US Treasury tax model file', *Economic Letters*, 31, 49–53.

Rehnberg, C. (1990) *The Organization of Public Health Care: An Economic Analysis of the Swedish Health Care System* (Linkoping: Department of Health and Society).

Rice, P. (1987) 'The demand for post-compulsory education in the UK and the effects of educational maintenance allowances', *Economica*, 54, 465–75.

Riley, J. (1979) 'Testing the educational screening hypothesis', *Journal of Political Economy*, 87, 227–51.

Riley, J. G. (1975) 'Competitive signalling', *Journal of Economic Theory*, 10, 174–86.

Riley, J. G. (1979) 'Informational equilibria', *Econometrica*, 47, 331–59.

Roberts, D. (1960) *The Victorian Origins of the British Welfare State* (Yale, Mass.: Archon Books).

Roberts, R. (1984) 'A positive model of private charity and public transfers', *Journal of Political Economy*, 92, 136–48.

Robertson, D. and Symons, J. (1988) *The Occupational Choice of British School Children* (London: Centre for Economic Performance, London School of Economics).

Robins, P. K., Spiegelman, R. G., Weiner, S. and Bell, J. G. (1980) *A Guaranteed Annual Income: Evidence from a Social Experiment* (New York: Academic Press).

Robinson, J. and Luft, H. (1985) 'The impact of hospital market structure on patient volume, average length of stay, and the cost of care', *Journal of Health Economics*, 4, 333–56.

Robinson, J. and Luft, H. (1987) 'Competition and the cost of hospital care, 1972–1982', *Journal of the American Medical Association*, 257, 3241–5.

Robinson, J. and Luft, H. (1988) 'Competition, regulation and hospital costs, 1982–1986', *Journal of the American Medical Association*, 260, 2676–81.

Robinson, R. (1979) *Housing Economics and Public Policy* (London: Macmillan).

Roos, L. L. (1979) 'Alternative designs to study outcomes: the tonsillectomy case', *Medical Care*, 17, 1069–87.

Roos, N. P. and Danzinger, R. (1986) 'Assessing surgical risks in a population: patient histories before and after cholecystectomy', *Social Science and Medicine*, 22, 571–8.

Rosa, J.-J. (ed.) (1982) *The World Crisis in Social Security* (San Francisco: Institute for Contemporary Studies).

Rose, M. E. (1972) *The Relief of Poverty, 1934–1914* (London: Macmillan).

Rosen, S. (1974) 'Hedonic prices and implicit markets', *Journal of Political Economy*, 82, 34–55.

Rosko, M. D. and Broyles, R. W. (1987) 'Short term response of hospitals to the DRG prospective pricing mechanism in New Jersey', *Medical Care*, 25, 88–94.

Rothschild, M. and Stiglitz, J. E. (1976) 'Equilibrium in competitive insurance markets: an essay on the economics of imperfect information, *Quarterly Journal of Economics*, 90, 629–49.
Rowntree, B. S. (1901) *Poverty – a Study of Town Life* (London: Macmillan).
Rowse, A. L. (1950) *The England of Elizabeth* (London: Macmillan).
Rutter, M. *et al.* (1979) *Fifteen Thousand Hours: Secondary Schools and their Effects on Children* (London: Open Books).
Sager, M. A., Easterling, D. V., Kindig, D. A. and Anderson, O. W. (1989) 'Changes in the location of death after passage of Medicare's prospective payment system', *New England Journal of Medicine*, 320, 433–9.
Saltman, R. B. and Otter, C. van (1987) 'Revitalizing public health care systems: a proposal for competition in Sweden', *Health Policy*, 7, 21–40.
Sandberg, S. I., Barnes, B. A., Weinstein, M. C. and Braun, P. (1985) 'Elective hysterectomy: benefits, risks and costs', *Medical Care*, 23, 1067–85.
Sanders, D., Coulter, A. and McPherson, K. (1989) 'Variations in hospital admission rates: a review of the literature', London, Kings Fund, Project Paper 79.
Sandler, T., Sterbenz, F. and Posnett, J. W. (1987) 'Free riding and uncertainty', *European Economic Review*, 31, 1605–17.
Schiff, J. (1985) 'Does government spending crowd out charitable contributions?', *National Tax Journal*, 38, 535–46.
Schiff, J. (1987) 'Tax reform and volunteering, *The Constitution and the Independent Sector Spring Research Forum* (Washington DC: CISRF).
Schiff, J. (1989) 'Tax policy, charitable giving and the non-profit sector: what do we really know?', in R. Magat (ed.) *Philanthropic Giving* (Oxford: Oxford University Press).
Schiff, J. (1990) *Charitable Giving and Government Policy: An Economic Analysis* (Wehart, Conn.: Greenwood Press).
Schultz, T. W. (1963) *The Economic Value of Education* (New York: Columbia University Press).
Sleeman, J. F. (1973) *The Welfare State* (London: Allen & Unwin).
Slemrod, J. (1989) 'Are estimated tax elasticities really just tax evasion elasticities?: the case of charitable contributions', *Review of Economics and Statistics*, 71, 517–22.
Smith, A. (1873) *An Inquiry into the Nature and Causes of the Wealth of Nations* (London: Nelson).
Smith, L., Rosen, C. and Fallis, G. (1988) 'Recent developments in economic models of housing markets', *Journal of Economic Literature*, 26, 29–44.
Spence, D. (1973) 'Job market signalling', *Quarterly Journal of Economics*, 87, 355–74.
Steinberg, R. (1983) 'Two essays on the non-profit sector', Ph.D. dissertation, University of Pennsylvania.

Steinberg, R. (1985) 'Empirical relations between government spending and charitable donations', *Journal of Voluntary Action Research*, 14, 54–64.

Steinberg, R. (1986) 'Charitable giving as a mixed public/private good: implications for tax policy', *Public Finance Quarterly*, 14, 415–31.

Steinberg, R. (1987) 'Voluntary donations and public expenditure in a federalist system', *American Economic Review*, 77, 24–36.

Steinberg, R. (1989) 'The theory of crowding-out: donations, local government spending and the new federalism', in R. Magat (ed.) *Philanthropic Giving* (Oxford: Oxford University Press).

Steinberg, R. (1990) 'Taxes and giving – new findings', Paper presented at the Independent Sector Research Forum, Boston 15–16, March.

Stigler, G. J. (1970) 'Director's law of public income redistribution', *Journal of Law and Economics*, 13, 1–10.

Stiglitz, J. E. (1975) 'The theory of screening, education and the distribution of income', *American Economic Review*, 65, 283–300.

Stock, J. H. and Wise, D. A. (1988) 'The pension inducement to retire: an option value analysis', National Bureau of Economic Research, Working Paper 2660.

Stoddart, G. L. and Labelle, R. J. (1985) *Privatization in the Canadian Health Care System: Assertions, Evidence, Ideology and Options*, (Ottawa: Health and Welfare Canada).

Stubblebine, W. C. (1965) 'Institutional elements in the financing of education', *Southern Economic Journal*, 32, 15–34.

Sugden, R. (1982) 'On the economics of philanthropy', *Economic Journal*, 92, 341–50.

Sugden, R. (1984) 'Reciprocity: the supply of public goods through voluntary contribution', *Economic Journal*, 94, 772–87.

Sugden, R. (1985) 'Consistent conjectures and voluntary contributions to public goods: why the conventional theory does not work', *Journal of Public Economics*, 27, 117–24.

Summers, L. H. (1989) 'Some simple economics of mandated benefits', *American Economic Review*, 79, 177–83.

Supplementary Benefits Commission (1976) *Annual Report* (London: HMSO).

Taubman, P. J. and Wales, T. J. (1973) 'Higher education, mental ability and screening', *Journal of Political Economy*, 81, 28–55.

Taussig, M. K. (1967) 'Economics aspects of the personal income tax treatment of charitable donations', *National Tax Journal*, 20, 1–19.

Temple, W. (1941) *Citizen and Churchman* (London: Eyre & Spottiswoode).

Thane, P. (ed.) (1978) *The Origins of British Social Policy* (London: Croom Helm).

Titmuss, R. A. (1968) *Commitment to Welfare* (London: Allen & Unwin).

Townsend, P. (1979) *Poverty in the United Kingdom* (London: Allen Lane).

Townsend, P. and Davidson, N. (1982) *Inequalities in Health* (Harmondsworth: Penguin Books).

UK (1942) *Social Insurance and Allied Services (the Beveridge report)* Cmd 6404 (London: HMSO).

UK (1963) *Higher Education (the Robbins report)* Cmnd 2154 (London: HMSO).

UK (1971) *Strategy for Pensions: The Future Development of State and Occupational Provision* Cmnd 4755 (London: HMSO).

UK (1974) *Better Pensions: Fully Protected Against Inflation* Cmnd 5713 (London: HMSO).

UK (1976) *Local Government Finance: Report of an Enquiry* Cmnd 6453 (London: HMSO).

UK (1985a) *Reform of Social Security* Cmnd 9517 (London: HMSO).

UK (1985b) *Reform of Social Security: Programme for Change* Cmnd 9518 (London: HMSO).

UK (1988) *Top-Up Loans for Students* Cm 520 (London: HMSO).

UK (1989) *Working for Patients* Cm 555 (London: HMSO).

Vaizey, J. (1958) *The Costs of Education* (London: Allen & Unwin).

van de Ven, W. P. M. M. (1990) 'From regulated cartel to regulated competition in the Dutch health care system', *European Economic Review*, 34, 632–45.

van de Ven, W. P. M. M. and van Vliet, R. C. J. A. (1990) 'How to prevent cream skimming in a competitive health insurance market? The great challenge for the 90s', Paper presented at the 1990 World Congress of Health Economics, Zurich.

van Praag, B. M. S., Hagenaars, A. J. M. and van Weeren, H. (1982) 'Poverty in Europe', *Review of Income and Wealth*, 28, 345–59.

Vickrey, C. (1977) 'The time-poor: a new look at poverty', *Journal of Human Resources*, 12, 27–48.

Wagstaff, A. (1991) 'QALYs and the equity-efficiency tradeoff', *Journal of Health Economics*, 10, 21–41.

Warr, P. G. (1982) 'Pareto optimal redistribution and private charity', *Journal of Public Economics*, 19, 131–8.

Warr, P. G. (1983) 'The private provision of a public good is independent of the distribution of income', *Economics Letters*, 13, 207–11.

Watson, H. (1984) 'A note on the effects of taxation on charitable giving over the life cycle and beyond', *Quarterly Journal of Economics*, 99, 639–47.

Weale, A. (1983) *Political Theory and Social Policy* (London: Macmillan).

Weisbrod, B. A. (1969) 'Collective action and the distribution of income: a conceptual approach', in Joint Economic Committee (ed.) *The Analysis and Evaluation of Public Expenditures* (Washington DC: US Government Printing Office).

Weisbrod, B. A. (1970) 'On the stigma effect and the demand for welfare programs: a theoretical note', University of Wisconsin, Discussion Paper.

Weitzman, M. L. (1977) 'Is the price system of rationing more effective in getting a commodity to those who need it most?', *Bell Journal of Economics*, 8, 517–24.

Wennberg, J. and Gittlesohn, A. (1982) 'Variations in medical care among small areas', *Scientific American*, 246, 100–11.

West, E. G. (1965) *Education and the State* (London: Institute of Economic Affairs).

Whynes, D. K. (1985) 'Markets and neo-liberal political economy', in P. T. Bean, J. S. Ferris and D. K. Whynes (eds) *In Defence of Welfare* (London: Tavistock).

Wilcox, S. (1991) *Macroeconomic Implications of Removing Mortgage Interest Tax Relief* (York: Joseph Rowntree Foundation).

Wiles, P. (1974) 'The correlation between education and earnings: the external-test-not-content hypothesis', *Higher Education*, 3, 43–58.

Williams, and Gordon, A. (1981) 'Perceived earnings functions and ex ante rates of return in post-compulsory education in England', *Higher Education*, 10, 199–207.

Wilson, C. A. (1977) 'A model of insurance markets with incomplete information', *Journal of Economic Theory*, 16, 167–207.

Winch, D. (1978) *Adam Smith's Politics* (Cambridge: Cambridge University Press).

Wise, D. A. (ed.) (1986) *Pensions, Labor and Individual Behavior* (Chicago: University of Chicago Press).

Zeckhauser, R. J. and Patel, J. (1987) 'Treasury bill futures as hedges against inflation risk', National Bureau of Economic Research, Working Paper 2322.

Zwanziger, J. and Melnick, G. A. (1988) 'The effects of hospital competition and the Medicare PPS program on hospital cost behaviour in California', *Journal of Health Economics*, 7, 301–20.

Name Index

Subject Index